THE
ROVER
STORY

THE ROVER STORY

A CENTURY OF SUCCESS

GRAHAM ROBSON

Graham Robson

PSL

Patrick Stephens, Cambridge

First published in 1977

British Library Cataloguing in Publication Data

Robson, Graham
  The Rover story
  1. Rover-British Leyland UK Limited — History
  I. Title
  338.7'62'922220941   HD9710.G74R/

  ISBN 0 85059 279 8

Text filmset in 10 on 11½ pt Baskerville
by Blackfriars Press Ltd, Leicester.
Printed in Great Britain on 115 gsm Fineblade coated
cartridge and bound by The Garden City Press,
Letchworth, Herts.
Published by Patrick Stephens Limited,
Bar Hill, Cambridge, CB3 8EL, England.

Contents

Note: Rover's financial year always opened in September. Any statistics quoted in the text — for instance 1936/37 — refer to the 12 months ending in August of the last year.

In almost every case, Rover's new models were revealed in the autumn of a year, and the model year then ran for 12 months. The new models were usually built from the end of one annual holiday to the beginning of the next. A 1955 model, therefore, might have been built between August/September 1954 and July/August 1955.

Author's introduction

This is not merely an enthusiast's book about a series of well-known cars. It is also a celebration, of 100 years of fascinating and wholly remarkable progress. Sometime in 1877 (and not even the Rover company themselves know the exact date) John Kemp Starley and William Sutton set up a business in Coventry to make pedal cycles. From such modest beginnings the prestigious Rover combine developed.

But since then, what changes! The modest little Coventry firm which was so proud of its pedal cycles became one of the world's most respected car makers. Rover cars are now just an integral part of British Leyland — but what a far cry this is from the Coventry Sewing Machine Company of the 1860s, which really started it all. The tiny company grew and grew, turned to cars in 1904, and almost sank into bankruptcy in 1931, but remained sturdily independent until the 1960s. Then, having started out on the takeover trail itself, it shortly agreed to capture by Leyland Motors.

In writing this book, I was privileged to look into confidential company records which had never previously been released. I am no less cynical than the next man, and expected some of these to throw up all manner of unsavoury 'skeletons'. There were none. But should I have expected any from Rover? How many other companies would supervise the education of a particularly valuable manager's son after his father had been killed in air-raids on the factory? And how many boards would solemnly study his school reports once a term? How many boards would consider every worker's retirement individually, and often increase a pension to well above the levels his contributions had assured?

Looking back on events, I can detect several crucial stages. Trying to take on the might of Austin and Morris in the 1920s with cheap cars was probably a mistake. To persevere with the £89 Scarab in 1931 would certainly have been fatal. The thinking which dreamed up those exciting gas-turbine prototypes was quite inspired, but hopes of production were over-optimistic. The same sort of people, however, thought of the Land-Rover, and *that* has been lastingly brilliant. Buying the rights to a rejected General Motors vee-8 engine did a lot for Rover's modernising image, and the Range Rover brought things thoroughly up to date. The one car that did most to change the firm's direction was the Rover 2000, only recently going out of production.

What we have already seen from the modern company is fascinating enough; the thought of what might yet follow is even more so. That is why I have chosen to concentrate more on Rover's more modern heritage than its ancient traditions. Will some of us be able to look back at Rover from the 21st century, and say that *this* was the most rewarding period. I wonder?

Graham Robson, March 1977

Chapter 1

From a humble bicycle . . .

People have short memories. There are those whose recall of Rover stops short at the Light 6 which beat the *Blue Train* in 1930. Others can remember the truly Edwardian Rovers, and some even know about that famous Tourist Trophy win of 1907. There are few, however, who realise that the whole thing really stemmed from success in marketing pedal cycles. There are even some tenuous links with Victorian sewing machines.

The Coventry Sewing Machine Company, founded in 1861, has a lot to be proud of. Most people now acknowledge that the British motor industry was born in Coventry, and evolved from the cycle trade. Not as many realise that the cycle business grew out of the sewing machine industry. That was more than a century ago, and that's where our story begins.

Not only Rover but others — Rudge, Ariel, Hillman, Singer, Lea & Francis, Swift, Excelsior and Humber — all are well-known marques which had roots in this same company. There were others, not so famous, which did not live for long.

More particularly, the Rover company originated with the Starleys — James and John, uncle and nephew. Not that they were 'Coventry kids' either; not, that is, at first. Starley the elder was born in Sussex in 1830, and was originally an apprentice gardener. He then moved on to being an apprentice engineer under one John Penn of Lewisham, South London. It was here, in Penn's marine engineering workshops, that the industrialisation of the Starleys began. Mrs Penn's sewing machine broke down and it was duly sent into the shops for attention. James Starley mended it, and Penn himself was suitably impressed.

Penn knew Josiah Turner (whose firm had made the sewing machine in question), mentioned how competent his trainee's repair job had been, and procured him a job with this firm — Newton, Wilson and Co. That would have been in the 1850s, and for a time Starley was happily engrossed in sewing machine design and manufacture. Before long he had developed a new machine of his own, patented it, and impressed Turner with its features. Turner, for his part, persuaded Starley to go into business with him and to sell the machines. For their new venture they chose Coventry.

But why Coventry, and why then? The decision, as we shall see, was crucial to the city's history for the next 100 years. Turner, not Starley, was at that time the entrepreneur, and knew that at the end of the 1850s Coventry's industries were in deep trouble. The city, which had relied on watch-making and ribbon weaving for so long was being battered by foreign competition, by adverse tariffs, and — dare I say it? — by strikes. There were several company bankruptcies, factories closed down, and a big pool of unemployed labour developing.

Turner took a chance, decided that a suitable factory would be easy to find, and that the built-in skills of Coventry watch-makers could easily adapt to making sewing machines. The Coventry Sewing Machine Company was therefore born in 1861, Turner and Starley moved up from London to guide its fortunes, and the commercial prospects for the still-small city were about to be transformed. Starley was then 31 years old.

The jump from sewing machines to bicycles was taken purely by chance, but for relatively obvious reasons. Josiah Turner had a nephew, Rowley Turner, then a student in Paris. In the best Victorian capitalistic style, his spare time interest in the French craze of velocipeding (cycling, in our language) eventually made him money as he took on a business interest in a French firm which made Michaux machines. Before long, too, he was also the Coventry Sewing Machine Company's Paris agent, after which his studies were conveniently forgotten. Shortly the two interests fused. Young Rowley Turner suggested that his uncle should start to make the Michaux Velocipedes in Coventry, and backed his argument by actually turning up in Coventry on one to prove his point. Although he had arrived at the offices on the machine, he had only ridden it from Coventry's railway station!

Uncle Josiah was soon convinced, as was Starley, but the company couldn't begin to make the cycles at once. This was not for any lack of resolve, but for the quaint and legalistic reason that the firm's Articles of Association did not allow it. No matter — the company was eventually wound up, and the Coventry Machinists Co Ltd took its place.

In 1869, therefore, Starley and Turner graduated to the wheeled-transport industry, and this is really the year in which the Coventry we know stepped hesitantly into the world. The bicycles — 'velocipedes' to the French, but 'boneshakers' to we British — were to be made at a factory in Coventry's Cheylesmore district, but before long Starley had moved on again. By comparison with his complex but effective sewing machines, these bicycles were crude. Starley was sure he could improve on the design, did so, and urged change on his partner. There was no response — were they not, after all, making and selling all the machines they wished? In 1870, therefore, James Starley left in a huff, taking with him a works foreman called William Hillman.

Hillman? Isn't that an industry name with a familiar ring? Indeed it is. Hillman's new partnership with Starley lasted for only six profitable years before he too drifted off to make his own cycles, and — in 1907 — the first Hillman car. The cars themselves would have much to do with the motor industry's future, but so would his daughters. Hillman fathered no fewer than six girls, two of whom were eventually wooed and married by bright young men on his car company staff — one was called John Black and one was Spencer Wilks. Both of these names, as we shall see, mean a lot to the rest of the story.

Shortly after, Starley was joined in Coventry by his young nephew, John Kemp Starley. Young John had spent his childhood in Ilford. By the time he was 18 years old he had developed the Starley love of machines, had been experimenting with steam engines, and had sent drawings to his successful uncle in Coventry. Realising that John was bent on a career in engineering, James Starley offered him a post in his partnership, which was accepted with some alacrity.

The story of the next few years gets complicated. In Victorian Britain, especially in the burgeoning cities where new products, new factories, new firms and buoyant enterprises were alive, there was much wheeling and dealing, even though it didn't get that disparaging title at the time. Starley and Hillman first established themselves in John Street, but before long had licensed production of their Ariel bicycles to Messrs Haynes and Jefferies of Spon Street. More important, with the Ariel move went young John Starley, who became works manager at Haynes and Jefferies.

It was the first factory in Coventry to concentrate entirely on building pedal cycles, and it gave the young man much scope for his experimental zeal. The Starleys, however, were nothing if not restless, and within four years John Starley was ready to move on. He wanted to make bicycles of his own.

In this he decided to join forces with William Sutton, a keen cycling enthusiast, who owned a haberdashery shop in the city. The new concern was called Starley and Sutton, a partnership with unlimited liability, and it took over the ground floor of a group of buildings in West Orchard, Coventry. Here, at last, we find the real origins of the Rover company, even though the name itself would not appear for another seven years. John Starley, in setting it up, was only 23 years old. But where was Uncle James in all this manoeuvring? Fear not — he seemed to have financial interests in most things. In this case he certainly helped John with money as initial capital, and his Compressus Ordinaries (which we now know as Penny Farthings) were the main product; Uncle James was shrewd enough to extract a royalty for every machine sold.

The factory itself, known even then as the Meteor Works, figures prominently in the Rover company's history. Even though an expansionist move was made to larger premises, just round the corner in Queen Victoria Road, after a few years, the original premises were kept on. However, don't bother to make the pilgrimage to Coventry to gaze on Rover's historical buildings, they were flattened many years ago. On the night of November 14 1940 the German air force had a very serious try at re-shaping the layout of Coventry, while the city fathers' ambitious post-war development plans did the rest. Rover had already sold the buildings before the bombing destroyed them in any case. If there are any Rover ghosts still around the area, I hope they are happy. Their old stamping grounds are now buried under shopping precincts and a retail market called the West Orchard, along with acres and acres of car parks. Only a façade on the eastern edge of the site remains.

Starley and Sutton prospered, even though their nearly hand-made machines were expensive. Tricycles were easier to control than the high and ungainly Ordinaries, but not as manoeuvrable, and much more expensive. John Starley's persistent aim was to produce a better two-wheeler, and he spent most of his spare time worrying away at this. His brainwave, one which eventually transformed prospects for the cycling business, was to reverse the accepted mechanical custom. He decided that a cycle's *rear* wheel should be driven, that a chain and gearing should reduce the rider's efforts, and that this meant that the wheel diameter could be dramatically reduced.

In the meantime, the first Rover machine appeared. This was a tricycle, and the name was meant to show that the machine could wander, or rove, around the countryside. The name surfaced in 1884, but made its own publicity in 1885 when it was applied to John Starley's first Safety bicycle. The Safety, of course, was really the prototype of the modern pedal cycle, and the ridiculous balancing problems of the ungainly Ordinaries had been solved.

To capitalise on the success of the revolutionary Safety machines, and taking account of the rapidly developing cycling boom in Britain, John Starley proposed to expand his company. His partner, William Sutton, was perhaps now feeling somewhat out of his financial depth, and was certainly not as buoyantly confident of the future. Accordingly, in 1888, the original partnership was amicably dissolved, and Starley took sole control of his new business, now titled J. K. Starley and Co Ltd. Thereafter, his fortunes took off with a vengeance.

Even at this stage, and long before the first petrol-engined Rover machine took the road, Starley began testing a spindly looking tricycle, electrically driven and battery-powered. The batteries were placed in a rather coy wicker basket above and behind the axle of the twin rear wheels, and the motor was tucked away underneath it. The range, reputedly, was pitiful, the performance likewise, and once the batteries went flat the dead weight of the machine would have daunted any but the strongest of riders. It was not a success, but it was only an experiment, and no attempt was ever made to sell replicas.

Starley's Safety bicycles caught on rapidly. Business went from success to success, sales rose rapidly on the back of the late-Victorian cycling craze, and before long John Starley was a wealthy man. Uncle James would have been proud of him, but was not around to witness it, having died in 1881. No one in Coventry doubted that Uncle James was responsible for their renewed prosperity. Since then he has become known as the father of modern Coventry, and there is a statue — near the site of the original Meteor works — to prove the point.

At last, at the peak of the cycling boom, Rover was included in the company's name. John Starley was still in expansionist mood, offered shares for new capital and proposed to call his new company The Rover Cycle Company Ltd. Its initial capital, in good solid British currency, was £150,000 with an additional £50,000 in 5 per cent Debentures. But by now he was no longer alone as Coventry's most prominent tycoon. More seriously, the now notorious Harry Lawson, his licence-built Daimler car, and his huge schemes for cornering the entire foundling British motor industry, had arrived on the other side of town. Starley was the Emperor of Queen Victoria Road, but Lawson seemed determined to be the Emperor of Coventry.

To start with, Lawson took over a disused cotton mill in the Radford district of the city. With a seemingly endless supply of shareholders' money, Lawson expanded by acquisition, and tried to induce Starley to join forces with him. He should have known better; predictably, there was no response from Starley. But Lawson's ideas, ill-considered as they might be, set Starley thinking, and it was from this incident that he first became interested in engines and their possibilities.

For his new company secretary, Starley chose Harry Smith, who would be linked with the firm for the next generation. He arrived, along with chairman Sir Frederick Dixon-Hartland, just in time to oversee the move from one Meteor Works to the next, and to see initial establishment under the roof that would witness such phenomenal developments in future years.

The New Meteor Works, with its main offices and gates facing out on to Queen Victoria Road and the Drill Hall, would house many secrets, successes, failures and experimental blind alleys before being sold off in 1932, but there was still a long way to go before the first car was built.

In June 1896 the Rover Cycle Co Ltd came into being. In its first year we know that about 11,000 cycles were built. The average price of a cycle was about £14.88, total turnover was of the order of £160,000 and the first profit was £21,945. It was a good and solid start for the public company.

Meanwhile, yet another member of the Starley family had arrived on the scene. John Starley's son, bearing the same christian names and therefore called 'Jack' by everyone to avoid confusion, had joined the company straight from school in 1892. Since then, of course, there have been other equally respected Starleys, but as far as the Rover was concerned, he would be the last of the line. In due course he would become managing director, and would stay until 1929.

So, with Rover profitably engaged in the pedal cycle business, was there any reason why they should seek to change this? Was Starley right to import a few Peugeot motor cycles from France in 1899, study them, and use them for experimental work? For an answer, we have to look round at the Coventry of the late 1890s, at its 60,000 population, and at the way business was developing.

By the end of the 19th century, the motor car phenomenon was already with us, and after 1896 it was even possible to run a private car on Britain's public highways without too much aggravation or official interference. Benz had started it all, in Germany, in 1885, and by the 1890s Panhard had joined him in popularising the 'horseless carriage' with its new-fangled 'explosion' engine. After Sir David Salomons had pressurised Parliament into changing the law, and Harry Lawson's publicists brought their own brand of publicity into the business, everyone seemed to know about the 'autocar'. *The Autocar,* Britain's very first motoring magazine, soon sprang into prominence.

Harry Lawson settled in Coventry, but Wolseley was in Birmingham. Lanchester was also in Birmingham, but the Riley family was already established in Coventry. The industry, without precedents, might have concentrated itself in either city, but because the existing 'transport' industry for cyclists was already booming in Coventry, it was the city of three spires which won the battle. Strangely enough, it was the four-wheel variety of motor vehicle which prospered first; the motor cycles, developed directly from the pedal cycles, followed a year or two behind.

Rover, and Starley, developed in an entirely logical manner. Following their study of the imported Peugeots, their first project was to motorise a Rover pedal cycle, something which Triumph, in Coventry, were also proposing to do. Triumph were of a similar, cautious, frame of mind, and were in no hurry to rush into doubtful commercial jungles. Their first motoring device ran in 1895, but was not marketed for another seven years. Rover were rather quicker than that, if we discount the electrically powered tricycle of 1888.

John Starley died tragically early, aged 46, in October 1901, while still the undisputed leader of Coventry's bicycle industry. Apart from being a successful businessman, he had also been a great philanthropist, and was a keen supporter of his local non-conformist Congregational church. In this connection, he arranged publication of the 'Starley Bible', where — unusually — the New Testament was printed at the beginning of the book.

Starley's death meant that wholesale management changes would follow. Sir Frederick Dixon-Hartland wanted no part in the day-to-day management of what was now a large (15,000 machines a year) business; accordingly secretary Harry Smith became the company's general manager, and Frank Ward became secretary in his place. This interregnum, with no managing director as such, continued for just one year, after which Harry Smith formally filled the post, the duties of which he had been carrying out for some time. When Smith became general manager in 1901, young Jack Starley was given his first executive post, as assistant works manager of the New Meteor Works.

There is nothing significant in the fact that motor cycle manufacture was avoided until after John Starley's death. Starley certainly had no prejudice against motor cycles *or* cars, but he was a cautious business man. After all, even in 1901, when he died, there was not a single example of a successful motor cycle made in Britain, and the cars themselves were still almost hilariously unreliable.

The decision to go motorised was taken by Harry Smith in 1902. Even though the works was bursting with activity (17,431 cycles built and sold in 1902), he had that laudable Edwardian ambition to expand yet further. Board meeting records tell us that the decision to market motor cycles was taken on October 10, while we know that the first public appearance of the 2¾ hp Rover was on November 24. We must assume from this that prototypes had been under development for some time, probably since 1900, and that board approval was formally necessary to commit money to tooling and facilities.

The motor cycles were barely in the hands of their first customers when Rover took their next deep breath, and expansionist move forwards. In spite of all its troubles, Britain's foundling motor car industry had begun to show signs of stability. Daimler, once rid of the rumbustious influence of Harry Lawson, had begun turning out good cars *and* showed signs of making money for him. More than this, some respectability had been gained when King Edward VII took delivery of his first car.

With profits recovering from a low point of £7,304 in 1900, Smith and his directors felt that they, too, should be a part of the new mechanised age, in spite of knowing nothing about it. Their motor cycles, after all, were merely extensions, in knowledge, of their pedal cycles. As far as cars were concerned, they had neither made chassis nor coachwork in the past. They were not even sure that their works were suited to building cars. No matter. On December 16 1903 the directors decided to start development of a light car, and they invited Edmund Lewis to design it for them. Lewis himself was 'poached' from Daimler, who were the acknowledged experts, and Rover were not at all ashamed of this move. 'Poaching' was rife then, and prospers even today.

Looking back, we can see that Rover's decision came only just in time. Already there was a lot of potential. Even in Coventry, Daimler and Riley had already been joined by Armstrong-Siddeley, Humber, Lea-Francis and Singer. Even as their decision was made, Standard (in Much Park Street) were about to join them. The directors decided. There would be Rover cars, and they were determined that there should be lots of them. It didn't matter that the New Meteor Works was probably the most famous cycle factory in the land — cars would soon be flooding out of its gates. The city's newest industry was well established, and Rover was all set to add to its achievements.

Chapter 2

Birth, growth, crisis

Board meeting minutes: April 24 1928

'As a result of negotiations with shareholders, it had been decided to invite Mr W. D. Sudbury and Mr Herman Jennings to meet the board today . . . It was resolved to co-opt Mr Sudbury and Mr Jennings to the board forthwith . . . The question of the chairmanship of the board was then considered . . . Mr Sudbury was elected to that position.'

If 1904 is a very important date in Rover's history, 1932 is even more so. 1904 was the year in which the story of the cars began, but 1932 was the year in which it very nearly ended. Not that there would have been anything very strange about that. The world-wide depression hit everybody, and Coventry's factories suffered as badly as most. Everything that could go wrong in the depression *did* go wrong — the miracle is that so few of Britain's car makers actually disappeared.

It took a quarter of a century for Rover to become convinced that they were making the wrong sort of cars. The cars were not badly designed, but they were not distinctive enough. The problem was really that Rover failed to establish any recognisable tradition.

By 1931 the company was losing money on every car they made, and selling fewer and fewer of them. It was definitely 'on the cards' for a time that Rover might have perished there and then. If so, they would have joined the distinguished company of Bentley, Lanchester, Swift, and others.

As car makers, Rover started slowly, built up well, but were never pre-eminent after the Great War as they had been before it. We must also not forget that the British motor industry was a very elementary affair at first, and that the science of mechanised production was still in its infancy. There were dozens of self-important little concerns, some with mechanical traditions and some without, who were quite convinced that *they* had the right formula for success. A well-established business like Rover's needed very little time, and only a restricted output, to become significant.

By 1914, certainly, there was no doubt that Rover had 'arrived'. Indeed, in terms of sales and prestige, the first ten years saw the company rise to a position of great importance in the industry. Even so, because of the number of cars actually sold, this has to be put into perspective. The last full production year before the war was 1913, with a total British output of around 26,000 cars. Ford, with about 6,000 Model Ts being shipped from Trafford Park, were way out in front of everybody else, and Wolseley, with between 2,000 and 3,000 cars built, were in a respectable second place. Rover, having made about 1,500 cars that year (and this discounts the motor cycles which were still important to work and to profits) were definitely well-up in the pack, and were matching the efforts of Austin, Morris, Singer and others.

This was both good news and bad news. It was good because it helped to establish the company's reputation and standing in the motor industry, but it was bad because it gave Harry Smith and J. K. Starley some big ideas. In the very different world of the 1920s, they were convinced that Rover could still match Austin and Morris in their endeavours, but could neither arrange the financial backing nor the factory resources to match this resolve. It was in the 1920s, as Rover gradually but persistently slipped back in the 'league table' of car producers, that the crisis developed.

The problem was that as Britain's motor industry boomed ahead from 1919 to 1929, Rover did not follow suit. The company was making no more cars at the end of the 1920s than they had been at the beginning, while at the same time industry production quadrupled. In 1922, with the cheap air-cooled 8 safely and successfully launched, nearly 6,500 Rovers were built — and that was a nine per cent share of the market. By 1928 only 3,800 Rovers were being sold, and since national output had soared to 165,000 this meant that the company's share had slumped to a miserable 2.3 per cent. This was tragic enough, but looks even worse when we realise that most of Rover's production was aimed at a developing mass market, which refused to be tempted.

The same dismal story was spelt out in the balance sheets. Profits surged ahead from 1912 and through the war years, reaching a peak of £146,754 in 1922. A year later they had crashed to a £36,752 loss. Between 1923 and 1932 the company only recorded profits in two years, and these were precariously achieved in the Searle-inspired 'dash for growth' period of 1929 and 1930. Worse still, in all that time the company was not actually expanding. Turnover stuck stubbornly at about £1.5 million, and declined steadily from 1924 onwards.

It had all started in 1904 with the Lewis-designed 8 hp machine, the first of several small-engined 'peoples' cars' which the company offered in an effort to build up sales. The original Rover car, however, was 'different'. It made no attempt to follow the fashion dictated by the French and German machines which still dominated our 1904 car market (so what's new about an imported-car invasion, after all?).

At the time it was commonplace to provide a car with a chassis frame developed from the horsedrawn carriage era, with wooden side members reinforced by steel flitch plates, or even by using a crude type of press-steel channel-section construction. But for Lewis this seemed far too easy. Choosing to ignore the lessons of the machines which he knew so well at Daimler, Lewis laid out the design of Rover's very first car with a technically advanced steel backbone frame.

The new car was born in an astonishingly short time, even by the brisker standards of Edwardian England. Lewis was not appointed by Rover's directors until December 1903, but his prototype 8 hp car was running by July 1904, and on sale by the end of the year.

By the standards of the day, and even by our present ones, the new car was remarkably advanced. Not only was a backbone type of 'chassis' construction chosen, but this was extended to include the back axle as well. Whereas it was, and is, normal for the mechanical parts to be chassis-mounted, and for the axle to be sprung, in the first Rover the axle was bolted up rigidly to the backbone and transmission. The only form of rear springing was between the body and the back end of the backbone/axle assembly, which must have assured this Rover of one of the highest unsprung/sprung weight ratios in the business. Only the fact that performance was very limited allowed the car's ride and handling to be anything but remotely acceptable.

The engine itself was a water-cooled vertical 'one-lunger' of 1,327 cc, with massive flywheels weighing a total of 120 lb, and a three-speed sliding pinion gearbox mounted inside the backbone and forming a part of it. One engine feature was that pedal pressure could move one set of cams, and bring into action another, which effectively turned the engine into a powerful air-compressor, and gave very efficient engine braking.

Within months the 8 was joined by a 6, also designed by Lewis but, significantly, much more conventional in concept. The 8 was complex, and was sometimes known to 'break its back', so when a cheaper 6 (there was a '100 Guinea' model on sale in 1905) was needed, the design was modified. The 8, in fact, was the first and last technically brave Rover until the still-born Scarab of 1931, and until the gas-turbine cars of the 1940s. The 6, much more in keeping with publicly accepted fashion, had a normally sprung axle, jointed propeller shaft, a wood-and-flitch-plate chassis, and half-elliptic road springs all round. In this last feature, at least, it was unique for a while, as all the other Rovers used a transverse front leaf spring.

1905 was a busy year for Rover and for Lewis, for the short-lived 10/12 model (with a monobloc four-cylinder engine) and the more significant 16/20 (which sired the TT-winning machine of 1907) were also revealed and put into production. Rover, like most of their rival firms, made very little of the cars themselves, preferring to buy out a lot of components; even so, production quantities were tiny by modern standards, and sales of more than 20 cars a week were a cause for rejoicing.

Lewis left the company to join Armstrong-Siddeley in a very senior management capacity at the end of 1905, but the cars he had designed were to serve Rover well for several more years. It would not be until 1911, when the legendary Clegg-designed 12 appeared, that another radically different design joined the Lewis-inspired products at Queen Victoria Road. Lewis, however, retained cordial links with Rover, and one result of this was that the 1912 Siddeley-Deasey 12 hp car was really a 'kit car', with an Aster engine in the current 12 hp Rover chassis.

I make no excuse for skipping fairly quickly through the Rover company's pre-war activities, as these have been well-documented by previous authors, and have little bearing on the way the company developed in post-war years. It is necessary to say, however, that once the Lewis-designed cars became obsolete, there was a period of unsettled design and business policy, when a bewildering variety of models were introduced.

The single-cylinder 6 and 8 models continued with few changes until 1912, after which the Clegg-designed 12 became so commercially important to Rover that most other models were ditched to make way for it. Even in 1905 it was obvious that standardisation of engine components was being considered, for the bare bones of the 6 — its bore, stroke, piston, connecting rods and valve gear — were used in the four-cylinder 16/20. Later, in 1908, the twin-cylinder 12 hp 'taxi' model arrived, and was also given the same basic engine dimensions. All were bored out to 97 mm, but the family of single-, twin-, and four-cylinder engines were well-established. Up to 1910 the only odd man out, with a 130 mm stroke, was the original backbone chassis 8.

The 16/20, introduced in 1905 at 3,119 cc, was related to the 6, with a lengthened version of its frame, but had a transverse leaf front spring and a steering-column gearchange control. Lewis designed it, of course, and it may be no coincidence that it resembled the 28-36 hp Daimler of the period. Whatever its merits as a touring car, the 16/20 will always be remembered for its exploits in the Tourist Trophy race. Not that racing cars were very fast in those days (at least not in the TT). A maximum speed of around 45-50 mph was all that could be hoped for, and on the long, rough and hilly Isle of Man circuit (52 miles a lap in 1905) average speeds of no more than 31 mph were achieved.

The 16/20's engine was typical of its day, with four separate cast-iron cylinders fixed to a light-alloy crankcase, and side valves. The engine braking feature pioneered on the original single-cylinder 8 was retained. The rest of the chassis was conventional, with a three-speed gearbox in unit with the engine, a right-hand gearchange, and torque tube location for the spiral-bevel back axle.

In those days, the Tourist Trophy's regulations also demanded a fuel consumption limit from the race cars. In the first year the cars had to achieve 22.5 mpg, and in 1907, when Rover's greatest triumph took place, 25 mpg in racing conditions had to be beaten.

In 1905, the first year the TT had been held, Rover entered two cars of the brand-new 16/20 type, both for publicity and for proving purposes, and backed their resolve by appointing designer Lewis and chief tester Ernest Courtis to drive them. In spite of the fact that the designs were very new, the two cars achieved a satisfactory result, with Courtis taking fifth place, and Lewis 12th. Courtis' average speed was 31 mph, and he finished 34 minutes (in six and a half hours) behind the winning Arrol-Johnston.

Improved and better-looking cars missed the 1906 race for no better reason than that they turned up late for pre-event scrutineering and were disqualified. A year later, with the same cars much modified to meet the stiffened regulations, the factory made no mistake. Lewis having now left the company, the cars were driven by the redoubtable Courtis, and by Edgar Folker. Regulations meant that the cars weighed in at more than 28 cwt, and even with a new four-speed gearbox to help the 20 developed horsepower, the four-cylinder car was going to have a hard time.

There were 31 entries, but only 22 starters. Both performance *and* fuel economy were going to be important, and it would be quite easy to run out of one commodity while exercising the other. This time the race was over six laps of a 40-mile circuit and the event was held in May, but weather and road conditions were atrocious.

History tells us that, although the Rover was by no means the most powerful car entered, nor its driver the most famous, car No 22 driven by Ernest Courtis took an overall victory, by more than 12 minutes, after a gruelling 8 hours 23 minutes 27 seconds. For Rover, it was a triumph, because the race cars were genuinely very closely related to the production machines, and they made great capital out of this, allied to the fact that a company employee had been driving.

Harry Smith and Jack Starley were delighted, but were wise enough to stop while they were ahead. There would be no more racing Rovers until the 1960s. Courtis' reward, incidentally, was a gold watch from the directors, and an extra week's holiday!

In the meantime, commercial expansion went on apace. At the end of 1905 a nod was given to the increasingly wide nature of business by having the company's name altered to The Rover Company Ltd — which would never again be altered until the Leyland mergers rendered a separate existence meaningless. Bernard Wright designed the Rover 15, built and sold between 1908 and 1911 and noted chiefly for its engine with cylinders cast in pairs, its heart-shaped radiator pioneered on the 1907 TT cars and for its general air of up-to-date design and refinement.

More interesting still, but very puzzling when trying to establish a design heritage, was the listing of two sleeve-valve engined cars for 1911 and 1912 models. The company's records make no comment on this, but it seems certain that nobody in Rover's employ could have designed the engines themselves, and as Daimler were the British patent holders of the Knight sleeve-valve patents it is probable that many components were actually supplied by Daimler for the purpose. There were two engines — a single-cylinder 8 (actually rated at 6.3 hp) and a twin-cylinder 12 (which was actually an 11.4 hp engine). They shared a common cylinder stroke of 130 mm, and cylinder dimensions to be found on contemporary Daimlers. The fact that the stroke was the same as the original Rover 8 is a coincidence.

There is no denying that the Knight-patented method of allowing a piston engine to breathe was a great advance over existing poppet-valve methods, but these engines could not hide the fact that they were deficient of cylinders. This was an inevitable result of the fact that Daimler would not consider sub-letting the rights to build them if it would cause competition with their own four-cylinder cars.

Demand for the Rover single- and twin-cylinder cars declined as the Edwardian era closed, while sales of the expensive four-cylinder 15s and 20s held up well. The remedy was obvious. A new and adventurous designer/works manager was needed, and his first brief should be to produce a new, smaller four-cylinder car. At the same time as Jack Starley, the last of the founding family members, became Rover's general manager in summer 1910, the search for a new man went ahead. It is at this point that the talented and important figure of Owen Clegg enters the story.

Clegg, like several notable people in the motor industry's pre-war expansion, had been employed at Wolseley for a time, and had risen to works manager after Herbert Austin had left to start his own concern. After a brief sojourn at another Vickers subsidiary in Glasgow, he moved south once again to apply his organisational talents to the Queen Victoria Road factory. There was plenty of scope for him, and for the rationalisation which he thought the place sorely needed. Pedal cycles were still an important part of the scene; the production of motor cycles, dropped in 1905, was about to be resumed; the sleeve-valve engines were about to be revealed to the public; and the 6 hp, 8 hp, 12 hp, 15 hp and 20 hp poppet-valve engined cars were all still listed.

First he began to rationalise the engines, while making sure that the new model he was being asked to design would slot in neatly. The magic figure of 130 mm for a common cylinder stroke was chosen, and the seven-year-old 6 hp 'single' was the last to differ from this. He looked askance at the sleeve-valve cars, decided that he did not like what he saw, but as these were new models he had to agree to giving them a fair trial. All the 'singles' and 'twins', as far as he was concerned, were already under sentence of death, and within a couple of seasons he was determined to populate the factory purely with smooth and modern 'fours'.

For what was, in effect, a brand-new model, Clegg achieved miracles of design, reliability, and speedy tooling up. He joined Rover in September 1910, obviously spent a short time finding his feet again, but had the new, and now legendary Rover 12, at the Olympia motor show and ready for production just over a year later.

Although the war later put paid to sales and production between 1915 and 1919, the new car was destined to be a thorough and long-lasting success. The last versions of the car, then called the 14 but without any change to the engine's displacement, was made in 1924. Clegg's new design was at once up-to-date, conventionally laid out, cheaper than its similar powered predecessors, simple, and reliable.

Although interest centred around the engine, many observers noted that the chassis frame and the underslung worm-drive back axle were derived from the 1911-model sleeve-valve 12, which must have cut down on development time quite noticeably. The separate three-speed gearbox and the brakes, with transmission footbrake and hand brake operating on rear wheel drums, were also familiar items.

The engine itself was rugged, simple, and very clean-looking. It was a monobloc 'four', with a three-bearing crankshaft, and a fixed cylinder head layout (post-war models had detachable cylinder heads). The SU-type carburettor, made under licence by Rover themselves, was bolted direct to the cylinder block, which had all the porting and manifolding cast into it. As the exhaust gallery was also integrally cast, that combined block and head must have been quite a work of the foundry-man's art. The engine had side valves, of course, and screw caps in the cylinder head through which they could be removed or re-inserted for maintenance.

The engine, incidentally, was rated as a 13.9 hp unit, though the car was billed as a 12 in every season except its last. There was nothing new, or unique, in this of course — it was merely indicative of the confusion often caused by the British government's taxation system. Rover, certainly, always looked on their car as a 12 by its size, and the market it was supposed to satisfy. The government was not impressed; all they were interested in, after all, was the cylinder bore which added up in their mathematical calculations to 13.9!

Alongside the new 12, and mechanically closely related to it, was another new model, the 18. Effectively this was the same car, but with a longer wheelbase and a larger engine. The 12's vital statistics were a bore and stroke of 75 mm by 130 mm (2,297 cc), while the 18 measured 90 mm by 130 mm (3,307 cc). The enlarged engine's crankshaft revolved in five main bearings, which made both block and crankshaft unique. The 12 retailed for £350 at first, and the 18 for £500. Although the 12 was popular, the 18's price always went against it. Only about 150 were made, in 1912 and 1913, after which it was discreetly dropped from the range.

With the 12 going into production at the end of 1911, every existing Rover model was unceremoniously dropped. As the 12 and the 18 were closely related, this meant that for the first time the company was beginning to follow an aggressive one-model policy. It had an immediate and beneficial effect on sales, profits and prospects for which Owen Clegg took the main credit.

From 1911 until private car production was closed down in 1915 to make way for the war effort, Rover never built any other cars. Sales boomed from 883 cars in 1911 to no fewer than 1,943 in 1914 and profits jumped from £7,100 to £137,000.

That was the good news. The bad news was that in March 1912, only 18 months after his arrival with such a flourish, Owen Clegg left the company. His master-piece had only been in production for a matter of months, yet he did not stay to engineer the successors and developments of the car which had done so much for his reputation. There was no question of a management disagreement, or of flaming rows between individual staff members. Quite simply, his success with the Rover 12 had suddenly made him a very hot property in the motor industry. Darracq, in France, persuaded him to join them, and to sort out their many problems, which he did with great success. The Darracq 12 and 16 models which followed his arrival had much in common with his Rover, even down to a similar monobloc L-head engine, and the worm-driven back axles.

Clegg's successor was Mark Wild, who was to double as works manager and as chief designer, but for a time he was not encouraged to make many changes. The 12 was selling well, and all the economies promised by the theory of rationalisation were coming to pass.

If ever Rover had been fated to become a quantity-production concern, the 12 might have provided the perfect springboard, but world events prevented this. With Europe sinking inexorably into total war in August 1914, the motor industry found that more serious things were expected of it. Even though private car production continued into 1915, it was soon clear that supplies of materials, and a demand for the cars, would soon run out.

In the meantime, too, Rover motor cycles had reappeared. The original Imperial Rover two-wheeler, announced in 1903, had speedily been overshadowed by the new car in 1904. Only about 1,250 examples were built before Harry Smith made the decision to close down the lines in 1905 and concentrate on the more prestigious and popular Rover cars. There were, it is true, many different makes of British motor cycle, most of which had been announced at about the same time, and it was not at all certain that Rover could have made good profits from their own products. Whatever the merits and the logic of this in 1905, the decision was reversed in 1910. A new 3½ hp motor cycle, rushed through under the guidance of J. E. Greenwood, was ready at the end of the year, and proved to be an immediate success, It was not technically advanced, and not at all related either to the original Imperial motor cycle or to the existing Rover cars, but it sold well without enormous backing or commitment from the company.

With final drive by belt, and only one gear (although a three-speed box soon became optional) it sold for £55 at first, and for £49 in 1912 and beyond. Maximum speed was about 50 mph, probably as fast as most of the company's cars, which was creditable when the simple design of the side-valve 499 cc engine was considered. There were 'TT' models for 1913, and works entries which achieved very little, and provision for side-car fittings (the company also made their own side-cars), but the model's biggest boost came in October 1914, soon after the outbreak of war, when an order for 350 motor cycles was suddenly received from the Russian government. British orders soon followed, though the War Office hedged its bets in two-wheelers (Triumph, in particular, benefited greatly from their dispatch rider requirements). Even so, Rover built more than 3,000 3½ hp motor cycles between 1915 and 1919, almost all of them destined to go to France and the Middle East on military service. It was enough to encourage further enterprise, and a 5/6 hp twin-cylinder machine soon followed, which the Russians adopted in a big way.

Although the outbreak of war was not unexpected — there had been sinister rumblings for months and years in Central Europe — it was not something to which the Rover company were looking forward. The 12 was a splendid light car, but light cars were not what the British forces would want for transport. Once it

was obvious that private car sales would have to stop, and with no military programme arranged to take their place, the company had a problem. How could they
keep their workforce busy?

The build-up of war material production took time to arrange (and — if the
truth be told — the government were not planning for a long war at first), so the
company took on a hotch-potch of contracts to make Stokes mortars, gas shells,
fuses, tank transmissions and the like. Motor cycle orders helped, but it still left a
nasty hole where hundreds of 12s had been made.

In the event, the company was asked to take over manufacture of two important
vehicles for military use — the Maudslay 3-ton lorry and the splendid 16 hp Sunbeam staff car — along with the use of a newly-leased factory at Helen Street,
Coventry to assist them. In neither case was Rover's design expertise involved (both
products were already in production before 1914), but in the hurly-burly of the
war effort the directors were not likely to take umbrage over that. The Maudslay
was a very ordinary machine, and none the worse for that, which was already being
made at Parkside in Coventry, only a few hundred yards from the Queen Victoria
Road works. Rover's efforts merely duplicated those of Maudslay, and speeded up
supplies. Just 500 of them were completed by the Rover company.

The Sunbeam 16, on the other hand, was much more suited to Rover's tastes. It
had been developed by the Wolverhampton-based company from the very successful 3-litre *Coupé de l'Auto* racing two-seater *voiturettes;* and would normally have
been manufactured by Sunbeam themselves. Sunbeam, and their chief designer
Louis Coatalen, were also fully committed to an aero engine programme as well
and, with both given high priority by the authorities, car production had to be
farmed out.

Rover, therefore, took on the Sunbeam contract, supplying these big 3-litre
machines in staff car and ambulance guise. Between 1915 and 1918 they built
1,781 of them, arguably far more than Sunbeam themselves, who were never
quantity-production car makers, could have achieved in the time.

With the arrival of peace, and a hurried re-conversion from war-time to peace-
time factory conditions, Rover had to take stock once again. At the time there
seemed to be an inexhaustible demand for new cars, so the company was very
happy to bring its 12 back into the market. Unfortunately the expenditure on war
material had led to serious inflation, and in November 1919 the Rover was listed at
£750 — double its 1914 price. Every other British car maker was in the same
position, which gave Rover a bit of breathing space, but imports (particularly from
North America) were much cheaper and suddenly very popular indeed.

The 12, inevitably, got itself involved in the price-cutting tactics of the early
1920s which were sparked off by Morris. This was all well and good, and kept the
production lines moving, but it would not have been enough to let the company
prosper. But that, and the expansionist ideas which lay behind Rover's post-war
plans, had already been dealt with. In spite of the fact that the company finished
the Great War with more Coventry-based factories than they had started with, they
were preparing to take on yet another one!

Harry Smith and his fellow directors had enjoyed their private little boom of
1911 to 1914, when turnover had rocketed from £320,000 to £707,000, and were
convinced that their company could keep pace with the expansion of Herbert
Austin in Birmingham, or William Morris at Cowley. They were wrong, we know
that now, but at the time prospects looked good. Like many engineering com-

panies, Rover had had 'a good war', and in 1920 it would break through the £1 million turnover barrier for the first time. They decided to go back into the small-car market that had been abandoned since 1912, and almost at the same time heard of a bright young Birmingham man called Jack Sangster who had a design to sell. The combination of Rover, Sangster and his air-cooled flat-twin 8 hp machine, and a new factory in Tyseley, Birmingham, was quickly forged.

The factory itself, now known as 'Tyseley 1' in British Leyland parlance, had been built before the Great War, used by the government-controlled Component Munitions Ltd to make fuses during the war, and was now on the open market, looking for a new peace-time occupant. Geographically and socially it was a considerable distance from Coventry, but Harry Smith was not perturbed by this.

A deal with Sangster was quickly struck. The novel design was committed for production, and Sangster became assistant works manager. The new 8 would not be assembled in Coventry like the other Rovers, but completed in rolling chassis form and delivered to Coventry for the bodies to be added.

If not by chance, but certainly by a lucky chain of circumstance, for the next few years Rover had settled on a winning formula. The British motorist, hard hit by higher taxation and inflation, was ready to buy a cheap and simple car. Apart from Ford, with their heavily taxed Model T, there were very few competently built cars of this type on the market. The cycle car breed (and the 8 was *not* one of those) was a short-lived joke.

From end to end this 8 was all new. A very simple channel-section chassis frame supported leading quarter-elliptic front springs, and cantilever quarter-elliptics at the rear. The engine itself was the principal novelty, being an air-cooled 998 cc flat-twin, wide enough to allow cut-outs which doubled as air-scoops to be needed in the bonnet panels. Although Jack Sangster had designed the machine, in production form it was certainly no coincidence that the basic cylinder dimensions (a bore of 85 mm and a stroke of 88 mm) were those of the successful 3½ hp Rover motor cycle. Valve gear, like that of the motor cycle, was at 'the side', which because of the layout of the unit meant that the valves and the camshaft were physically on top of the engine.

With an output of about 14 bhp, the little 8 was a sturdy machine and, although its wide-ratio three-speed gearbox allowed it to tackle just about every hill on the public road, the car was no great performer. Anything above 35 mph was a rather resourceful adventure, as the engine peaked at 1,800 rpm which corresponded to about 30 mph.

This willing little car went into production early in 1920 after £400,000 was reputedly spent on tools and fixtures for making it in quantity, a great deal of money measured in 1920s hard currency. For the next four years the 8 and the modernised 12 comprised Rover's entire range, and this sensible concentration on two models paid off. Sales, certainly, shot ahead. In 1920, with the 8 struggling to get established, only 1,400 cars were built. After a further year, the same number of 12s had been made, but 3,175 air-cooled 8s were delivered. The total rose to 6,466 in 1922, dropped back slightly in 1923, and peaked in 1924 at 6,749. In that last year, more than 5,000 sales went to the air-cooled car.

It was all very fine, mostly profitable, and encouraging to staff and shareholders alike, but there were snags. Since Owen Clegg had gone off to work for Darracq in 1912, Rover had effectively been without a specialist designer. Mark Wild, Clegg's successor, was more of a works manager than an innovator, and Sangster left

Rover in 1922 to become assistant managing director of the Ariel motor cycle works in Birmingham. Production, too, was fragmented, with the air-cooled cars effectively being built at Tyseley and the 12 in Coventry.

There was another problem, and his name was Herbert Austin. Having made the biggest possible error in 1919, by deciding to make the Austin company a one-model firm with the wrong, expensive 20 hp car, Austin decided to break into the marginal-motoring business with a new design. The result, of course, was the Austin Seven, announced in the autumn of 1922, and that, potentially, was very bad news indeed for Rover and its air-cooled cars. The problem was two-fold. Austin's dealer network, and his potential output of Austin Sevens, was far greater than that of Rover. Worse was the fact that the Austin Seven was cheaper than almost every other car on the market, and undercut the Rover 8 by £15. That doesn't sound important today, but when the total sum involved was only £165 or £180 it was critical.

In the meantime, Harry Smith retired with failing health, and J. K. Starley was appointed managing director in his place. Starley, in spite of his 25 years with the company, and in spite of the experience and traditions handed down by his illustrious forebears, was not a successful managing director. He was appointed in 1923, and resigned at the beginning of 1929, and in that time the company never made a yearly profit. Its losses, in fact, piled up to the tune of more than £400,000.

For all that, the company jumped precisely the wrong way in 1923 when they decided not to fight Herbert Austin with improved small cars, but to add a massive and expensive (£1,050 for the saloon) 3½-litre car to the range! It was sheer folly, a prestige car which happened rather than was designed, under the guidance of works manager Mark Wild. The engine was really one-and-a-half 12s, sharing the same cylinder dimensions and many details in a big monobloc fixed-head engine of 3,446 cc. The four-wheel brakes were an advance for Rover (they had not been fitted to other models at that stage), but the rest of the car was heavy, conventional and commonplace. The public found it almost unnoticeable at the Olympia motor show in 1923, and declined to place orders. The car, therefore, failed and only three were made!

Starley, as the 'new broom', began to make other changes. Like his pre-war predecessors, he could see the dangers of dispersed resources and, in spite of the company's multiplicity of factory buildings, decided to do something about it. The New Rover Cycle Co Ltd, whose function is obvious, was closed down, and for a short time the parent company took direct control of pedal cycle and motor cycle production. In 1924, however, two-wheeler production was ended altogether — more than 400,000 pedal cycles having been made since 1896, and more than 10,000 motor cycles in the two periods of production which began in 1902/3.

In the same 12 months, Starley also approved two new models, and set the company on its course to the late 1920s. Had he but known it, that course would be stormy and very dramatic. First, and most logical, was the evolution of the 8 into a 9. It was by no means as simple as it sounds, for the 9 had an entirely new little four-cylinder water-cooled engine to replace the well-loved air-cooled flat-twin. Air-cooled units had somehow become stigmatised in the cycle-car boom and there was no doubt that a little 'four' would be quieter, more refined, and more salesworthy

Nobody takes individual credit for the engine — it was probably a 'committee' job guided by Mark Wild, still works manager in Coventry — which was a thoroughly conventional overhead valve unit of 1,074 cc, with a bore and stroke of 60 mm by 95 mm. It produced about 20 bhp at 3,000 rpm and at 329 lb was both heavier than the air-cooled twin and heavy for its purpose. It was a completely unexceptional engine which is precisely what Rover needed at the time and it was to find a place, in developed form, in every yearly programme until the summer of 1933, when it was at last replaced by the Wilks-inspired '100 mm' 10. When announced in the spring of 1924 the 9 was nothing more than a re-engined 8, though considerably more expensive. The 8s price had been cut to the bone (£160) to fight back at the Austin Seven, but was losing that battle. It ran alongside the new water-cooled car for a year or so, then retired gracefully with more than 17,000 sales to its credit.

The 9, for all the fact that it was heavy, under-powered, and mechanically out of date with the 8 chassis, propped up the firm for years. Later, in 1927, there would be a year when all but 200 of the cars built were 9s. Nevertheless, the design was a wasting asset, as its bodies (in the Weymann style, from the Rover company's Parkside body factory) were by no means perfectly built, and the car's quality reputation began to suffer.

The other new Rover, which really ensured that financial upheaval would be certain in later years, was the 14/45 — a replacement for the long-running and still well-liked Clegg-designed 12. Its origins, and its arrival at Rover, make up a curious story. Its designer was none other than Peter Poppe, whose name had already been made in connection with the 'Bullnose' Morris, but his own firm of White and Poppe was not involved!

White and Poppe had come together in Coventry in 1899, and soon began building engines in Lockhurst Lane, Coventry. In 1919, however, Alfred White (who had financial control) sold out to Dennis Brothers of Guildford. Dennis, for their part, felt justified in dictating policy matters, Poppe submitting to this direction for a time. By the beginning of 1924, however, his patience had come to an end and he resigned.

Now comes the astonishing postscript. Poppe's contract, such as it was, did not bind his ideas to the firm which had employed him, nor preclude him from joining a rival. Poppe therefore took with him a complex overhead camshaft four-cylinder engine design on which he had been engaged since 1918 for possible use in a W & P car of his own! He marched down to Starley's office in Queen Victoria Road, offered his services, his engine and his reputation, and was promptly hired by the Rover company. The fact that Alex Craig, a director of Rover, was also a personal friend of Peter Poppe, no doubt helped this along.

In a true fairy tale, Poppe would then have produced the new medium-size Rover in double-quick time, everything would have been sweetness and light, and the financial corner would have been turned. In real life such things rarely happen and, in the case of the 14/45, the opposite was nearer the truth.

Although Poppe had been working away at his new engine design for some years, and there was no doubt that it was very advanced, it produced no more than 20 bhp per litre and there were teething troubles, complaints of valve gear noise and heavy fuel consumption. In short, the 54-year-old Norwegian had produced an engine which looked classic, but which was by no means fully proved.

All the interest in the 14/45 is in the engine, which was a really interesting four-cylinder three-bearing design of 2,132 cc, with a bore and stroke of 75 mm by 120 mm. Combustion chambers were truly hemispherical, and the valves were inclined to each other at an included angle of 90 degrees. The camshaft was actually in the cylinder head, running alongside and outside the inlet valves. The inlets were directly operated (via rockers), while the exhausts were worked through push rods and rockers, the pushrods being threaded horizontally across the head, inside the casting, between the cylinder chambers.

It sounded, and looked, like a recipe for high performance, but such hopes were never realised. The car itself was heavy enough to feel definitely underpowered, so much so that for 1926 it had to be enlarged to an 80 mm bore and 2,413 cc to become the 16/50. The two cars ran together for a couple of seasons, but the engine itself was only to have a complete four-year life. It was, above all, expensive to make, and it is doubtful if the company ever made a profit on the 14/45s and 16/50s actually delivered. In four years — from 1924 to 1928 — less than 2,000 examples were made.

By 1927 the company's finances were in serious disarray. The loss recorded in 1926/27 was £77,945, better than the £123,450 of a year earlier, but still serious for a firm with a mere £1 million turnover. No shareholders' dividends had been paid since 1923, and the situation was beginning to look desperate. At this point the shareholders set up an action committee, and a revolt got under way. They were not prepared to sit back and watch their investments melt away. Dewar trophy awards for publicity achievements by the 14/45 would not pay the wages, nor the company's creditors. Shipment of cars to Australia had been very disappointing, and the company was seriously over-stocked.

Poppe, meantime, had been striving to rescue the company's and his own reputation. To replace the troublesome, handsome and complex overhead-cam 'four' he designed a simple 'straight-six'. This unit, of 2,023 cc, was launched in the autumn of 1927. It was at one and the same time cheaper to build, simpler to service, smaller in displacement, and probably no less powerful than the 14/45 unit, while it had the sweet-running qualities of a 'six' that the 14/45 could never have provided. It was an advance, and it would be a useful engine until 1934, but it could not save the company.

At the beginning of 1928, a shareholders' committee, headed by Herman Jennings and W. D. Sudbury, met Colonel Wyley (Rover's chairman since 1909, and a director since 1907). It was a frigidly conducted meeting, with an unfortunate sequel. Hurt so much by the attitude of the people who had invested in the company, Colonel Wyley resigned and went into retirement. The rest of the directors, realising that they were in serious difficulties, invited Mr Sudbury and Mr Jennings to join them at once. Sudbury, from Matlock, and Jennings, from Sheffield, were both hard-headed north country men with their own ideas about running a car firm, for which, incidentally, neither was particularly qualified.

Sudbury was elected chairman at once and shortly, on the advice of a fellow director, approached Colonel Frank Searle from London, who also had no motor industry experience of any sort, and appointed him a director. Searle's original appointment was as managing director, jointly with J. K. Starley, but it was clear to all that Starley's name would not remain at the head of the list for long. Searle, at least, realised that they could not make a success of reviving the Rover company without the injection of some genuine industrial management talent, and it was at his insistence that the position of general manager was founded. The man interviewed to fill that position in 1929 was Spencer Wilks, and his arrival marked a turning point in the company's affairs.

Chapter 3

Wilks brothers to the rescue

Board meeting minutes: September 3 1929
'On the recommendation of Colonel Searle, Captain S. B. Wilks was interviewed by the board, and it was resolved to appoint him as general manager of the company.'

Board meeting minutes: December 21 1938
'Mr Wilks reported that the programme entered upon by the company in 1932 had been completed in the early part of 1938, and that future development was held up owing to the general trade conditions of the country.

'He considered, however, that it was now necessary to enter upon a plan for the future development of the company's manufacturing facilities, with a view to steadily increasing turnover during the next four or five years . . .'

It is not overstating the case to say that Spencer Wilks saved the Rover company. Not only did he save it, but he also transformed it. Before his arrival in 1929 Rover was in a very rocky state. Within ten years the company's reputation, its financial standing, and its prospects, had been completely transformed. Between 1929 and 1931 Wilks could only take orders, but from 1932 onwards the orders were his. The steady surge forward from then was all inspired by him and — eventually — by his brother Maurice. Without his influence I doubt very much if the company could have survived the Depression.

As already shown, by 1929 the company's problems were serious. There was no single black spot. It was a case of the wrong models at the wrong time, poor quality control, erratic sales forecasts, and inexperienced management. The boardroom revolution of 1928 had not really solved anything. One management team without a clear future strategy had been replaced by another with unsettled ideas. There was a frightening lack of specialised industrial experience. Stability and a bit of forward planning were badly needed.

In hindsight, Colonel Frank Searle certainly made a short-lived impact on the Rover company's affairs, though it was not the sort he would have wanted. He should be remembered, however, for making one vitally important move — it was on his recommendation, in September 1929, that Spencer Wilks was appointed as general manager. Rover had not previously needed such a person, and this was a tacit admission of failure. The board might have been revised, with a new chairman and a new managing director, but actually they knew very little about cars. To hold a substantial shareholding in a company does not guarantee expertise in running it. Sudbury, a Yorkshire-based food importer, had hoped he could.

Management quarrels had also decimated the company's senior staff. The unfortunate Starley had been dismissed in January 1929 without ever coming back from his extended overseas business tour, while Searle clashed with the engine designer Peter Poppe, who was forced to leave in September.

Spencer Bernau Wilks, already a top man in the motor industry, was an ideal choice for Rover's new job. At the Hillman motor car company in Coventry, he already had a formidable record. By the end of the 1920s, he was joint managing director of Hillman along with another ex-military man, Captain John Black. Although a barrister by training, Spencer Wilks had joined Hillman at the close of the Great War.

Both Rover and Standard should have thanked the Rootes family very sincerely. Rootes had bought in to the Hillman company in 1928, as a first step to forming the Rootes group in the early 1930s, and had immediately begun to make their own vigorous and personal impressions on it. Neither Wilks nor Black were happy about this, and looked around for a change. The industry, which recognised good men quickly, was not slow to react. Black moved across town to Standard, where he became managing director in the 1930s, and Wilks moved a couple of miles up the road to Rover.

Although the astute, judicious and very analytical Wilks was not given a seat among the directors at first, he had almost a free hand to make improvements. It wasn't long before other ex-Hillman employees joined Rover — Geoffrey Savage and Jess Worster among them.

One of Wilks' first acts was to commission ex-Hillman engine designer Major B. H. Thomas (who had just completed the Hillman 'straight-eight' engine project) to produce a new, small 'six' engine — as a gap filler between the 1,185 cc Wild-designed 10 and the 2,023 cc/2,565 cc Poppe-designed 'six'. Thomas dealt with this request very competently in the fashionable end-of-1920s manner — effectively by making a 'six' out of the existing 10 hp 'four'. True, both bore and stroke were different, because of the need to get the engine neatly inside one of the RAC's disliked 'taxation horsepower' limits, but the engine's lineage is clear. Detail consideration of its place in the scheme of things comes later — it was, after all, an engine which was important to Rover throughout the 1930s — but at this point we must mention it as an example of Spencer Wilks' foresight and long-term planning. The first model for which he intended it might not have been a great success (and indeed, in the event the Pilot was only to run for a couple of years), but he was already looking beyond it.

As soon as Colonel Searle had hired him, Spencer Wilks became involved in the Searle-inspired rear-engined Scarab project (its history is fully described in Appendix 1), but it was never the sort of new car over which he could enthuse. His younger brother Maurice, a gifted engineer who had moved over to Rover from Hillman at the same time as Spencer, and Robert Boyle were attached to the Scarab, which was to be designed and built in experimental form at Searle's private house near Rugby. Both were back in the factory before the end of 1931.

There was a watershed in the company's affairs near the end of 1931. It came when Colonel Searle set sail for New Zealand (and a visit to Rover's new factory there), and when Spencer Wilks took charge of the day-to-day running of the entire business. Searle was never to return to Rover, while Wilks would officially become its managing director 13 months later, in January 1933.

The company's ups and downs during the Depression can be summarised in two ways — either by looking at events which occurred before and after December

1931, or by looking at the product before and after conception of the entirely new range of cars which would appear in August 1933. The two dates are very closely related. The excellence of Rover in the 1930s is directly related to the troubled times of Searle and the Scarab in 1931.

When Spencer Wilks took up his post at the end of 1929, the 1930 models were already on sale, and the 1931 range was being prepared. He could only grit his teeth for a while, concentrate on minor improvements that his cash-starved company could afford, and look ahead to 1932 and beyond. As he saw it, 1930 though potentially a profitable year would have to look after itself. Unfortunately for him, his standing in Rover was not yet high enough for him to get his own way. The Wilks philosophy, which was to become very clear in the next 30 years, was that quality should always take precedence over quantity. Colonel Frank Searle and his associates thought otherwise — that more and more production would lead to higher and higher sales.

In prosperous times, Searle's philosophy might have worked. In depression-hit Britain, it never stood a chance. British motor industry production hit a new peak in 1929, along with Searle's confidence. More than 180,000 cars were made, of which Rover's share was about four per cent. A year later, industry sales were down to 170,000, but Rover had built 3.5 per cent of them. That was an omen which Searle seemed to ignore. With 1931 the very worst year so far, total car sales sank to 159,000, but Rover built 10,144 — more than six per cent of the total. You will notice the word 'built' — not the word 'sold'.

More Rover cars were built in 1931 than in any previous post-war year, but there were, if anything, fewer genuine Rover customers than ever. Since 1928, quality had sagged, and the cars were piling up, unsold, in dealers' showrooms. Not that the directors had been ignorant of this. They had been warned at one point in 1930 that cars were being made at a rate of 280 a week, while orders totalled only 55 cars. The manufacturing programme for 1930/31 was higher than ever before, though orders continued to be low. It was not surprising that by mid-summer Sudbury and Searle had quarrelled over various matters.

But what of the cars themselves? The 10/25, itself a descendant of the 9, and even of the earlier air-cooled 8, was a car on which Frank Searle pinned many of his hopes. Small family cars, selling faster than previous Rovers, were what he wanted, and he thought the ageing 10/25 could do the job for him.

In 1930 the car was given the backing of greatly increased facilities at Tyseley, a wider and lower chassis frame (the first change, in pedigree, since Jack Sangster designed it in 1919), and a cheap all-steel body from Pressed Steel at Cowley. This was the first such Rover shell, and was supplied in painted and ready-trimmed form for the car finally to be assembled at Tyseley. It set some sort of a record, as the only Rover model to be built there in its entirety. The price, partly due to the less expensive body (quantity-produced Pressed Steel shells were much cheaper than craftsman-erected Weymann bodies), and partly due to Searle's deliberate policy, was down from £250 to £189, which was all very well, except that the car's appearance and performance were disappointing. No matter, until the Wilks plan began to work through, the company had to have a fairly small car, or so they thought, and, perforce, it had to be this one.

A year later, for 1932, the 10/25 was continued with no important changes except that — as was the case with many cars struggling for sales in the Depression — its prices were cut by £10 or so. The revolution came in August 1932, but almost by stealth. The existing 10/25 was continued, without important changes apart from the specification of half-elliptic leaf springs at the rear (quarter-elliptics had graced that chassis, and its ancestors, since 1920), and the use of the new 'corporate-standard' radiator shell; it also got a new name — 'Family 10' — and suffered a slight price increase.

The 'other' 10/25, the '10 Special', shared the same basic four-door body shell, supplied by the Pressed Steel company, but was almost entirely different under the skin. Apart from its well-known engine (and that would only last for another buying season), everything else was new. It was, in many ways, the precursor of the whole series of Wilks-inspired improvements to find its way into production. The chassis itself was straight-sided and channel section, but still kicked up over the back axle. It had half-elliptic front and rear springs, 4 foot 3 inch wheel tracks at front and rear, and an 8 foot 8 inch wheelbase. There was a four-speed gearbox (the old 10/25 had used a three-speed box for a long time) with constant mesh top, third and second gears, and a dramatic innovation for Rover — a driver-controlled roller-and-incline freewheel mounted immediately behind the gearbox. The combined gearbox/freewheel unit was flexibly mounted to the frame by a big circular collar with rubber inserts, and the front of the engine was also rubber-supported. A brand-new Moss spiral bevel final drive replaced the old 10's worm drive, to complete the transformation.

Incidentally, if you think that Spencer Wilks might have done a deal with his old employers at Hillman, so that the '10 Special' could share body panels from the Hillman Minx (both bodies being pressed and assembled by Pressed Steel), you would be right. He had pleaded poverty over the cost of unique press dies. Quite a bit of this sort of unnoticed standardisation went on in the 1930s to keep down costs, but you could be sure that neither Rover nor Hillman would ever admit to it!

The Poppe-designed '2-litre' six-cylinder equipped cars were introduced after the 9/20, actually in the same year that this little car was up-engined to become the 10/25. The smaller of the two engine sizes, the 15.7 hp RAC-rated 2,023 cc version, was dropped officially in the summer of 1934, and the 19.3 hp RAC-rated 2,565 cc unit was carried on into 1935, but it is doubtful if any more than 'old stock' machines from 1933 were ever delivered. There was therefore a gap without a six-cylinder car in the range, before the first of the Maurice Wilks designs appeared in July 1936. A four-speed gearbox became optional on the 2-litre in 1930, but apart from this the chassis was little changed until Spencer Wilks dropped it in 1932. It did, however, lead to two offshoots — the short-lived Light 6, and the rather more successful Meteor models.

The Light 6 cars — either a two-door Sportsman's Saloon or a four-door saloon — were odd machines, with a shorter wheelbase than the 2-litre. The Sportsman saloon had cycle-type front wings and no running boards, a longish bonnet and a dumpy and well set-back two-door body. As a cheaper (by £43) alternative to the 2-litre, it had a point, especially in the unhappy 1930 season, but it never sold at all well, and was dropped after a year. The cynics mark it down as another of the Sudbury/Searle mistakes.

Ironically enough, however, it was the 'Light 6' two-door, crewed by publicity manager Dudley Noble and a couple of journalist friends, which made the headlines in January 1930, by racing the famous French express, the *Blue Train,* from St Raphael on the French Riviera to its destination in Calais. Not withstanding a crash on the way to the start from Nice, the car did everything that was asked of it, the crew managed to find their way and stay awake, and the car eventually won the 'race' by 20 minutes. With 750 miles completed in less than 20 hours, Noble had some cause for celebration, though his brash stunts did not go down too well with the cautious and civilised Spencer Wilks.

The other 2-litre 'offshoot' was the Meteor and its derivatives. Meteors, which also became Speed 16s and Speed 20s before 1935, were more luxurious, better-equipped and considerably more costly than the 2-litres, though built on the same chassis and suspensions. Between 1930 and 1933 the company, in common with most other firms of the period, indulged in a good deal of wheelbase length, engine size and bodyshell re-shuffling. Most Meteors, though, were built around the majestic 9 foot 10 inch wheelbase chassis with wide 4 foot 8.5 inch wheel tracks, and cost around £400 depending on the coachwork chosen. The 'Special Speed Tourers' first built in 1931 had the big 2,565 cc Meteor engines in the short-wheelbase 2-litre 'Light 20' chassis.

New for 1932, and rather an oddball of a car in the same way as was the Wolseley Hornet, came the Pilot. Like the better-known Hornet, it involved the squeezing of a six-cylinder engine into a scarcely altered four-cylinder chassis — in this case the Rover 10/25 frame. Body styles were not altered, nor the wheelbase and axles. The engine, as already noted, was Major Thomas' effort for Spencer Wilks, and was a nice if quite gutless 1,410 cc unit.

For 1933 the Pilots and the Meteors were given a thorough design overhaul by Maurice Wilks and Robert Boyle. Lilke the new 'Ten Special' they were much-changed mechanically, with many features which Spencer Wilks intended to standardise in future years. The Pilot's chassis, as before, was shared with the 10/25, and was the new straight-sided type already described. The Meteors, 16 and 20, shared a 9 foot 10 inch wheelbase version of that frame, along with the suspensions, four-speed constant-mesh gearboxes, free-wheels and spiral bevel axles.

All models, incidentally, benefited from flexible engine mountings, new radiator shell designs pioneered on Scarab, and the weird and complex Lucas Startix electrical system. This last, incidentally, meant that the starter would always come into operation (when suitably switched) every time the engine stalled — a very creditable and worthy feature which produced hilarious results in an unattended car with the choke out!

As in 1931/32, there were many approved examples of special coachwork on Rover chassis, and their abundance tended to disguise the significance of one machine — the Speed Pilot. For 1933 this was given a raised compression ratio and, more importantly, a unique underslung chassis frame. It was, if the Press had only realised it, a very important pointer to the future. The underslung frame at the rear might limit available axle movement, but it also allowed much lower and more sporting bodywork to be fitted. One particular body, the closed two-door four-seater coupé from Carbodies, of Coventry, used this low-slung frame to advantage, and caused quite a stir. An early example, fitted with the newly developed three-carburettor 1,577 cc six-cylinder engine, was fine enough to take the coachwork prize in the RAC Rally, which finished at Hastings. Rover were so inspired by this achievement that they decided to offer it as a catalogue model, and naturally called it the Hastings coupé.

The Hastings' shape, with a four-window cabin, and a notchback shape including a spare wheel bootlid impression, made a big impact on the Wilks brothers.

The 'New Deal' from Rover was almost ready for complete release, but the last piece in the jig-saw — a new range of four-cylinder engines — would have to follow later. In the meantime the Pilot unit was enlarged from 1,410 cc to 1,577 cc by increases in bore and stroke.

Meanwhile, there were big changes behind the publicity screen. In 1930 the company had kept its financial head above water, with a net profit of more than £30,000, but there was still no shareholders' dividend. Greatly increased production in 1931, in defiance of world trends, had led to cars being built and not sold. The result was predictable — in 1931 the company turned in a loss of nearly £80,000, and dealers like Henly's, no doubt worried about their future supplies, were obliged to take delivery of hundreds of obsolete cars at greater discounts.

When Colonel Searle left for Australia and New Zealand at the end of the year, he left Spencer Wilks in charge of Rover's affairs. The Scarab project had been cancelled, and he was desperately hoping that things were already becoming better. He was wrong. By the New Year, the situation was so nearly terminal that Lloyds Bank suggested that an independent financial adviser be appointed. It is at this point that the powerful influence of Howe Graham came on the scene.

Graham, a partner of Messrs Gibson and Ashford, an accountancy business in Birmingham, was appointed to the board as financial director, incredibly enough the first person to hold that specific job in the Rover company. Almost immediately he made it clear that only he and Spencer Wilks should have executive powers, and made sure that Wilks was appointed to the board at once. So far, so good. The next problem was to stem the serious out-flow of cash. Wilks decided to cut production, mount a blitz on quality matters, and to begin a policy of production rationalisation. Graham, for his part, cut a swathe through wasteful expenditure, installed much more rigid costing and cash-flow control, and within months had produced annual cost savings of more than £100,000. Expertise, sadly lacking in recent years, produced almost instant results.

Cars were being made, partly made, and finished in too many places, and Spencer Wilks proposed to put an end to this. Although sentiment suggested otherwise, he decided that the original factory off Queen Victoria Road, sadly under-utilised since the last bicycles and motor cycles had been dropped in mid-1920s, should be sold off. As much work as possible should be concentrated under two roofs — at Tyseley in Birmingham, and in Helen Street, north of Coventry's city centre. Helen Street therefore became the New Meteor Works, and was the centre of all final assembly of Rover cars from 1932 to 1939. The Helen Street buildings, leased from English Electric for so many years, had been purchased for £30,000 in 1929 — and since this price included nearly 13 acres of land, much of it undeveloped, it was a bargain. Tyseley would concentrate on making engines and transmissions, while the practice of building rolling chassis of the 10/25 before delivering them by road to Coventry for body fitment was stopped.

In the middle of this turmoil, Colonel Searle left the company, and for legal reasons connected with the fact that Lloyds were now squeezing their overdraft provision very hard indeed, Howe Graham resigned from the board but continued as an independent adviser. If there was ever a time when Rover might have folded completely, this was it. Losses for the year's trading ending August 1932 were nearly a quarter of a million pounds, and at one stage it looked as if the bank's receiver might have to be called in. Wilks and Graham, who had established a remarkable rapport in no time at all, resisted this move strongly, and almost from that moment the turn round began to take effect. The greatly-improved 1933 models had been introduced early, a few days before the end of July 1932, and once it became clear that the company had much needed successes on their hands the atmosphere cheered up considerably.

Once again Spencer Wilks had cut back the production programme (not entirely from choice, though — there was a limit to the newly concentrated production of Helen Street, after all) — and he only expected to sell 5,000 cars in 1932/33. That target was comfortably achieved and, although it represented little more than two per cent of the British total, Wilks did not mind that. It was the particular two per cent he wanted, and a profitable share at that.

In the winter of 1932/33, too, long-term management stability was finally established. Alex Craig, who had been Rover's chairman on a meeting-by-meeting basis since August 1931, gave way to E. Ransom Harrison, who had joined the directors in April 1931. A few weeks later Spencer Wilks was formally appointed managing director. It was the end of transition, and a happy close to the years of drift and dissent. With profitability restored, Howe Graham was able to rejoin the board in 1934, and for the next 20 years the quintet of Messrs Harrison, Wilks, Graham, Jennings and Frank Ward made an unchanged team.

In August 1933, the 'New Deal' cars were finally ready to be launched, and after seeing them the Press and public were duly impressed. Although existing body styles were little changed, there were new sports saloons which leaned heavily on the Hastings coupé for inspiration. The mechanical transformation was complete. All chassis frames (as presaged by the Speed Pilot) were underslung, but the kernel to the new cars' triumph was the entirely new three-bearing overhead-valve four-cylinder engine.

Students of 1930s motor car construction will realise that it was a deliberately 'stretchable' design, capable of being made in various sizes. It was also arranged so that a 'straight-six' version could easily evolve from it, but that development, at least, would have to wait for a couple of years. The 'family identification mark' which can usually be picked out in any such engine was its 100 mm stroke, a dimension which remained unchanged until the entire design was replaced in 1948. At first, for the 1934 season, there were two variations — 66.5 mm or 69 mm cylinder bore sizes giving 1,389 cc or 1,496 cc — which neatly allowed RAC-rated 10s and 12s to be marketed.

All the previous mechanical fittings — constant-mesh gearbox, freewheel, flexible engine mountings and other details — were carried forward to 1934, and the company also made much of a new feature, the Wilmot-Breeden harmonic stabiliser. This was more of an admission that the chassis design was defective, than an advance in itself. The theory was that chassis frame weaving at the front of the car (more prevalent now that engines were flexibly mounted, and overall rigidity had been lost), could be countered by a high-inertia damper. The stabiliser was nothing more than a very long transverse leaf in spring steel, with heavy bob weights fixed to its extremities. These, in turn, were hidden inside the end rolls of the front bumper. Its effect was certainly over-emphasised at the time, but in overall terms it was a better gimmick than an engineering improvement. That said, it has to be admitted that other manufacturers followed Rover's lead, and that Rover themselves were faithful to the stabilisers until 1947. The last series of post-war P2s had conventional bumpers.

As far as the six-cylinder cars were concerned, the 1934 model news concentrated on coachwork. Among them a four-seater sports tourer and a four-window four-door sports saloon made the biggest impact. The Meteor name, incidentally, had been abandoned. The four-door sports saloon was sold only through Henly's, Rover's London distributors, and, like the Hastings coupé, had coachwork by Carbodies. The notchback shape pioneered on the Hastings was carried through unaltered, and was already fast becoming a recognisable Rover feature.

With one part of his master plan revealed, Spencer Wilks could now turn to the other — the question of his larger cars. Should he push Rover ahead straight away with new 18s and 20s, or was the market too restricted? Work had already started in 1933 on such cars, and the six-cylinder version of the brand-new 'four' was already in existence, before commercial prudence caused the projects to be slowed down. After all, it was barely a year since the traumatic weeks when the arrival of the receiver had seemed to be imminent, and the country's economy as a whole was still pulling itself painfully out of the worst of the Depression.

After a successful first year, the latest range of cars was carried on without change. Bijur automatic chassis lubrication was a feature of 1935 models. The 12 was given an alternative longer wheelbase, while the 14 also got an extra three inches in that department. The only important innovations, held back until October, were the brand-new Streamline cars — a 14 hp six-window saloon and a 14 hp four-window coupé, the latter on the Speed 14 chassis as well as the normal one. Rover, like other car makers, had decided that wind-cheating body styles were becoming fashionable but, like everybody else who didn't really understand aerodynamics, they confined their attentions to the tail! The fronts of these cars (Triumph and SS produced similarly influenced styles) were as bluff as ever, while the tails were smoothly shaped. An almost incidental feature was a useful boot with downward hinging lid, in the base of which the spare wheel hid coyly from view. The slightly lengthened wheelbase helped to make the cars really splendid shapes.

The mystery to Rover enthusiasts was that when the Speed 14 model was first mooted, it was earmarked as the first Wilks-designed car to have independent front suspension. The dealers were told about the feature in the summer, and early brochures certainly boasted of it, but there was a delay. All other 1935 models appeared on schedule in August, but there was no Streamline car. Six weeks later the company had lost its commitment to the technical advance. Independent suspension was confined to Helen Street's 'might have been' cupboard, and the car was sold without it. There was no ifs on a Rover sold to the public before 1948, and that was on the P3 which Gordon Bashford designed.

Incidentally, the splendidly detailed *Autocar* cutaway drawing of the coupé was, and is, incorrect. The familiar engine was shown as having only a single carburettor, when of course it should have had the triple SUs used since the 1933 Hastings prototype was built.

Rover publicity at this time made much of the various engineering features, one of which was 'graded frame stiffness'. What that actually meant was that the chassis frames were weak in torsion, and tended to twist and rack, in spite of the presence of the 'stabilisers'. Virtue was therefore made out of a shortcoming! But we must not mock Rover too much — the whole of the motor industry tended to talk in euphemisms in those days.

For 1936, the biggest news was that there was no news. Existing models were carried forward for another season with little to be talked about. 1936 models could be identified by the slim horizontal grooving in bonnet panels. Serious observers of the scene inferred from all this that something was brewing at Rover for 1937, and they were quite right.

Even though Robert Boyle had gone off to work for Morris Engines (also in Coventry) by then, he and Maurice Wilks had made sweeping improvements to the existing cars, and had been able to pick up the 'frozen' six-cylinder engine programme again. The results were so far-reaching that, although many standard 'building blocks' like the four-cylinder engines and the freewheel transmissions were retained, they became new cars. Styling was considerably changed, and in this form the cars really became the well-loved P2s.

But why P1 or P2? Rover never bothered to explain this at the time, but it seems certain that P stands for project, and that the Wilks-designed cars of 1933/34 had been the first phase. P2, therefore, made sense for the really substantial redesigns.

Spencer Wilks had been thinking about the future 'shape' of his model range for some time, and once told his colleagues that he would rather see a 12-16-20 line-up than a 12-14-18 range. In neither case was he anxious to keep the 10, though it continued to sell well, in spite of having had few important body improvements since the beginning of the 1930s. He could afford to be expansive, after all. The company's record was looking much more healthy, and all his sales projections told him that the expansion would continue. At this point a few statistics might help, and so below is a summary of Rover's activities from 1933, up to the beginning of the Second World War:

Year*	Number of cars built	Total British car production	Rover share (%)	Company net profit
1933	4,960	220,779	2.2	£7,511
1934	5,964	256,866	2.3	£94,439
1935	7,253	311,544	2.3	£152,910
1936	8,335	353,838	2.35	£165,282
1937	10,183	389,633	2.6	£200,921
1938	10,516	342,390	3.1	£168,938
1939	11,103	350,586	3.2	£205,957

Rover's 'year' was calculated from September to the following August, being neatly started and finished by the firm's annual summer holiday.

The recovery since the dark days of 1932 had been quite unprecedented. Debts piled up during the Depression were cleared by 1935, and the first shareholders' dividends for 13 years, apart from a single distribution in 1929, were paid out in 1936. It was all going according to the master plan. The 'New Deal' models of 1932 and 1933 had been produced with the very minimum of capital, but much more was being spent on the new P1 cars. Even so, the profit margin on the P1s and P2s was not excessive — about £14 a car to the company, when the average selling price was in the order of £300. That worked out at less than five per cent.

Perhaps the market could have taken slightly higher prices in 1937, but one must remember that at that time Rover were facing strong competition from firms as diverse as Triumph, Wolseley, Lanchester and Armstrong Siddeley, not to mention the ever-growing threat of the smart SS-Jaguars from Foleshill. To restore liquidity, and to finance the replacement of the ageing 10 body shell in 1938, a further £260,000 capital was raised in 1937. The directors were agreeably pleased to see how readily this was found; it was yet another indication of what the world was beginning to think about the Wilks regime.

The range of P2s was very logical indeed. Every engine but one — the Thomas-designed six-cylinder 14 — was derived from the well-conceived 100 mm stroke family. The new six-cylinder cars, with their 2,147 cc and 2,512 cc displacements, were rated at 16.9 and 19.8 hp by the RAC method. The big 'six' cars had a new chassis with a 9 foot 7 inch wheelbase, a front-mounted steering box, and were considerably more rigid than the older design, but shared many common components. Apart from the dear old 10 with its upright six-window saloon body, as supplied by Pressed Steel since the end of 1930 with only two significant up-dates, all the other 1937 models except the 20 — the 12s, 14s and 16s — shared a choice of saloon body styles. These were on either a 9 foot 4 inch or 9 foot 7 inch wheelbase, the difference being accommodated in the bonnet length, and had either six-window or four-window shapes. Further, the rear doors on the 'six-light' had curved cut-outs, which gave the styling a slightly odd look. Tails, in influence, were almost pure Hastings coupé, so Carbodies were no doubt flattered. The 20 was supplied only in four-window form. Harry Loker had shaped these cars to Maurice Wilks' instructions and the panels were supplied by outside specialists, but erected around ash frameworks at the recently extended Helen Street building in north Coventry. Sadly, because they had not sold as well as hoped, the Streamline cars were dropped. Incidentally, the rival cars from Triumph and SS had also flopped. The public, it seemed, were not yet ready for that type of styling.

This sort of design activity was achieved with very few staff. Jack Swaine did much of the 1930s design work for Maurice Wilks after Robert Boyle had moved on, and considered himself lucky if he even had one junior to help out. 'But we worked on Saturday mornings then, of course,' Jack recalls, 'and I often used to take drawings over to component suppliers one evening on my way home from work, leave them for the night shift to tackle, and sometimes picked up the new parts at breakfast time the day afterwards! It seemed easier, somehow, to get things done.'

Gordon Bashford, who is now fast approaching retirement as a very important member of the Leyland Cars advanced engineering team (and the man who, as we shall see, takes credit for the initial layout of every one of Rover's post-war products), put everything into perspective.

He joined Rover's design department, then at Queen Victoria Road, as an office boy in 1930 for the princely sum of 10s (50p) a week, and remembers vividly then that when he secured a 2s 6d (12½p) rise it felt like riches to him. He moved on in 1933 to Alfred Herbert Ltd, the Coventry-based machine tool makers, but accepted an offer from Rover's drawing office chief Roland Seale to return to the company in 1935.

'By then,' remembers an amused Gordon, 'the design department had moved to Helen Street, into a sort of leaky shed-type building, but we were all very happy. The total drawing office staff, which included all engines, body and chassis people, was probably no more than 15!'

He also makes the point, which became more and more obvious as the Wilks' range developed, that there was a great degree of standardisation right through from 10 to 20. This, unavoidably, meant that the 10 was over-engineered in places, and therefore heavy and none-too-lively, but at least it was impressively reliable.

By 1937 the Wilks brothers had realised that the 10 body was fast reaching obsolescence, and decided that an all-new shell was needed. This would cost nearly £60,000 in new press tools from Pressed Steel, and the car could not possibly be ready before the autumn of 1938. To hold the line, however, they introduced a very smart two-door four-seater coupé 10 at the 1937 show, priced at £280 compared with £255 for the four-door saloon. Its lines were similar to the latest P2s, though the nose would be restyled within a year to fall in with corporate thinking for 1939. All the other 1938 models were given fixed bonnet sides which meant that only the bonnet tops opened, but otherwise it was 'the mixture as before'. A year later, as might have been forecast from the silence in autumn 1937, there were more big changes. Spencer Wilks had already told his fellow directors that with the introduction of 1939 models his six-year plan for Rover's rejuvenation would be complete. The car to complete the jigsaw was the rebodied 10, and at the same time there would be a new engine for the 14.

Perhaps the 1,901 cc six-cylinder engine for the 14 was even more important than the new 10 body shell. It meant that seven years after design had been initiated every Rover car was being made with the same basic design of engine, transmission and chassis, and that the entire family had 'look-alike' styling. The six-year-old 1,577 cc engine had been a 'cuckoo' in the line-up for a couple of years, and its demise was expected. In its place was yet another version of the ubiquitous 100 mm stroke family, an under-bored version of the 16 which, really as a bit of cheat, was RAC-rated as a 14.9 hp car.

Standardisation was now impressive. One basic engine design from Tyseley, in four-cylinder or six-cylinder form, with five different cylinder bores and piston sizes, catered for every Rover from the 10 to the 20. They all shared the same, new transmission, the same freewheel and the same axle. Frames, in three wheelbase lengths, were of two related types. Bodies of all but the 10 were based on the same cabin, either in six-window or four-window guise.

Behind all the engines was the new synchromesh gearbox. This was several years late by comparison with companies in the industry's 'Big Six', but at least the old non-synchromesh change had had constant-mesh gears, and was made easy by the provision of the freewheel. For no good reason, Rover omitted to provide synchromesh on second gear — a feature which would have to wait until 1953, when it was first applied to P4 and was offered to the Rover customer.

Maurice Wilks, like other British designers, was now paying more attention to a car's roadholding and, although he was not prepared to offer independent front suspension at that stage, he did develop anti-roll bars for the front *and* rear suspensions of all the six-cylinder cars. A year later, when announcing the abortive 1940 programme, the anti-roll bars were also fitted to the 12, but never offered for the 10. The main changes to that 1940 range were power increases for six-cylinder cars through carburettor and manifolding improvements, and the standardisation of pressed steel disc road wheels which had been optional to the wire-spoke variety since 1938. All except the 10 had their rear track increased to 4 feet 6 inches, and rear seat space was enlarged appropriately.

Perhaps war came at exactly the right time as far as Rover's private car sales were concerned. Nothing now could sully that splendid reputation for quality in design and construction. The company's advertising slogan 'One of Britain's Fine Cars' was no exaggeration, and in that fiercely contested middle-class British market the Rover was certainly a leader. Rover sentimentalists would never admit this, even today, but there were signs that the rationalised design would shortly begin to lag behind the industry. SS-Jaguar, in particular, might only have needed another couple of years to finalise their own new developments, and with the performance image they already held that could have posed serious problems. But Spencer Wilks and his brother Maurice were not worried about conjecture. From September 3 1939, they had more world-shattering things to think about.

Chapter 4

Underground, overground — Rover's war machines

Board meeting minutes: April 27 1939

'Mr Wilks reported that discussions had taken place with leading officials of the Air Ministry and suggestions made by the Ministry that we should undertake the erection, equipment, and management of a factory for the manufacture of complete aeroplane engines.

'He pointed out that in the event of war this scheme would mean the stoppage of manufacture of motor cars by us, and that our *entire organisation* would be dislocated . . .'

Board meeting minutes: November 26 1940

'A report was made that our Coventry works had been severely damaged in the raid by German aeroplanes on the night of November 14. It had been necessary to transfer the offices, and these were now being located in that portion of the Chesford Grange Hotel which was available . . .'

Even in 1936, to many people another war looked inevitable. After years of vacillation, and of sticking its collective head in the sand, our government finally recognised the possibility, and set about re-arming on a big scale. This, although they did not suspect it at the time, was going to affect Rover in a big way.

At the time, certainly, the Wilks brothers looked on it all as a chore, a diversion away from the master plan that was still being developed in Coventry, but eventually it would be looked on as a period of which the company could be proud. Even three years earlier, Rover would certainly not have been asked to co-operate in a major government innovation; the company's standing was still too rocky for that. When the opportunity arose in April 1936, it was something of an honour. Spencer Wilks knew that his new policy had helped to work wonders for the company — now his success had tacitly been approved by outside bodies. After all, if Rover could now be bracketed with Austin, Daimler, Rootes, Standard, and a few others, was this not recognition of a remarkable transformation?

The Air Ministry's proposal was simple and straightforward. Would Rover, along with a handful of other car makers in the Midlands, be prepared to join in a 'shadow factory' scheme? Further, would they be willing to divert resources, mainly management and systems, at once to get their part of the scheme under way?

The board's first, impulsive, inclination was to turn the government down, particularly as at that time there was no immediate conflict in prospect, and they had quite enough on their corporate 'plates' already. A more mature judgment was that they should accept the task as a duty to the nation, to help build up its defences, and hope that motor car development would not be disrupted too much. It is fair to say that most firms approached in the first instance went through the same processes of doubt. Only Lord Nuffield, who was angrily in dispute with that Ministry over Wolseley aeroplane engine schemes, turned them down flat.

But what was this new invention — the 'shadow factory'? What sort of shadow exactly? Shadows have no substance, and are impossible to touch. They disappear when the sun goes down, when the lights go out. Was that the sort of factory involved? It was nothing quite as romantic as that. The 'shadow' in this case meant that the new buildings would live in the shadow of the aero-engine specialists. Their problem was that their own production facilities could not suddenly cope with the increase in military orders, and that new government financed factories would have to help solve the problem. The new buildings, in every way, would be 'shadows', with the same type of machinery, the same products, and the same standards.

Certainly there was nothing secret about them. The world knew about the 'shadow factory' scheme before a single part had been made, and the government wanted to use this knowledge as a deterrent to further war-mongering from abroad. At least once the Rover management welcomed an official delegation of Germans to inspect their production methods!

The scheme was a triumph of foresight because it was so rare. Here was a plan thought up by government, one which worked, and one which was in operation before the need actually arose. In every way, the setting up of the new factories proved to be a great boost to Rover's prospects. Whereas the other motor industry participants all welcomed their 'shadows' very close to existing plants, Rover were asked to take over management of a new building about 20 miles away!

Standard, for instance, saw the new building they were to manage erected alongside the Canley plant, and the Daimler-managed factory rose behind their Radford buildings. The first Rootes 'shadow' was at Stoke Aldermoor, behind the Humber-Hillman assembly lines. Rover had no spare land to make that possible. Helen Street's buildings were hemmed in on three sides by housing, and the Parkside plant leaned heavily on Armstrong-Siddeley anyway. For better or worse (and to Spencer Wilks, in 1936, it was 'worse') they were offered a building at Acocks Green, just a few miles from the Rover components factory at Tyseley.

Acocks Green, now an engine-manufacturing plant servicing the tracks at Solihull, was to be constructed on a green-field site near the outskirts of Birmingham, and would not involve Rover in providing any risk capital. It would be erected, equipped, stocked and even provided with labour by the government themselves. Rover, for their part, would undertake the organisation and management of the plant, which would initially be readied to make parts for Bristol Hercules radial engines. Production would be at a low level at first, even though the factory would be completely equipped to accommodate many more workers. The rate of production could rapidly be built up in the event of a serious national emergency, when it was assumed that the motor industry's involvement in private car production would be rapidly run down.

Once started, the scheme rapidly took shape. The first confidential approaches reached the company in April 1936, the news of the scheme was made public in July and building started in October. Production commenced in July 1937, and deliveries to Bristol began at once. Incidentally, the other car makers involved in the initial scheme were Austin, Rootes, Daimler, Standard and Singer — all but one, be it noted, being centred in Coventry, which was very much the hub of the motor industry at the time.

The Rover management, like any other clear-thinking British citizen, would have been happy for all threats of war to be swept away, and from time to time they made no secret of their distaste for the aggravation caused by management of Acocks Green. The Munich crisis of 1938 died down so quickly that it had little effect on the aero-engine manufacturers' demands, but by the spring of 1939 all hope of continued peace seemed to have gone. In April, therefore, Spencer Wilks was once again approached by the Air Ministry, who were planning the second, and much more ambitious phase, in the 'shadow factory' scheme. The new proposal was that Rover should undertake the erection, equipment and management of another plant — the purpose on this occasion being to look after the manufacture of complete Hercules radial engines, in association with the Rootes group.

This sounded like, and was, a much bigger undertaking. The new factory would be at least three times as large and complex as the Acocks Green plant, and up to 7,000 workers would be employed. By Rover's existing standards it was a vast project, and the directors were, at first, alarmed by the implications. Once again, however, considerations of national security and patriotism outweighed mere commercial caution, and the proposal was accepted. The new factory, to be called Rover Shadow Factory No 2, which automatically meant that Acocks Green would be retitled 'Shadow Factory No 1', was to be on farmland immediately north of Solihull. The requisitioned area totalled 65 acres. Very prudently, too, the company decided to take the opportunity of buying nearly 200 acres of agricultural land surrounding the new site — a brilliant long-term move for which latter-day management should have been eternally grateful. Without it, and if other development had taken place on the land instead, Rover's two largest pieces of expansion at Solihull — the Rover 2000 North Block and the latest SD1 factory — would never have been feasible.

Once the company had agreed to take over management of the Solihull project, things got under way very fast. General site excavation began in June, foundations were initiated in July, and the first Hercules components were machined in January 1940. In spite of the severe winter of 1940, which meant that outside building work was often impossible, that conditions inside the unfinished factory were arctic, work was well and truly under way in the spring. The building, including a batch of test beds, was virtually finished by September 1940, and the first completely Rover-built Hercules was being tested in October.

In the meantime, the crises, and the Air Ministry's requirements, had doubled and redoubled. By July 1939 Spencer Wilks had been approached to see if he could find space in Helen Street and Tyseley for repair and servicing work of Armstrong-Siddeley Cheetah aero engines — with the proviso that *if* war broke out — the Air Ministry was still praying for a miracle! — Rover would consider manufacturing these as well. Around the same time, components for Pegasus engines were sourced from 'No 1' along with increased orders for Hercules parts.

The international situation in the summer of 1939, and all its horrific undertones, had made logical planning of a car programme for 1940 almost impossible. On September 4 1939, the first Monday after Neville Chamberlain's historic radio broadcast to the people of Britain, the directors were almost relieved to be able to discuss their company's proposed war efforts. All was not clear, except that 'shadow factory' work would be kept clear of motor car factory work. The Cheetah maintenance contract went ahead, and preparations were made for any air-frame construction work which would be allocated to the firm.

Re-equipping the motor car factories took time, even under the feverishly active pressure of wartime emergency conditions. Much of the existing car making equipment, the production lines, and allied facilities had to be moved, but by July 1940 the body-erecting shops had begun making airframe parts for Albemarle aircraft (and later would be involved in making wings for Lancasters and Bristol war planes). Surprisingly enough, some 1940 model cars *were* made after the outbreak of war — mainly from existing stocks — as there was little point in the factory being completely idle while new jigs and fixtures for aircraft work were still being made. The last 'pre-war' Rover was built in May 1940, after which all possible priority was given to war work. A service facility was maintained throughout the conflict, as many of the long-lasting Rover cars were being used on essential business.

However, there were more upsets to come. The war had only been under way for a few months, when Spencer Wilks was again approached by the government and asked to give support to a radically new and very secret development — Frank Whittle's gas turbine 'jet' engine project. Wilks, an urbane and equable man at all times, was really rather flabbergasted by this, not only because he sensed that his engineers knew nothing about the subject (it had been, after all, highly secret up until then), but because it was an entirely new type of venture for him. No matter. He was nothing if not patriotic, and entered into discussions on the subject at once. An interesting point is that the government were so terrified there might be security leaks somewhere along the line, that they instructed Rover and all other people involved in the work to refer to Whittle's invention as a 'supercharger'.

Whittle's little company, Power Jets Ltd, was based in a converted foundry in Lutterworth, only 16 miles from Coventry. Although they were the world's leaders in turbo-jet design (and their first Whittle-engine flight would be in 1941) they were chronically short of production facilities. Power Jets at Lutterworth was purely an experimental workshop, and a pilot-build plant at Whetstone, near Leicester, was not even being considered at that stage, though it followed later in the war. Parts for Whittle jets had come mainly from BTH, who made big industrial turbines at Rugby, and from Joseph Lucas in Birmingham.

The original scheme was that Rover would develop a Whittle design to production state, and might then begin manufacture of the engines for RAF use. Rover were happy to know that Gloster Aircraft, for whom they were already tackling Albemarle airframe work, would be designing the first 'jet' fighter, which eventually became known as the Meteor. It is important to realise that at this time Rolls-Royce had absolutely no interest in gas turbines, since they were fully committed to vee-12 piston-engined Merlin production. Their name, however, will soon re-enter the story.

From the spring of 1940 work went ahead cheerfully enough, but soon it became clear that there were going to be serious personality differences between Frank Whittle and the Rover engineers. Whittle, whose Power Jets concern's main task was to act as innovators, soon became convinced that Rover engineers were altering ('improving' was not a word he used at any stage) his designs, both in detail and in basic concept, without consulting him or his staff. His own autobiography *Jet* makes this quite clear.

Before gas turbine work at Solihull became an important part of Rover's war efforts, however, the German Luftwaffe took a hand in events. The night of

November 14/15 1940, a Thursday night, has long been notorious as the one on which the bombers concentrated their venom on Coventry. Much of the city's historic centre was razed, or burnt, and elsewhere in the district many factories received attention. Rover's Helen Street plant, north of the city centre, was badly damaged by blast bombs and incendiaries, so much so that Albemarle production was halted, and the Cheetah section gravely inconvenienced. This sort of calamity had already been foreseen and dispersal of many activities was being planned. The raids merely made it more urgent. Within days the offices had been moved away from the industrial squalor of Helen Street to the calm of the expensive Chesford Grange Hotel, near Kenilworth, But as Gordon Bashford relates: 'It wasn't as luxurious as all that. Most of us were in the ballroom — a great barn of a place without much light, and with a very high ceiling. But at least we weren't bombed again!'

As far as production was concerned, the dispersals were far flung. Principal among them was a group of disused cotton mills in Lancashire, and the requisition of other mills in nearby Yorkshire. By the time expansion was complete in 1942, Rover's control extended to 18 different factories, of which six were 'shadow' premises owned by the government.

The north-west group comprised Waterloo Mill in Clitheroe, Grove Mill and Soughbridge Mill in Earby, Carleton Mill near Skipton, Calf Hall, Butts Mill and Bankfield Shed in Barnoldswick, along with administrative offices in the splendour of Bracewell Hall. There was also a mill in Nottingham, where work on behalf of Rolls-Royce was carried out, smaller premises dotted around the Midlands, and a remarkable and highly-secret underground factory at Drakelow near Kidderminster.

The size and scope of the much-expanded Rover companies was this — in 1944 their own employees, including all staff, totalled 3,780, but through the dispersals and the fee-contracted work for the Air Ministry, they controlled a further 20,000 workers. A far cry, indeed, from the run-down concern which Spencer Wilks had joined in 1929.

The underground 'shadow factory', one of several built in the Second World War, should more accurately be described as an 'underhill factory'. The object, obviously, was to make it invisible and impregnable from air attack. It had first been discussed with Rover managers in the spring of 1941, and 27 different sites were studied before a choice was made. Blakeshall Common, near Kinver Edge, north of Kidderminster, was earmarked for the purpose. The factory floor space comprised a network of large corridors cut into the hillside. Excavation began in July 1941, machinery was installed in September 1942, and production actually began during the winter. The site covered more than 50 acres and it was intended as a back-up and as a feeder plant for Acocks Green and Solihull.

Parts for Pegasus and Hercules engines at first, and Centaurus engines later, were all machined underground at Drakelow, but the factory was speedily run down in 1945 when victory had been gained.

All this, of course, paled into insignificance compared with the secrecy, the excitement, and the technological challenge of the new 'supercharger'. Unbelievably, the government had removed all priority from this work in the late spring of 1940 because the need to build up conventional arms was thought more important, but from November 1940 this situation was reversed. From then on there was never any doubt that improvement and proving of the Whittle machine was of great national importance. Dispersal to Clitheroe and Barnoldswick was decided

Above *Plan view of the original 1904 8 hp Rover car, with single-cylinder vertical engine, and backbone transmission/chassis.*

Below *One of the victorious 16/20 Rovers entered in the 1907 Isle of Man TT race — a passenger had to be carried on race day.*

Above *J. K. Starley posed on a typical Rover product of the late 1890s.*

Below *Starley's first motor-driven machine, really a pedal tricycle with a feeble electric motor in the back axle. The batteries were carried in the wicker container.*

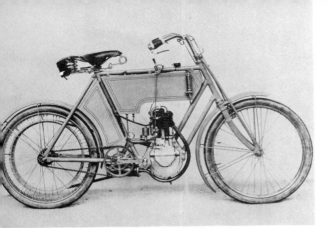

ROVER 12 h.p. FOUR-CYLINDER CAR

300 Gns.

Tax. 14 b. B.H.P. 22

Three speeds, gate change, worm drive back axle, Bosch magneto, full inside splashers to front and back guards, and wheels made detachable.

For full Specification see p. 15.

Chassis · · £275
complete with 4 wheels only, tyres and spares

Complete Car · · · · · £350
Including hood, screen, two acetylene head lamps with separate generator, two side and one tail paraffin lamps (electric extra), horn, spare wheel and steel studded tyre.

Above *A 1913 advertisement for the Clegg-designed Rover 12 hp.*

Above left *Rover's first engine-powered machine — the 2 ¼ hp Imperial motorcycle, which retailed for £55.*

Left *The 15 hp of 1910 — here in landaulette form — which cost £375 in chassis guise and £510 with this particular coachwork. The spare wheel was an extra for £20.*

Below *The 'vintage' years in Coventry. Building bodies on the larger-engined cars in this case, was so much simpler then.*

Above *Well-known picture of Rover air-cooled 8s outside the Tyseley works. But they are not on 'road test'! They are on the way to Coventry, on Coventry trade plates, for the bodies to be fitted.*

Right *The Hertford Street frontage in Coventry during the 1920s, with a 14/45 Rover parked outside. The frontage still stands in this much-redeveloped area.*

Below *The 14/45 of 1925, with — hidden away — the complex Poppe-designed four-cylinder engine.*

Above *The Meteor 20 of 1930, looking slightly sleeker in this artist's rendering than it was in fact.*

Left *A rare and formal portrait of Colonel Frank Searle, Rover's managing director for three years, 1929-1932.*

Below *The Hastings Coupé car of 1933 which started a trend to sleek Rover sports saloons in the 1930s and 1940s.*

Above *Building 1930s P1 models at Helen Street — the final finish area.*

Right *P2 elegance at its height — the 1939 model six-cylinder 14 hp model in six window form. There was also the four window four-door sports saloon version on the same chassis.*

Below *The Ten Special for 1933 — same basic bodywork as the ageing 10/25, but much improved chassis and details under the skin. This body shared many panels with the contemporary Hillman Minx.*

Above *Helen Street during the Second World War — Albemarle centre sections being assembled (foreground) along with wings for the Lancaster bomber.*

Left *The dark doorway leads to Rover's underground 'shadow factory' near Kidderminster, used in the 1940s.*

Below *A mixture of post-war and pre-war. The scene is Solihull but the cars are P2s designed in the 1930s. The date — 1946.*

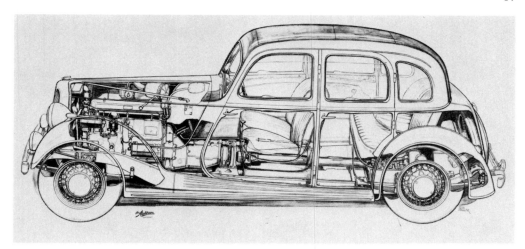

Above *Typical of all P2s was the 1939 14 hp model, with its six-cylinder 1,901 cc engine. Note the freewheel behind the gearbox, the underslung rear chassis frame, rear-mounted batteries, and front anti-roll bar. There was also a four window version on the same chassis.*

Right *The underground Drakelow factory consisted of a series of long corridors. There was no assembly on this site, which was completely given over to machining operations.*

Below *The mess left by the bombing in November 1940 at Helen Street, Coventry.*

Above *Rover's own jet turbine design and the world's first 'straight-through' layout, which is the true ancestor of the first Rolls-Royce 'production' jets. It was this design which caused such disagreement with Frank Whittle.*

Above left *1945, and one of several attempts to marry a full-width nose to the classic P2/P3 passenger cabin. These were not a success.*

Left *The Rover Meteor vee-12 engine, developed from the supercharged Merlin aeroplane engine, and tailored for use in British tanks.*

Below *Thornycroft's 'Mighty Antar' tank transporter.*

upon at once and completed in 1941. Bankfield Shed at Barnoldswick had been closed in the gloomy days of the 1930s textile trade depression. Later, it became even more famous in Rolls-Royce's hands and even today modern R-R engine type numbers such as RB211 carry the designation 'RB' for Rolls-Royce Barnoldswick.

The first development engines, made to Whittle's W2 design, used Rover expertise in the area of accessory drives, but was otherwise unchanged. In spite of close links with Lucas over combustion and fuel systems, there was serious trouble from surging and the failure of turbine blades. Misunderstandings, and the difficult atmosphere between Power Jets and Rover, did nothing to improve the situation, which was rather embarrassing to one of Whittle's staff, J. C. B. Tinling, as it was his initiative at social level with the Maurice Wilks' which had brought about Rover's involvement in the first place.

The W2 proved to be seriously underpowered, and Rover were then asked to go ahead with development around Whittle's W2B design, which meant that they undertook considerable mechanical design of their own. The first Rover-built W2Bs were running, in the Lancashire factories, by October 1941, even though Whittle himself was furious at design changes made from his own firm's layout.

In view of the complicated political situation which has only become clear in recent years, it is rather miraculous that jet engines were developed at all. Vauxhall Motors, for instance, were also to have been involved at one stage, but withdrew when faced with other priority contracts. Why on earth Rover should have been asked to undertake development, when an aero engine firm like Bristol or Armstrong-Siddeley, not to mention Rolls-Royce, were so ideally qualified, is a mystery still lodged in Whitehall.

Although Rover were asked to plan for quantity production of W2Bs at Clitheroe and Barnoldswick, they also asked for, and received, permission to begin design of a rather different layout. Project work was carried out in great secrecy — so secret that not even Frank Whittle was informed — on a new engine called the B26. Rover's engine designers had reached the conclusion that Whittle's W1 and W2 engines were aerodynamically inefficient internally because of the counterflow arrangement of compressors, combustion canisters, and turbines. Their B26 would be a straight through design, while retaining the best of the original centrifugal compressor layout. The prototype B26 ran for the first time in November 1942, and almost immediately showed a great improvement in thrust and reliability. It is gratifying to all students of aviation to realise that the world's first 'production' jet — the Rolls-Royce Welland — was based on a motor car company's design!

By the end of 1942 Rover were the most prolific of the jet engine developers which now included de Havilland, whose own project was not nearly as far advanced. In August one of the Whittle-type W2Bs had been installed in the tail of a Wellington, and flown from the Rolls-Royce flight test field at Hucknall, near Nottingham. More than 30 engines of all types, mainly developments of W2Bs, had been built. With a government decision about to be made on quantity production of gas turbine engines, and Gloster all ready to begin manufacture of Meteor fighter planes, Rolls-Royce threw their hat into the ring. After years of saying that they were far too busy to do more than watch other people's progress in gas turbine development, they now announced that as a matter of policy they would want to get involved in such work as soon as possible. However, because of their all-pervading commitment to the Merlin vee-12s, they would need extra factories in which to do this.

With this sort of commitment made public to the authorities, and with Rolls-Royce's obvious claims to lasting fame in the aero engine business, their wishes clearly had to be taken seriously. It was not too much to say, after all, that their legendary Merlin engines were helping to win the aerial war for Great Britain. The fact that the Rover management, in spite of its acknowledged successes with the new technology engines, was not at all sure that it wished to continue with aircraft engines on a long-term basis, made the situation intriguing.

The solution, proposed, accepted and implemented very quickly at the end of 1942 was a masterly compromise which left both Rover and Rolls-Royce happy. It was really very simple — Rover would hand over their gas turbine work, and in exchange Rolls-Royce would present them with a large and vital tank engine contract. Rolls would get the gas turbine technology to play with, while Rover would occupy themselves with mass production of a splendidly advanced piston engine. In fact Rover were asked to complete their existing development contracts before handing over all the prototype engines, the rest of the hardware, and the premises. It was not until July 1943 that Bankfield Shed and Waterloo Mill were officially released. Then, and only then, could Maurice Wilks, Robert Boyle, Jack Swaine and Roland Seale move back from Lancashire to the Midlands.

In exchange, Rover took over the entire Rolls-Royce Meteor engine project. This, of course, was a much-modified and unsupercharged version of the vee-12 Merlin unit, and was intended for the latest heavy allied tanks. Meteor, incidentally, was a name already given to the engine before it was handed over to Rover — the fact that the same name applied to the Coventry factory was no more than coincidence. It was, by a long way, the most powerful piston engine with which the company has ever been linked. Something like 700 bhp was available — all very necessary when the weight of the tanks using the engine is considered. Major B. H. Thomas, already noted for Rover engine work in peace-time, and now managing the Birmingham-based 'shadow factories', had much to do with the Meteor's development. The engine, in Mark IV form, sprang to prominence as the world-famous Centurion tank's power unit, and later the fuel-injected M120 type powered the even bigger and more impressive Conqueror.

Since 1943, when the company started work on the Meteor, it had been assigned all rights to the design, and its evolution. In all its production forms, therefore, the Meteor was a 'Rover' engine. From the end of the hostilities, the Acocks Green factory was designated as the home of fighting vehicle engine research in collaboration with the Fighting Vehicle Research and Design Establishment (FVRDE) at Chobham. It was partly their desire to encourage a family of heavy duty engines, using many common parts, which led to Rover's ingenious Meteorite engine range being built. Meteorite came into the world in the late 1940s, and was, in essence, two-thirds of a Meteor engine. That is to say that it was a vee-8 (the Meteor was a vee-12), with a 60 degree included angle between cylinder banks. This, naturally enough, was not normal for a vee-8, but it did at least mean that the complex cylinder block machining could be carried out on the same production lines.

Meteorites were built in petrol and diesel engine forms, for vehicles, for marine use, and as stationary power units. The Mighty Antar (from Thornycroft) was powered by a Meteorite, often when dragging Meteor-engined tanks around the world. Rover's association with the defence ministries in this critically important engine project carried on for 21 continuous years into 1964 and work was always centred at Acocks Green.

Gas turbine engines usually take all the glamour in references to Rover's war-time activities. Even so, the piston engines, all radials apart from the Meteors, which poured out of the 'shadow factories', and the thousands of airframe parts built in the damaged Helen Street works, were much more numerous. Not to be forgotten were the Army webbing contracts completed at Hinckley, overhaul and repair of aircraft magnetos at Lutterworth, vehicle body manufacture and the building of aero engine test stands at the London Seagrave Road service buildings.

No one who lived through the feverish excitement, fear, gloom, and exhilaration of the war years will ever forget it. To take part, and to strive for success, became second nature. Working hours tended to become horrifyingly extended, and the pressure was continuous. By 1944, with a bridgehead firmly established on the continent, it was obvious that an end to the fighting was in sight. This, naturally, would immediately mean stopping most war-production work, and the company would be able to think about its normal peace-time activities again. But Rover, as a car making firm, would never be the same again. For one thing, its Helen Street premises in Coventry were still badly damaged. For another, its staff were dispersed among several factories, and, most important of all, it was now a much larger business than ever before. Post-war conditions would be different from the 1930s, and depending on the political climate the demand for Rover's type of quality middle-class cars might be greatly changed. Spencer Wilks was not at all sure what awaited him in peace-time but, as usual, he was looking forward to the challenge.

Chapter 5

'One of Britain's fine cars' — the 'Auntie' era

Board meeting minutes: July 4 1947

'Mr S. B. Wilks outlined to the board the features of the P3 models, including independent front suspension, new sloping-head engines, and wider bodies . . . Mr Wilks also outlined the development that had so far taken place on the P4 models which would follow the P3 . . . He said that the tendency was towards wider and roomier bodies which necessitated taking the body out to the full width of the existing running boards, and that this in turn necessitated altering the shape of the body.'

Wartime activities had proved quite a lot about the Rover company. Work on the gas turbine engines, on the aircraft engines, and the fuselage sections to match them, had proved that Rover were not so staid and backward looking as its cars in the 1930s might have suggested. It was merely that Spencer Wilks had preferred his cars that way.

On the other hand, the weapons of war had been complex, ultra-modern and terrifying, but that didn't mean that the post-war cars would be the same. Indeed, it was not until 1944 that Spencer and Maurice Wilks could begin to think about their future in any detail.

The brothers had many bright ideas to develop, but they were in no hurry. At first, for sure, the post-war products would have to be like those of the 1930s — smooth, peaceful, refined and utterly conventional in every way. Should we really have expected anything more, at first? The firm, after all, had been engaged in total war. Even so, in the relief brought about by victory, and by peace after nearly six years, the world of motoring was a more frivolous place. The wags took a long look at Rover's offerings and the sort of buyers they attracted and made a firm decision. Rovers were 'Aunties' — and so they remained. It would be nearly 20 years before anybody had any reason to recant.

Rovers of the 1940s and 1950s were 'Aunties' because of their looks and the way they did things. Aunts and great aunts were usually dignified, their skirts were always too long, and they sometimes smelt endearingly of camphor, coal fires and country tweeds. Could anything define a P3 or a P4 better?

Spencer and Maurice Wilks were highly amused; they thought it was all great sport. In a changing world where Rover needed to keep its traditional customers, what reputation could be better? They advertised it as 'One of Britain's fine cars' — and it was. Rover cars began to be discussed with the same sort of deference as a Daimler or even a Rolls-Royce.

A car like a Rover which didn't appeal to the trendies, the young, and the brash was just what the professional men rushed to buy. The trendies usually didn't have much cash anyway; the professional men had enough. Rover's immediate future was assured. That was what Wilks had been working for throughout the 1930s. He had almost forged this reputation for 'his' company by 1939, and the nostalgia caused by six car-starved war years did the rest. Selling the post-war Rovers, therefore, didn't look like being a problem. But precisely what sort of cars should they be, and where should they be assembled? The hustle and bustle of getting any sort of car into production again solved the first problem. With no more than minor changes the 1940-model cars, which had barely started to be produced in August and September 1939, would have to be sold.

The 'where' and the 'how' was complicated by the efforts of the German air force. In November 1940, and again in the spring of 1941, the bombers had made a very good job of damaging the Helen Street premises. Hasty and temporary repairs had allowed most of the plant to carry on turning out useful war material — aero engines and airframes — but much would have to be done to make it a proper peace-time car-producing plant. The other 'satellite' factories in Coventry were much too small, and Tyseley was purely a components machining and assembly building. Fortunately, a speedy run-down in the war effort provided an answer. Spencer Wilks, ever the forward planner, had already been assured about the future of the Solihull 'Number Two' shadow factory; if and when the time came for the government to give it up, then Rover would have first refusal as to its future. On the other hand, it was made clear that a licence to rebuild Helen Street would probably be refused . . .

By the end of 1944, the die was cast. The company decided that its peace-time operations should be centred on Solihull, and that the Helen Street works should be patched up and sold. For the first time, since the 1870s, the company's centre of gravity would move out of Coventry.

Is was a momentous year in many ways. On a personal note, company secretary Frank Ward resigned from his position, though he remained on the board of directors well into the 1950s; in 1944 he had already served Rover for 55 years, having been with John Starley since the very early Rover Safety cycle days. Of more importance, commercially, was the fact that the company had applied for government permission to resume post-war private car development and production — and had been refused. There was confusion and consternation about this because, at the time, the company was sure that its competitors would be allowed to establish a lead which could not be overtaken. The smartest operators, who had been carrying on post-war work 'under cover' for some time, were Austin, who announced their range of immediate post-war machines in November 1944. Austin, of course, had carried on producing 'utility' cars throughout the war. Rover had not built a car since 1940.

In the face of this enterprise, which Spencer Wilks regarded as 'rule breaking', Rover could only advertise — 'The policy of producing cars of the highest possible quality will be continued when manufacture is resumed'. Fortunately for the board's collective blood pressure, the appropriate government ministry changed its mind and granted permission to begin car manufacture again. But there was a snag, steel allocations were so low that the quantities envisaged were ludicrous. That first permit allowed for precisely 500 10 hp cars, 500 12 hp cars, 100 six-cylinder machines and eight new development cars!

But it was a start, and within weeks S. B. Wilks was able to give his views on an immediate post-war programme. It ought to be possible, he thought, to plan for 20,000 cars a year from Solihull, 5,000 of which would be a new 6 hp machine (described more fully in Appendix 1). Helen Street was put up for sale, and even before the end of the war it had been snapped up by Messrs Alfred Herbert Ltd, the big Coventry-based machine tool manufacturers who own it to this day.

To get things going a very small 'pilot line' was set up at the Clay Lane factory, just around the corner from the bombed-out Triumph premises, where a mere handful of four-cylinder cars were made. All efforts, however, went into the conversion of Solihull from an aero engine plant to a car maker's delight. And, once the machine tools had been cleared away, a delight it was. There was so much more space than Helen Street had ever enjoyed that it was almost overwhelming. However, Spencer Wilks' hopes of a speedy build-up to volume deliveries were soon dashed. Not only were supplies of sheet steel rationed according to a company's export potential, but the little M-Type small car project had to be cancelled. Even in 1947 there was no sign of the company's 1939 effort of building 11,000 cars being exceeded. The vast open spaces of Solihull, and the Land-Rover which was speedily produced to fill them, are a story in themselves, covered in Chapter 7.

The first Rovers to leave the company in post-war years were two 10 hp saloons dispatched in December 1945, and the newly converted Solihull premises were officially opened by the President of the Board of Trade, Sir Stafford Cripps, in February 1946. He made his usually gloomy references to Britain's prospects and the world at large, emphasised the country's need for exports, and talked airily about a 'one model' policy from each car maker. As far as Rover were concerned, they were already committed to this policy. If by one model Sir Stafford Cripps really meant one model *range,* then the cars he saw at Solihull were very dutiful and correct. With the single exception of the prestigious 20 hp car, all the 1940-model Rovers — the 10 hp, 12 hp, 14 hp and 16 hp machines — were back in production. Six-light four-door saloons were normal wear, but four-light sports saloons were soon back on offer for the 12, 14, and 16 hp cars. An open tourer 12 followed, but was theoretically reserved for export.

In the meantime, Maurice Wilks was not exactly idle. Along with Robert Boyle, Jack Swaine and Gordon Bashford, he had had a very busy war, spending much time dodging exploding jet engine turbine blades at Waterloo Mill in Clitheroe, and later concentrating his team's efforts on the 600 bhp 27-litre vee-12 R-R Meteor tank engine. Having been effectively bombed out of Helen Street in 1940, the design team was installed in the ballroom at Chesford Grange Hotel, just south of Kenilworth, for the duration. It was here, at the beginning of 1945, that new work began, and each man involved remembers it for different reasons. Tom Barton, or 'Mr Land-Rover' for so many years. 'I spent a lot of time there working on the tank engine, but I moved back to Helen Street for a short time to design the first left-hand steering system for export cars. Up to then, quite literally, there had never been a left-hand-drive Rover, and we had been making cars since 1904.'

Gordon Bashford, about to begin his post-war career of the basic shaper and schemer behind every Rover car. 'Immediately after VE day, Maurice Wilks sent for me, and said, quite simply, that he wanted me to go off to Chesford Grange and start thinking up ideas for post-war cars. Except that he briefed me about the tiny M-model, it was as wide-ranging as that. I could have a drawing board — just one — a mock-up shop, and a photographer.'

Jack Swaine, still turning Maurice Wilks' engine ideas into fact. 'Over at Chesford, a very pleasant place to go to work incidentally, I first of all designed the M-type engine, then we got down to finalising the sloping-head engines for post-war cars which I had originally devised for a pre-war vee-6 engine.'

Gordon Bashford's brief was very wide; he should merely produce ideas for a completely new post-war Rover car, and apart from making sure that it followed the established Rover traditions there were very few restrictions as to the way he should work.

What happened in 1945/46 is, in retrospect, slightly confusing. Nobody could know just how difficult it was going to be to ensure supplies, nor how long it was going to take for new tooling to be completed. The car which Bashford first conceived was not the one which actually appeared. 'I started work on a new P3, which was really P4, but only half way to it, if you know what I mean!'

P3, as we now know it, should never have happened. The post-war car which began to take shape in the autumn of 1945 had a new box section chassis, coil spring independent front suspension as patented by Girling (the basic geometry had already been well proven on Lanchester Roadriders in the 1930s), and a much-modified P1/P2 body shell with a full-width nose.

The 'chief stylist', as he had been for some years, was really Maurice Wilks, and it was his principal body designer Harry Loker who had to interpret his ideas. In that little wooden hut on the banks of the River Avon, Loker and his clay-shaping craftsmen slaved away to produce alternative styles for Maurice Wilks to inspect. The new 'hybrids' were not a success. Maurice Wilks, it seemed, had a sure eye when the elegant, 'classic' shape of car was involved, but it took him years to come to terms with the full width styles. This disappointment, added to a growing realisation that a new car could not possibly be ready before 1949 in any case, caused Wilks to halt the project, and to make speedy tactical changes.

The little design office at Chesford Grange was closed down, the team returned temporarily to Helen Street, and eventually they were installed in a new department at Solihull. With the move came firm decisions. P3 — the new Rover car — would progress as a second priority, and would be named P4. In its place, and wanted as quickly as was decently possible, would be a half-way modernised car, coded P3.

Visually, P3 looks very similar to the P2s which it would replace in February 1948. Most of the panels, shaped by Pressed Steel but assembled by Rover, were unchanged. However the interior was 2½ inches wider than before, the wheelbase was chopped back by 4½ inches, and the wings and bonnet from the P2 12 were used. The nose was decorated with a single central pass lamp and twin horns. As usual, six-light and four-light bodies were available.

All the radically new engineering was hidden. Bashford's time spent experimenting with new chassis structures had not been wasted. The new frame not only accommodated independent front suspension, but had fully boxed side members, and was chopped off short of the rear axle. The P1/P2 cars had always suffered from badly restricted rear wheel rebound movements because of their underslung chassis side members but chopping away this section of the frame solved that problem at a stroke. Bashford then found to his amazement and pleasure that the rear of the half-elliptic leaf springs could be shackled up directly to the steel bodywork with no more than local reinforcement.

The front suspension was a great step forward for Rover, as they had never offered such a system before. Only the Scarab, and the mythical 1935 Speed 14 coupé with i f s, pre-dated it and neither went into production. The linkage was as patented by Girling, but carefully modified to Rover's requirements. In particular the lever-type hydraulic shock absorbers which also formed the top wishbone were angled to build a degree of anti-dive action into the geometry. There was also an anti-roll torsion bar, and great attention had been given to sound suppression.

Paying lip service to government policy, but also with an eye to maximum production with the minimum of aggravation, Rover decided on a 'one-chassis' policy. Not only that, but the new engine, to be sold in four-clinder and six-cylinder forms, was just the start of a single integrated family. It was a remarkable design, and deserves much study.

Its origins lie in the 1930s (as designer Jack Swaine makes clear in Appendix 1). There were many good reasons why a sloping head joint, with a combination of overhead inlet valves and side exhaust valves, should be adopted but, as often happens in car making firms, the theoretical advantages did not become obvious until the layout had been invented! Jack Swaine has already said how the head evolved so that a vee-6 unit could be made as compact as possible inside the existing slim P1 bonnet.

What started out as a considerable modification of the Wilks-Boyle 100 mm stroke family in the 1930s, however, matured in post-war years into a completely new family of engines. Bores and strokes are all different, as are the basic parameters of cylinder block and head dimensions. It was, in all truth, a more complex block than that developed by Rolls-Royce for a similar i o e v layout. With a common stroke of 105 mm, the 1,595 cc four-cylinder and 2,103 cc six-cylinder engines were RAC-rated at 11.98 hp and 15.81 hp respectively. To keep a common cylinder bore would have meant an 18 rating for the big car, which Maurice Wilks refused to consider as taxation weighed very heavily against such cars. There was no overlap with the old engines, which disappeared immediately.

Mated to the new engine was the existing P2 transmission, including the freewheel which was by now almost a trademark of Rover engineering. It all added up to a very smooth, very refined and silkily silent way to go motoring. The new suspension worked well enough on P3 but when the engine was pushed further forward for P4, that car soon built up a reputation for heavy understeer for which there was no real solution.

Not even the new and more spacious factory at Solihull, however, could allow the company to get back to pre-war production levels. Cars were trickling out of Solihull at the rate of six cars a day in January 1946, and at 20 cars a day by June, but the first 200-car week was not achieved until the beginning of 1947. The traditional post-war explosion in costs had much to do with this, though a world-wide shortage of everything didn't help. Even so, the change in popular 12 hp car prices tells its own story. The 1940 six-light model had found plenty of customers at £300, but by 1946 (with the help of purchase tax) this had rocketed to £646. When P2s were replaced by P3s in February 1948, the 12 hp car had become the new 60 and the price had leapt yet again to no less than £1,080. Equivalent prices for a 16 hp car were £360 to £742 in 1946, and a staggering £1,106 for the new model 75. Nevertheless, the Wilks brothers were no longer willing to make anything as humble as a 10. This was phased out at the end of 1947, and with the agreement of Pressed Steel the redundant body dies were actually offered to Alvis for possible use in one of their post-war models. This offer was not taken up, as Alvis decided to carry on with a re-worked version of their own 1930s-style 12/70 shell until the new 3-litre car was ready.

P3s should have been ready for release in the autumn of 1947, but the public did not get a glimpse of them until the following February. In the event, they were in production for less than two years, for by October 1949 the true post-war model was, at last, tooled up and ready. Pressed Steel would supply the complete body shell from Cowley, tools for which cost nearly a quarter of a million pounds, and Solihull, fed from Tyseley and Acocks Green, would manufacture most of the rest.

According to Maurice Wilks' plans laid in 1946, P4 would follow on logically from P3, and would pick up its then-new chassis components. Murphy's Law, naturally, made sure that this did not happen. The Bashford designed chassis and suspension, while it worked well enough, had already shown problems before P4 design came to be frozen. At the front, for instance, it was discovered that piston-type dampers were not at all effective in controlling small movements, and at the rear poor quality post-war pressed steel managed to rust away in spite of Rover's best efforts, with potentially disastrous effects on rear spring shackle location. With that in mind, and suspecting that the P4 design might just be destined for a very long life indeed, Bashford laid out a massively strong and heavy chassis frame, with box section side members sweeping over the back axle. The front suspension had already been modified on P3 for 1949 when the piston-type dampers were discarded and a simple two-piece wishbone was specified in its place, and telescopic dampers had been added just to the rear of the coil spring support pressings. In addition the lower radius arms were made even longer than before, and pivoted from the cross member which supported the gearbox.

The body style, over which Maurice Wilks and Harry Loker had spent so much time, looked for the first time as if a Rover project had actually started life as a clay model instead of as a panelled mock-up, which of course it had. It was notable that the interior was placed even further forward, relative to the road wheels, than ever before, so much so that the back door's trailing edge was straight and barely intruded on the rear 'wing' pressing. It was the first Rover not to have obvious running boards, though these remained, hidden by the doors when closed. The P3 centre spot lamp feature was retained, but built into the grille in a 'Cyclops' position. The boot had a sharply sloping top which ensured very little stowage space (and would eventually be improved on later models).

There was no four-cylinder version of the car at first — only the six-cylinder 75 engine, with a new aluminium cylinder head and a twin-choke Solex carburettor. The four-cylinder engine was not dropped altogether, as it continued to find a home in the Land-Rover, which had already become Solihull's most important single product. The P4 propeller shaft was divided, with a centre bearing, and — horror of horrors — Maurice Wilks had fallen for the fashion which dictated that export-conscious cars should have a steering column gear change.

Although the new car was received with mixed feelings by Rover devotees, there were still plenty of customers prepared to put up with the crazy British delivery situation, allied to the notorious 'Covenant' scheme, which meant that many people who ordered in 1949 would have to wait until 1953 or 1954 before they could take delivery of their cars. The price in Britain, for the fortunate few, was £1,106 — exactly the same as had been asked for the obsolete P3 75.

Changing over from one model to another, especially where there are technical differences, particularly regarding body shell construction, is always a traumatic experience. With Pressed Steel supplying complete body shells, and with Rover gearing themselves up more and more towards quantity production, it was hoped that output would rise rapidly. In the event, that first financial year — 1949/50 — saw only 3,563 P4s built, a considerable drop compared with P3s final year. 8,821 cars were built in 1950/51, which was better, but it wasn't until 1953/54 that the pre-war record was finally broken with an output of 11,991 cars.

Getting P4 into production by the autumn of 1949 had been a great achievement, helped along by the speed with which Maurice Wilks arrived at the full-width body shape after he had 'bought' time with P3. It is no secret, now, that two of the Raymond Leowy-styled Studebaker cars were purchased as soon as possible and shipped to Solihull for study. One of them was used as a works hack for some years, but Maurice Wilks was so impressed with the general shaping of the cars that he was plainly influenced in what he chose for P4. The 1947/48 Studebaker placed side-by-side with an original P4 is certainly a distant relation, if not quite a blood brother. If Wilks had not been tied to the concept of a traditional vertical-type nose that resemblance could have been closer and more obvious.

The Studebakers were so useful, in fact, that the body from one of them was mounted on a prototype P4 rolling chassis frame, so that proving could proceed apace — thus the legendary Solihull 'Roverbaker' was born. Details like the front bench seat, and the rectangular instruments were also Studebaker influenced, though the use of light-alloy skin panels was inspired by the desire to save weight and to economise on the use of sheet steel.

With P4 in production, and with volume building up, the industrial scene at Solihull began to settle down. The new car consolidated the 'Auntie' image, and was to be improved, steadily and conservatively, over the years. But on September 28 1949, when P4 was launched, even Spencer Wilks could have had no idea how much the car was going to mean to his company. It was not really technically advanced, even in 1949, but it ran and ran. The last did not roll off a Solihull production line until May 27 1964 — and made a total of 130,342 built since 1949. In the most prolific financial year — 1955/56 — nearly 15,000 were sold. By then, of course, it was high time that Maurice Wilks' work was recognised. Spencer Wilks, with an eye to the succession, duly had him appointed to the board of directors in the spring of 1950. For the very first time, Rover's technical chief had a seat on the board.

For another nine years, the P4s were the only private cars to be made by Rover, and their shape barely altered. As far as the public was concerned, all the technical excitement centred around the gas turbine prototypes, and around the amazingly prolific Land-Rovers. At a casual glance you might think that P4, an established success, was left to make its own way in the world, but this would be quite wrong.

It is important, even in a history of this nature, to know 'why' as well as 'what' and 'how'. A change looked at out of context may seem illogical, but when viewed against the overall corporate picture might make more sense. P4's changes, however, can be summarised in two areas — the body and the mechanical improvements. What happened to the styling was never influenced by other Rovers, but the same could not be said about the engines. The Land-Rover's demands, and marketing re-alignment dictated by the bigger P5 (from 1958), were both important. Without either, P4 might not have developed in the way that it did.

There were only two significant styling changes, neither introduced purely as a marketing ploy. Rover, somehow, were above that sort of thing. Most of the pressings, in steel or in light alloy, were the same in 1964 as they had been in 1948 when Pressed Steel were given the tooling order. At the front of the car, the 'Cyclops' centre lamp layout was not a success, and was dropped in March 1952. The new nose included a plain but neatly proportioned grille with vertical bars, and no extra lamp. There were two further modifications. From September 1956 the line of the front wing was raised and 'sharpened', with flashing indicator units incorporated in their tips (semaphore arms had been discarded two years earlier). From September 1958 the radiator grille was again re-styled, with recessed bars and one prominent centre one, along with different-sectioned bumpers. At the rear, the sloping tail with its restricted boot space, came in for much criticism. William Martin-Hurst, whose sister had married Maurice Wilks in the 1930s, was a persistent opponent of this feature:

'I used to say, "Look Maurice, this 75 is a splendid motor car, but you really can't get anything into the boot unless you put your clothes into a sack! Anyway it slopes from the seat back down to the tail, and you've got some ugly bulges which stick up, and they rub holes in cases", and I know this helped to change his mind.'

Even so, it was not until October 1954 that the rear was revised. Not only was the tail restyled, with a less sloping line, but it managed to look smarter as well, and was linked to a much larger semi-wrap-around rear window. That style remained unchanged for a decade, and died with the demise of the car itself. Mechanically, work done on the car centred round a range of engines, all of which were developed to broaden the appeal of the range. Both Maurice and Spencer Wilks could remember, with great pride, how they had been able to market anything from a 10 hp to a 20 hp car at the end of the 1930s, from one basic chassis. When the time was ripe, and supply restrictions had eased, they wanted P4 to develop the same way.

What happened over the years is complicated enough to need explanation by a chart. This shows the models, and the years in which they were sold, along with the numbers built.

P4 chronology with numbers built

Model	60	75	80	90	95	100	105R	105S	110	
Engine	4-cyl	6-cyl	4-cyl	6-cyl	6-cyl	6-cyl	6-cyl	6-cyl	6-cyl	**Total**
Financial year	1,997	*2,103	2,286	2,638	2,625	2,625	2,638	2,638	2,625	**built**
1949/50		3,563								3,563
1950/51		8,821								8,821
1951/52		8,090								8,090
1952/53		9,224								9,224
1953/54	1,997	4,037		5,957						11,991
1954/55	1,488	3,220		8,728						13,436
1955/56	1,807	3,178		9,870						14,855
1956/57	828	1,087		3,299			1,889	1,504		8,607
1957/58	1,498	1,418		4,167			1,610	3,667		12,360
1958/59	1,643	1,039		3,870				2,030		8,582
1959/60			2,797			6,873				9,670
1960/61			2,483			5,878				8,361
1961/62			620		3	3,870				4,493
1962/63					2,387				2,802	5,189
1963/64					1,290				1,810	3,100
Totals	9,261	43,677	5,900	35,891	3,680	16,621	3,499	7,201	4,612	130,342

*From 1954 2,230 cc.

This chart makes clear that the first big expansion came in the autumn of 1953, and the next in the autumn of 1956. One model was dropped in the autumn of 1958 (significantly enough this was at the time of P5's release) and much-needed rationalisation followed a year later. Changes in 1962 were really an upgrading of existing machines, though engines were further rationalised at the same time.

One has to say that attempts to popularise 'cheap' four-cylinder P4s failed. In nine years only 15,161 60s and 80s were sold, just 16 per cent of the total, and none is remembered with any great nostalgia by Rover enthusiasts. Four-cylinder cars, of course, were marketed to bring down the P4's 'cost base'. When launched in 1953, a Rover 60 cost £820 before tax whereas the 75 cost £895 and the 90 £915. In 1962, when the last of the Rover 80s was made, it sold for £985, compared with £1,095 for the 100, and £1,288 for the P5 3-litre. In the 1930s, perhaps, when the customer expected to see wide model ranges offered by everybody, such a ploy might have worked; in the 1950s when they viewed a Rover or a Jaguar as a particular 'type' of car, it didn't. The fact was that refinement and performance was taken out of the car faster than the price could be lowered, and not enough potential buyers could be persuaded that they were getting good value for money from the 'fours'.

The engines themselves, and their pedigree, need some sorting out. Apart from the Rover 80's unit, which was nothing more than an unmodified overhead-valve Land-Rover 'four' of 2,286 cc, the same in every detail, and quite unrelated to anything else, every other P4 engine was a member of the sloping-head family. Of these, only the 60 had four cylinders, and was a much-modified and over-bored version of the 1,595 cc P3 unit, with repositioned cylinder bores and a new aluminium cylinder head with integral manifolding and an SU carburettor. It is a Rover oddity that the Land-Rover got its 2-litre engine before it was ever offered in a P4, but it was a rather different version (with a cast iron head and different carburation for example), and even this engine was then modified in 1955 to bring it more in common with the new P4 60 unit.

Although all the 'sixes' stemmed from the same basic layout, there were several important differences in the breeds. The principal reason for changes in cylinder dimensions, introduced from time to time, was to rationalise as much as possible, often with other ranges in mind. If we accept this, a rather confusing picture begins to look more logical. We can also sum up the changes in terms of the Acocks Green/Tyseley machining installations. From the point of view of expense, it always made sense to standardise on the same cylinder bore dimensions where possible, and to let the crankshaft throw and thus, the stroke, look after itself. The fact that P5's engine, because of its larger cylinder bore and revised cylinder block casting, also had different cylinder centre spacings, was important. It is interesting to recall that Maurice Wilks and Robert Boyle had laid down the 1930s/40s engine family with a rigidly enforced 100 mm stroke in mind, whereas for the P4/P5 unit, which is still in production for the six-cylinder Land-Rover, both bore and stroke could be varied.

The first major engine change came in September 1953, with the announcement of the 90 bhp Rover 90, which had the bored-out 73 mm by 105 mm 2,638 cc engine. That made three bores and a single stroke, but for reasons already stated, and to allow the engine to turn over faster, the 1955 model 75 was given a revised engine with the 90 cylinder bore and a unique 88.9 mm stroke making 2,230 cc.

All was peace until September 1958, when P5 was launched, combining the largest 60 cylinder bore with the usual 105 mm stroke, and 2,995 cc. A year later, in the middle of a big reshuffle of P4 models, the 2.6-litre engine was again revised, this time to fit in with the 3-litre's cylinder block, and was given dimensions of 77.8 mm by 92.1 mm, 2,625 cc, a capacity which continues to this day in the Land-Rover.

There were, of course, many variations of carburation, compression ratio and engine tune which add up to a spectrum of power outputs from 60 bhp for the first Rover 60, through 75 bhp for the first 75, to 123 bhp for the last of the Rover 110s. When rationalised with P5 in August 1959, the cylinder blocks inherited seven main bearings instead of the original four, along with the other details. In September 1962, when the 3-litre was substantially improved after attention to the breathing by air-flow expert Harry Weslake, the same treatment was given to the new 110, whereas the old-type engine was retained for the 95.

This must not detract from the very real improvements made to other areas of the cars. The Studebaker-style instruments were dropped in favour of circular instruments in 1950, and at the same time full hydraulic brakes replaced the original hydro-mechanical system. However, the Panhard rod, in the original specification, was dropped after a short time as the company had considerable trouble keeping the location bracketry in one piece. The well-liked Rover gearbox was given synchromesh on second gear (it had only been fitted on top and third since 1938) in autumn 1953, bigger brakes arrived a year later, optional Laycock overdrive 12 months after that, and the twin 105S/105R models another year later.

The 105S and 105R cars were mechanically identical except in their transmissions. The 105S ('S' for sporting?) was a tuned-up version of the 90 with 108 bhp instead of 90 bhp, and came with overdrive as standard. Incidentally, any car fitted with overdrive could not, by definition, have the freewheel, as the two items fought for the same space behind the gearbox. The freewheel, in any case, was dropped when disc brakes and a servo were standardised.

The 105R ('R' for what? Some say 'refined' and others say, with tongue in cheek, 'retired', or even 'retarded') was a much more gentle machine. It was given the 108 bhp engine, but the transmission, called Roverdrive, was a unique semi-automatic device. Working backwards from the flywheel there was a torque converter, a single-plate clutch, a synchromesh two-speed gearbox, and a Laycock overdrive. Like similar systems (Standrive, Manumatic and Easidrive among others) this was intended to give all the advantages of two-pedal motoring without the cost or complication of a full automatic transmission. The lower of the two manual ratios could be used for climbing steep hills, but normally all motoring was done in 'top' gear with the help of the torque converter. The overdrive was calibrated so that it normally cut-in automatically at higher speeds, the speed depending on the throttle opening, and to cut-out again as speeds dropped. Although the system sounded cumbersome, it worked very well. The problem, a serious one, was that acceleration was severely restricted, and both performance and fuel economy were badly affected by inefficiencies in the torque converter. With 3,499 sales in two years, after which it was dropped with relief by the company, it has to count as a qualified failure.

Front wheel disc brakes were fitted from 1959 and these, apart from the Weslake-inspired engine changes of 1962, were really the last major modifications applied to P4. Connoisseurs of the model will know that the steering column gearchange was replaced by a floor change (ingeniously adjustable for alignment) in

September 1953 and this coincided with the introduction of synchromesh on second gear. When overdrive was standardised the freewheel which was so much a part of Rover's tradition finally disappeared.

As the P4 gradually and inevitably became a profitable 'fixture' at Solihull, the company's finances benefited because of it. After-tax profits in the year P4 was introduced — 1948/49 — were £158,098 — a figure which was doubled in just three years. The Land-Rover's contribution, of course, was considerable. Both models contributed enormously to this fiscal improvement and by 1955 the figure had risen to a splendid £938,482. National and company problems then set in — there was the Suez crisis of 1956/57 to be considered, and the fact that P5 was *very* expensive to introduce — so the 'Magic Million' mark was not to be reached until 1960.

Management, too, like the company they ruled, was remarkably stable. Geoffrey Savage, the production genius with such charisma that he had most of the workforce eating out of his hand, was knighted in 1952, but died only a year later. George Farmer became commercial director in 1953, and thus continued a steady climb to the chairmanship. Ransom Harrison retired in 1954 after 22 years in the chair, and was replaced by long-serving Howe Graham until 1957.

At this point things began to change. Spencer Wilks, after a quarter of a century in complete control of the company's destiny, stepped up to become chairman, leaving George Farmer and Maurice Wilks as joint managing directors. It was a very comfortable period for the company, whose bosses were well known to shareholders, workers and Press alike. It has to be said, also, that it was a time of great placidity for the motor industry as a whole, when companies could plan ahead for years knowing that external forces would hardly be likely to drive them off course.

By the mid-1950s Maurice Wilks was beginning to think of broadening the company's private car range. His first thoughts were for a smaller car to slot in underneath the successful P4s for the failure to establish a 'cheap' P4 still rankled. Then he wondered about replacing P4 with a more versatile machine, and finally he thought he should add to Rover's range a larger, more luxurious saloon. Jaguar's success in producing and selling their big and fast Mark VII model had a lot to do with this, allied to the fact that neither Alvis, Daimler nor Armstrong-Siddeley were making a go of selling cars just that important bit more expensive than his P4s. For this purpose, and because he knew that specialist knowledge in shaping cars, and designing interiors, was now needed, he decided to open a styling office. Thus it was that Rover's now illustrious reputation for producing modern-looking and practical cars was established.

David Bache had joined Austin as a student engineering apprentice in 1948 and spent six years at Longbridge, interspersed with courses at Birmingham University and the Birmingham College of Art. At 26 years of age, with little more than his Austin experience and a burning desire to design the best cars in the business, he came to work at Solihull. His first task, to shape P5 to Maurice Wilks' wishes, was as daunting as any which followed.

The problem, as has already been made clear, was that Maurice Wilks did not really know at that stage (1954) what he wanted to produce next. There was no product planning force to guide him, and the sales department deferred to whatever the omniscient Wilks brothers thought was good for them. At first he wanted to see P5 as a smaller car than P4, certainly with a four-cylinder engine, perhaps 8 inches smaller in length and wheelbase than the P4 cars. Robert Boyle, as already mentioned, along with Gordon Bashford, had already formulated his ideas on that subject in April 1953. It was to weigh no more than 22 cwt (2,464 lb) at the kerbside, and it would have what we now know as a 'base unit' type of body structure. This, mark you, was more than two years before Citroen launched their DS19.

The engine to power P5 would have to be new, and as Wilks' thoughts on the car swung to and fro, so did the engine's requirements. In Appendix 1 Jack Swaine explains how the vee-6 engine project was very much dependent on the vagaries of P5's progress.

Probably the biggest factor weighing against a P5 'small car' was the demand that would exist for it. It was useless to produce a fine car in the best of traditions, for which there would be large sales, when Solihull's facilities were quite incapable of producing that number. Rover were going through a period of great frustration. Although they owned hundreds of acres of land adjacent to the existing Solihull factory, their requests for planning permission to build extensions were being repeatedly turned away by government edict. A new factory? Certainly . . . in Scotland, on Merseyside, or in South Wales. But in the Midlands, sorry, no!

At the very time when P5 was being planned, the company had been forced to buy nearly 130,000 square feet of existing factory space in Percy Road, Birmingham, to deal with yet more expansion in Land-Rover transmission production, and that had been the fourth such purchase in as many years.

A bigger car, more highly priced, and therefore aimed at a more restricted market, would still be a viable proposition, *and* could find a place in the Solihull factory. On that basis, and with rather less time than they would have liked, both Robert Boyle and David Bache were urged to proceed. This would be in 1955, and by then the 2.6-litre Rover 90 was in production and the 105s in their final development stages. P5 would have to be bigger, faster, grander, and more expensive than the 105s, which almost automatically meant that it would have to have a full 3-litre engine. The vee-6 engine, an 'on-off' project for more than five years, was by no means ready and was suspended yet again. In its place, and with very little time or tooling money to back him, Jack Swaine was asked to produce a 3-litre engine from the old P4 design — and to do it quickly.

The 2.6-litre engine already in production measured 73 mm by 105 mm. Lengthening the stroke was not even considered as it would have increased connecting rod angularity too much and restricted the revving capabilities, so the only alternative was to enlarge the bore. One of 77.8 mm was already in use for the four-cylinder 60 and Land-Rover engines, and could be used for the new version of the engine except for one basic snag — there wasn't space in the existing cylinder block to include it! A bore increase was not possible in any case without adding to the thickness of the cast cylinder walls, and this would mean unsatisfactory 'siamesing' between the bores. Rover were not in favour of such things . . . impasse?

The only solution was to go back to first principles, ask the production engineers if it was even feasible to juggle with cylinder centres, and proceed on that basis? It was feasible, if not desirable (changes are *never* desirable to a production engineer!), and Jack Swaine's team eventually squeezed 2,995 cc out of the cylinder block without changing the overall dimensions.

This is an example of the way in which engineering change is rarely as simply achieved as it may seem, nor at so little expense. The P5 3-litre engine 'conversion' became even more expensive when it was decided to incorporate a seven-bearing crankshaft, which made the cylinder block completely, instead of partially, unique.

The rest of the car took shape in a less restricted manner. David Bache eventually got approval for a big and impressive new car with a 9 foot 2.5 inch wheelbase, actually a half inch shorter than P4, but about 4.5 inches wider and 3.5 inches lower. More efficient use of the wheelbase was gained by pushing the back seat rearward towards the line of the axle, and the scuttle forward. The result was an extra 8 inches length inside. P5 was smoother and more integrated than P4, as one would expect of a full-time professional styling engineer. Wrap-around screens and rear windows were in the current vogue, as was the general proportion, but the new Rover had no swivelling quarter windows. Small plastic wind deflectors were fitted at the top of each window frame. Bache's touches applied to P4 since 1954 would declare their authorship in 1958 when we all saw P5, because several 'signatures' were repeated — the wing-tip indicators, the recessed grille bars and the vertical tail lights among them.

Robert Boyle and Gordon Bashford, on the other hand, had not been idle. After scheming P3, P4, Land-Rover and the 'killed-off' Road Rover (see Appendix 1), Bashford had been detached from the main-stream of engineering, given a very small team to back him up, and told to start planning well ahead for Rovers of the future. P5, and the interesting touches which went into it, was the first fruit of that directive, and the much more exciting P6 would follow it, though the even more intriguing rear-engined T3 turbine car would find a place in his working hours as well.

P5, as one would expect by the mid-1950s, had a monocoque pressed steel body shell, but it was a monocoque with a difference. Instead of a mere cross-member at the front of the car to support the front suspension and engine/transmission, there was what amounted to the front third or so of a box section chassis frame. This carried the suspension, steering engine mounts, and gearbox mounts in a neatly integrated whole, and was terminated by rubber mountings under the front seats.

The front suspension itself was also unusual. The wishbones and geometry were normal enough, but suspension was by laminated leaf torsion bars that were really long thin leaf springs arranged to twist rather than bend. Only Daimler and their offshoots had previously used this layout, which gave all the advantages of torsion bars without the expense of machining the normal circular-section variety.

The one oddity, for autumn 1958, was that the car was released with an all-drum braking system. Gordon Bashford has said that this was done because the company was still cautious about the performance and prospects of disc brakes, even though at least a dozen British manufacturers had standardised them on some models by that time. There was sales resistance to this right from the start, and within a year the company was forced to specify Girling discs at the front at the same time as they were standardised for the new model Rover 80s and 100s.

With P5, the Rover company found out how expensive it was becoming to stay in the vanguard of motor car manufacture. Whereas body tools for P4 had cost about a quarter of a million pounds, and that was shocking enough, the bill for P5 was nearer the million mark! There is no question of criticism against Pressed Steel here, who certainly made no more than a fair profit out of their operations — it was just a measure of the way costs were rocketing, and complication was setting in.

Tooling costs, and the problem of having more than one type in production at once, were the main reasons for the late appearance of the smart and rakish 3-litre coupé. This car, with a lowered roof line and other distinctive touches, had been styled in the mid-1950s by David Bache, but would not appear until 1962.

As with P4, so did P5 production take time to build up, but in the second year —

Top *Solihull as originally built, pictured immediately after the war, in 1946. Those are still the head offices, but the engineering design block now stands where the thistles grow in this picture.*

Above *P4 in quarter-scale model form, with an early nose design, but with a close approximation to the final style.*

Below *The P3 showing the 'classic lines' which meant so much to the customers.*

Above left *The Pininfarina interior of the 1953 P4 convertible with steering column gearchange. The car proved too expensive to be put into production.*

Above right *P4 nearly there! This looks good enough to be the real thing but is actually a mock-up, and note that at this stage (1948/49) it might have been called a Viking.*

Below *P4 in production at Solihull in 1950, the original sloping-tail model with the 'Cyclops' nose.*

Above *George Mackie (left) and Peter Wilks smiling hopefully in front of their Marauder sports car, which used a P4 chassis and many body parts. The date is August 16 1950 when hopes were high, but only 15 examples were sold.*

Below *Pininfarina built this fixed-head P4 which, for 1953/54, has very attractive lines indeed.*

Above *The 1959 production P5 3-litre. The recessed grille was a Rover trade mark between 1958 and 1964. The original P5 had no opening quarter windows, but had louvres above the drop glasses.*

Below *Full-size mock-up, and first thoughts on a new P5 in 1955. Yes, you really can see through to the other side of the 'car' behind that front wheel.*

Above *Small-scale P5 models photographed against a real background. The trick was to stand the model and tiny walls out on the terrace of a house owned by the company. Note that saloon and coupé styling were carried out at the same time — both are to David Bache's credit.*

Below *The original automotive turbine engine on test, with the exhaust taken straight up out of the roof of the cell. This would be in 1947.*

Above *The third rear-engined turbine car — T2A — which, apart from its vast turbine exhaust spout, looked very much like a standard P4.*

Below left *Rover's first automotive gas turbine engine, built in 1947 and first shown in 1948. Air intakes were low down at the rear (left) and the exhaust was vertically expelled. Note the small size (from the inch scale). In this form the unit was intended for front-mounting.*

Below right *Frank Bell (left) the first Rover turbine project engineer, and his technical chief Maurice Wilks, alongside JET 1 at Silverstone in March 1950.*

Above *First public appearance of JET 1 in March 1950. Spen King is at the wheel, Frank Bell is getting into the passenger seat, while the Wilks brothers look on.*

Below *T3 laid bare. This was a completely designed turbine car concept, where the rear engine position, the four-wheel-drive and the suspension layout were all done with turbine car motoring in mind. The car was conceived in 1956.*

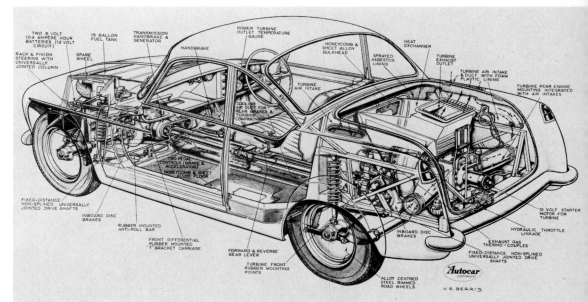

Above *Prelude to the record runs at Jabbeke in 1952, with Spen King about to unleash the car, now with its restyled nose, and his great friend Peter Wilks leaning on the door.*

Left *T4 with its front-mounted turbine engine on view. Structurally this car was based on a P6 body/chassis unit, but had front wheel drive. It was built in 1961.*

Below *An historic photograph — four Rover turbine cars formating at Silverstone in 1963 a few weeks after the Rover-BRM (foreground) had performed so well at Le Mans. Graham Hill is driving car 00.*

1959/60 — it sold 7,460 copies compared with 9,670 P4s. This, right away, justified Maurice Wilks' desire to get into the bigger and more expensive stratas of the market. Even the arrival of Jaguar's Mark II saloons in 1959 did little to harm P5, which was an altogether bigger and more dignified machine. Even better news for the company was that Armstrong-Siddeley had decided to drop out of the car-making market altogether, Alvis were wedded to making two-door coupés, and Daimlers were getting bigger and even more expensive.

What Jaguar had in mind to replace their ageing Mark IX was more worrying, and even before the sleek Mark 10 was revealed the engineers at Solihull were beavering away at improvements to P5. The basic problem was not that the car was heavy and cumbersome because power steering had, after all, become optional from autumn 1960, but that it was quite simply not fast enough. A 3-litre engine boasting only 105 bhp (net) was none too advanced by current standards. P5, even in its overdrive form, was not a 100 mph machine (the Borg Warner automatic version was even slower and added to its 20 mpg fuel consumption) and its £1,700 price tag was not really competitive. The changes, which turned the car into a 'Mark II' in 1962, were therefore concentrated on the engine.

The company had always managed to produce refined and very reliable units, but they had no true airflow experts. One of the continuing problems with the vee-6 engines that might have powered the P5 and its successors was a lack of power, speedily identified as a breathing deficiency. For the 3-litre 'six', therefore, Maurice Wilks decided to call in one of the acknowledged experts — Harry Weslake.

Weslake had made his name many years earlier with the performance development of engines as distinguished as the Bentleys, and later with mundane little units like the post-war BMC 'A' and 'B' series designs. In his day, Weslake was as famous as Keith Duckworth is in the 1970s, and he was the ideal choice.

There is, however, no such thing as 'Weslake magic'. His attention to engine breathing is based on many years' experience and practical results. His remedy for P5's problem was straightforward. From the cost-saving but inefficient integral manifold casting of P5's head, he proposed to return to the more efficient and simpler system of P3, which had separate inlet manifolds with more sinuous contours. In the Mark II P5's case, however, the water-heated feature would be retained, something which P3s and earlier P4s never had.

Maximum power went up from 105 bhp to 121 bhp, and this, together with revised gear ratios, and the new remote-control gear change, made the car altogether more spritely. Maximum speed was up to more than 105 mph, with improved acceleration to match. Technically, however, this was nearly the end of the story for P5, even though David Bache's team would be encouraged to improve the car for 1966 as a Mark III. If not a successor, P5 was soon to be joined by a companion. Since the end of the 1950s, Solihull has gradually become completely immersed in P6 — which was an entirely new type of Rover. With it, Rover's traditions would be stood on their heads, and the 'Auntie' era ended. If P5 was the last of the old-style Rovers, P6 would be the first of the new. The Rover company, and its standing in the business, would never be quite the same again.

Chapter 6

World pioneers — the gas turbine cars

Board meeting minutes: November 1 1945

'Mr S. B. Wilks reported that he had had several discussions with Leyland Motors Ltd on the advisability of carrying out development on gas turbines, as there were strong indications that this type of engine might be suitable for motor cars.

He considered that a change from the present piston-type engine to the gas turbine, if it came about, would be so revolutionary and would have such far reaching consequences that it would be in the best interests of the company to keep pace with any developments on these lines . . .'

It was a cold day, and passers-by were not too keen to stand and stare. The car which whined its way out of the gates at Solihull looked much like other Rover 75s — or did it? It didn't have a roof, and it only had two doors, which made it special enough — but what about the noise? It sounded rather like a harsh vacuum cleaner, and as it disappeared up the road there were no discernible pauses for gear changing . . .

It was a historic occasion, and even if the Rover company and its marque name were to die tomorrow, they would be remembered for it. Until the Russians rewrite history yet again to suit themselves, Rover will always have the distinction of being world pioneers — the builders of the very first turbine powered car.

JET 1, that trend-setting machine, is now honourably retired and on display in the Kensington Science Museum, looking remarkably old-fashioned by the standards of the 1970s, but it was the first flowering of the genius of Spen King and Frank Bell. No other gas turbine cars, not even those built in Detroit, were as practical or as advanced as the prototypes built at Solihull.

The pity of it all is that the technical problems known to Bell and King in 1946 were still problems in the 1960s, and that tells us almost the complete story. Rover knew how to make automotive gas turbines work well by the 1960s, but they still hadn't solved the problems of fuel consumption and costs. But there is no shame in this — neither has anyone else.

40 years after Frank Whittle laid down the principles of gas turbine engines, and getting on for 30 years after Rover decided to put a prototype engine into a car, no gas turbine powered cars have yet been sold. There are those, now, prepared to bet that none ever will be. The fuel consumption problem was serious, but this would not have deterred the rich and the status-seekers from buying a car. However, the problem of costs was insurmountable.

None of this, of course, mattered in the 1940s. The problems then were concerned with making a gas turbine car feasible. Rover, in spite of their automotive reputation for being staid and conventional, were ideally placed to be world pioneers. Spencer

Wilks, despite his cautious and judicious background, was prepared to back a hunch. The spark for this probably came in 1942.

At the beginning of the 1940s gas turbines were brand-new and *very* secret. In the thick of a war that might be expected to settle the world's destiny for another century, the development of entirely new types of engine was a closely guarded military secret. Rover, because of their links with Frank Whittle and Power Jets Ltd, were at the very core of new developments.

Maurice Wilks and Robert Boyle began work on Whittle-type prototype gas turbines in 1940, and found it all very strange at first. But engineers are engineers, and once the basis of Whittle's brilliant concepts became familiar they began to look for improvements of their own. With full ministry approval they designed the world's first straight-through combustion 'jet', and took it to a remarkably high state of development before handing it over, as the forerunner of the 'Welland' jet engine, to Rolls-Royce in 1943. That was the end of Rover's war-time involvement with gas turbines, but it had proved to them that they, as motor car designers, could tackle the new subject without fear and without making huge, expensive mistakes. The seeds of future activities were sown, whether they knew it or not.

Between 1943 and 1945, as Rover put the Rolls-Royce Meteor tank engine into production, there was close liaison at all levels between the two companies. In 1945, just after the war had ended, the Wilks brothers got together to consider their future. Although at first they had been appalled at the potential dislocation which would result from war and their work on unfamiliar products, both Spencer and Maurice had become fascinated by the new machines they were asked to build. It was Maurice who first tentatively broached the subject of a post-war gas turbine programme at Solihull.

Spencer Wilks was cautious at first, but then there was nothing unusual in that. He had seen how smoothly his own staff had 'taken' to gas turbine work, but he also knew the nature of the costs involved. If Rover were to interest themselves in a peace-time programme there would be no benevolent government departments to pay the bill. But the implications of vibration-free engines, cheap fuels, and what looked like limitless development prospects, made the idea attractive. Perhaps if Rover could get a partner for the work . . .

In the next few months, Spencer Wilks had several talks with his great friend Henry Spurrier of Leyland Motors, and the result was that Leyland agreed to be associated with the Rover company in any automotive gas turbine projects they might have. By the end of 1945, in conditions of great secrecy, work had begun at Solihull. Leyland, though financially involved, never took any active part in the experiments, and would not see an engine in one of their trucks until the late 1960s.

Project Department 'C', set up at Solihull at the beginning of 1946, was not completely wrapped up in gas turbine work — early experimental work was carried out on diesel engines and on sleeve-valve units. Its two original employees however, were Frank Bell and the youthful Spencer King, both of whom had been working on the new-fangled gas turbine technology with Rolls-Royce at Derby, and who were in the words of an admiring colleague, 'as near to the textbook definition of boffins as anybody I've ever met.'

Bell was an established aero engine expert (he was to leave Rover in 1952 to join Blackburn Aircraft in Yorkshire as chief engine designer), but King was only recently out of his apprenticeship, and was to become a very important part of the Rover (and, later, British Leyland) scene. Spen King's mother was a Wilks' daughter, which made Spencer and Maurice Wilks his uncles. He had been educated at Hailey-bury public school, and completed a war-time apprenticeship at Rolls-Royce where, as he says: 'I always wanted to be a mechanical engineer . . . I got deeply involved in turbine engines and jets because Rolls-Royce was then in the process of learning all about them. In a way it was a terribly good "university" — it was fundamentally new, no one had a text book, and there were lots of bright people wrapped up in a new subject; one learned an awful lot.'

Their problems, at first, were not technical, but financial. Tony Poole, who joined the department as a fitter in 1949, remembers:

'We always had budget problems. I was once asked to make a rig to hold up the 40-gallon test bed fuel tank, so I went out to a dump around the corner to 'borrow' some scaffolding, made a hell of noise about it and came back with some of the wrong clips. My boss, Charlie Hudson, went out the next evening to get the clips and was nicked by the works police who thought he was a common thief!'

Poole even raided the local second-hand bicycle shop in Solihull for bits and pieces. To this day, JET 1 has a brake to stop the power turbine rotating when the transmission is in neutral, which started life as a tandem brake!

Bell and King soon found that apart from finance, and the fact that they were having to write their own textbooks, the technology needed for automotive gas turbines was far removed from that of aero engines. To get power outputs down to reasonable levels — they thought something like 150 bhp would be ample — the turbines had to be scaled down considerably. This was all very well, but it was impossible to scale down the jet engine clearances as well, and efficiency suffered. The other major problem with which they all had to live was that exotic aero engine materials could not be used. For one thing there was the question of material priorities to be argued out at every turn, and for another there was the always vexing question of costs. In no way could the materials used in a multi-thousand pound aero engine be considered for automotive applications.

This said, and in spite of post-war restrictions on all supplies of non-essential non-export-orientated components, Bell and King had their very first prototype engine running at the beginning of 1947. The historic day came on February 3 1947, just before a nationwide shortage of coal caused a complete shutdown at most fac-tories for two weeks!

This is certainly not the place for gas turbine technicalities to be plumbed, but a few comments are necessary. Original gas turbines, of course, relied purely on jet thrust for their power. Air was compressed, burnt in combustion chambers, fed through turbine wheels which drove the original air compressor, and expelled at high speed through a jet pipe, where the properties of Newton's Law did the rest. Pure jet thrust for road vehicles was never considered. Apart from being inefficient and noisy, it would also have been uncontrollable, anti-social, and potentially dangerous to following traffic. Some way would have to be found to link the availa-ble power to driven road wheels. The method chosen, and one universally employed by all those who copied Rover in later years, was that already earmarked for propeller-turbine aero engines. After passing through the 'gasifier', the title nor-mally given to the compressor-combustion chamber/compressor turbine combina-tion, the hot gases were passed across the blades of a second power turbine, itself geared to the transmission. If everyone had done their sums correctly, there would be very little residual thrust, and the gas could be exhausted to the atmosphere.

As far as this system was concerned, there was both good news and bad news. The good news was that the power turbine could act as its own clutch as there was no question of a solid drive line in this concept, but the bad news was that it would be rotating far too fast.

Gas turbine engines are not subject to reciprocating forces in any way, and if perfectly balanced can run at whatever speed their designers find suitable. Small units, with little inertia but with a sizeable air flow always revolved at more than 40,000 rpm, even in the early days. It meant that a car designer had to start by adding another 'nought' to all the figures he understood, and then work out how to gear the output down to usable levels. That, of course, was really a 'chassis' or 'transmission' problem, and neither Bell nor King bothered themselves with its implications at first. In the initial stages it was something of a miracle if an engine could be persuaded to run properly, and for any appreciable amount of time. Anything over 30 minutes before disaster was cause for a celebration!

The engines were, of course, air-cooled, or self-cooled to be more accurate, and a major problem was keeping the shaft bearings lubricated and the lubricant in the correct state. Test bed work tended to be a bit of an adventure, and most of the operators were volunteers and unmarried! A typical test bed sequence, as noted in one of the fitters' notebooks, was as follows. 'First run, satisfactory light-up, no oil pressure. Second run, no light-up. Third attempt, engine exploded . . .' It was that sort of project, where everyone was learning hard all the time, and experimental runs often had spectacular results. Test bed work was usually carried out behind a row of protective sandbags, and if things got out of hand a turbine blade would often depart through the casing at high speed and dig another hole in the long-suffering cell walls. As Tony Poole recalls.

'We once had a fire which got out of hand, and it even got to a new car that was passing outside the test cells. There was a hell of a row about that . . .'

Work began on T5, a small engine with ribbed casings, and this was the unit first 'leaked' to the Press in a most intriguing way. Spencer Wilks was by no means ready to show his new toys to the world, but in April 1948 an unfinished turbine from Centrax Power Units of Acton was shown at the British Industries Fair with the claim that it could be used in a car. The fact that the engine had not been completed, and was certainly not proven, goaded the normally reticent Wilks into action. The greatest of the specialist journalists in this field — Geoffrey Smith of *Flight* and *Autocar,* who had been introduced to T5 some months earlier, was given leave to describe Rover's work in *The Autocar* on May 7 and May 14 1948. These detailed and informative features are another land-mark in the history of the gas turbine — they were the first to describe actual as opposed to projected engines for automotive use. Geoffrey Smith even suggested that 'the Rover unit is so far advanced that it could be fitted into a car' though nothing of this nature had then been proposed. Nothing came of the Centrax proposal, which was most certainly never fitted to a car or a truck (and would have been far too bulky in any case), and never found other commercial uses.

T5 is important because it was the *first,* even though it was never used outside the Solihull test beds. Its 100 bhp were produced at 55,000 compressor turbine revs per minute, and it was certainly light enough, weighing 200 lb less than the most powerful of the P3 units, but it was also very inefficient in its use of kerosene. As with any gas turbine, there was a great deal of residual and therefore waste heat in the exhaust gases. It was logical that this heat should be used to warm up the incoming air, but no suitable exchangers which could be carried on a car were available.

By 1949 a decision was taken to design a more powerful engine. T5 was side-lined and T8 was born. T8 made its first appearance in a machine, not in a car as some might think, but in Spencer King's long-suffering boat *Torquil*. By the winter of 1949, however, it was clear that a motor car installation was practical, and Gordon Bashford was winkled out of the normal design areas to produce the first turbine car.

For its base, Bashford chose the company's newest product, P4, chopped the chassis about to accept its strange power unit and arranged for it to be installed behind the driving seats. JET 1, as it was soon registered by the company, was therefore the first mid-engined car they had ever built, and the first with its engine behind the occupants since the still-born Scarabs of 1929/31.

The engine was ahead of, and rather above, the normal back axle, driving forward to a simple transfer gearbox which then powered the normal spiral bevel back axle through a propeller shaft under the engine. The front suspension, steering, and brakes were all standard P4, as were the lines of the body, though of course a four-door saloon had been converted into a two-door 'sports' car. Even the 'Cyclops' nose was retained, but it is interesting to note that when P4 was updated with a conventional grille in 1952, so too was JET 1.

The first turbo-car's engine, the T8 type, was an altogether more powerful example than those first T5s. Maximum compressor turbine speed was 40,000 rpm, at which the power turbine could run up to 26,000 rpm, and produce up to 230 bhp. The first unit to be installed in the car, however, was limited to not more than 100 bhp as it was not known at the time just how far the engine could be stretched before turbine blade failures occurred. There was no question about one thing — with the full-power engine JET 1 was going to be an extremely fast car, and certainly much the quickest Rover had ever built.

JET 1, still unregistered, made its first runs at an airfield near Solihull on Saturday, March 4 1950. Four days later, on March 8, it was demonstrated very convincingly to the RAC's technical committee for five laps of MIRA's original perimeter track, and reached speeds of up to 85 mph. The day after that the car was taken to Silverstone for a driving session in front of Press, radio and TV crews.

On that day the car was certainly not extended, and the company retained an intriguing air of mystery by refusing to have the engine lid raised. Spencer Wilks went to great lengths in his statement to emphasise that sales and production of such cars could not possibly begin for some years. How many years? He was not to be drawn. Maurice Wilks went even further, saying: 'The present engine is really a piece of test bed apparatus and, in consequence, does not bear much resemblance to what the company has in mind for a motor car . . . in any case, in any future production car we would certainly not put the engine where one expects to find the back seat!' He then went on to admit that prototype engines rarely stayed together for more than a few minutes, and lavished great praise on Henry Wiggin and Co for inventing Nimonic materials, and on Lucas for all their help in combustion chamber designs.

An interesting quirk is that the car remained unregistered for the simple reason that British authorities had no administrative machinery for licensing a car designed to run on paraffin! A way was speedily found round this ruling, because the turbine could equally well run on petrol, and was registered on that basis.

After the razz-ma-tazz, back to business. JET 1 was set to work as a mobile test bed, and very little more was heard about the project for a couple of years. Nevertheless, everything was not sweetness and light. Rover (Gas Turbines) Ltd was set up in 1952 to separate all the pioneering work from that of Rover's normal engineering activities, but around the same time Frank Bell abruptly resigned and went back to his native New Zealand for a long holiday. With this departure Spen King took over all activities on the engineering side.

In June 1952, however, Rover thought it appropriate to bring the further-developed T8 engine out into the open and prove something. Even though the projected heat exchanger fitment was still not considered reliable, which restricted fuel consumption to 6 mpg at best and more often to 4 or 5 mpg, the engine output had been boosted to 230 bhp. At this rating it even idled at 13,000 rpm, a speed controlled by the fuel settings, but 'light-up' was established from about 3,000 rpm on the gasifier shaft.

Maurice Wilks no longer trusted Rover's normal drum brakes to keep the car in check, so a set of prototype Girling disc brakes, which would not actually be fitted to production cars for several more years, were used instead. The transfer gearbox on the original 'low power' JET 1 enclosed a 7.55 step-down ratio, but for high-speed testing this was raised to 4.875. The back axle ratio in each case was 3.64-to-1. Internal details of the T8 engine were released for the first time, showing that the gasifier consisted of a centrifugal compressor fixed to an axial compressor turbine. There was a single Lucas-designed combustion chamber mounted on top of the unit, and a single stage axial power turbine fixed directly to the step-down gears. In the original JET 1 a reverse gear was provided, but for the record runs this was discarded, and a Rover freewheel assembly installed in its place.

The car was taken to the new and fashionable Jabbeke highway in Belgium, now part of the completed Ostend-Brussels motorway, and on June 25 and 26 was unleashed up the concrete straights, with Spen King at the wheel. On the Wednes-day, with a 3.64 axle installed, the car achieved a two-way flying kilometre speed of 140.422 mph. Overnight the axle ratio was dropped slightly to 3.275, and on the following morning, while the air was still cool, the car notched up a splendid 151.96 mph. It was in any case a turbo-car world record (no other turbo-car had been built, after all) and an excellent standard for the competition to aim at.

Frank Bell wrote a long and fascinatingly detailed description of 'his' engine in *The Autocar* of July 4 1952, and revealed that the company had already built a second turbine car. This was T2, of which no-one is very proud, and of which no trace remains. It was a front-engined machine, based on a P4 saloon, but with all the exhaust gases designed to be taken out to the rear through chassis side-members. It was soon realised that the through-put of hot gas was so high that enormous side members were needed to keep gas velocities within bounds. There was also a dis-tressing tendency for unburnt paraffin to collect in the side members (this was passed through the system before 'light-up'), and then to self-ignite! By the time the members had been sufficiently lagged to prevent them setting fire to the rest of the car the vehicle had become impracticable. One run was enough, and in Gordon Bashford's words 'we therefore cast it into the canal!'

T2A, which followed, was so strange that no mention of it ever appeared in the press, and the picture I have been allowed to use was marked 'Confidential' even in 1976! This looked very much like a standard P4 saloon, except for the vast exhaust funnel built up behind the rear window to take the hot gases away from pedes-trians and the air intakes of following cars. The gas-turbine engine was rear-mounted, behind the line of the rear wheels (unlike JET 1), and drove a propeller shaft which ran forward to a conventional Land-Rover gearbox mounted in the normal position in the P4 chassis. From here a propeller shaft drove a live axle, suspended on half-elliptic leaf springs. Like T2, T2A was a short-lived experiment which was quickly discarded. As far as the public were concerned, Rover gas turbine activities had once again gone back 'under cover', but there was no slackening of effort behind closed doors at Solihull itself.

Frank Bell had left the company when it became clear that pure development was to be restricted, and the commercialisation of the engines was about to begin. The Neptune engine was developed (more formally known as 1S-60) for all manner of applications, including use as an aircraft auxiliary power unit (APU), for stationary power plant usage, and related functions. Another unit mentioned prematurely in 1954 was to be a two-shaft engine with a heat exchanger, suitable both for 'vehicles and boats', which shared common parts with Neptune.

But all this was a prelude to the birth of one of the most astonishingly original cars the world of motoring has ever seen. Spen King, no longer content with the installation of his precious turbines in modified production cars, and with an unshakeable conviction that sales of true turbine cars would soon be feasible, had decided to do the job properly at last. In 1956, whenever he got the chance, he began to think about a completely new car — T3 — which would be specifically designed around a gas turbine engine. Not only was this astonishing because it was clever, but because of the way it was designed. The company's designers were busy enough without such diversions, as they had only just finalised P5, and were now beginning to get involved in P6. The budget for frivolities like T3 was very restricted, and chassis designers simply could not be spared from their daily tasks.

Not to be foiled, therefore, Spen King and Gordon Bashford, with suitable asides from Peter Wilks, embarked on the design of T3 in Bashford's own home. For weeks, three nights every week, the dining room table became a designer's board between about 8 pm and 1 am. This drove Gordon's wife frantic and ruined several social lives, but T3 progressed at a very satisfactory rate.

'Don't ever forget,' Spen King once said, 'that T3 as a *car* was really done without a budget at all.'

T3, in Rover's history, is both interesting and extremely significant. Not only did it prove, for the first time, that Spen King was already one of the industry's deepest thinkers about overall vehicle design, but it pointed the way to several features which future Rover production cars would use. We have, in fact, to go back even further into history for a few pointers — to the single-seater Rover Special with which King, Peter Wilks and George Mackie had all been involved. Their thinking and their successful development of a de Dion rear suspension with fixed-length drive shafts was very important and looked at in context of experience, and of current motoring fashions, T3 was an extremely logical design. It would have been easy to expect a front-engined car to be designed, but after the inflammatory experiences of T2 the company were in no hurry to comply with tradition. T3, like JET 1 before it, would have the engine behind the seats. The engine itself would be the latest two-shaft design called Type 2S/100 which meant 'Two shaft 100 horsepower'.

Apart from the engine, which will be described shortly, the two most outstanding new features in the design were the suspension layouts, and the drive. Not only was de Dion suspension adopted for the rear, but the car was also given four-wheel drive.

Some form of fixed-differential rear suspension was essential as the transmission and final drive were all to be in unit with the gas turbine engine, and knowing the success that had been achieved with the single-seater Rover Special it was easy to see why a similar de Dion layout was chosen. Four-wheel drive was chosen as an important and desirable feature to tame the torque characteristics of the turbine, and this also explains why four-wheel inboard disc brakes by Dunlop were chosen.

The basis of the whole car was a fabricated sheet steel chassis frame, suitably stiffened by light alloy honeycomb and bulkhead cross-members; the body, styled by David Bache himself, was built of glass-fibre. Tony Poole, still a gas-turbine department fitter, made several sketched suggestions for badges and other details, and on the strength of this found himself nominated for a permanent job in the styling studios.

The 2S/100 engine was a development of that prematurely 'leaked' in 1954, and as used for T3 developed 110 bhp at a colossal 52,000 compressor turbine revs per minute. The starter motor in this case could spin the gasifier shaft up to 15,000 rpm or so, and after 'light-up' would settle down to idle at a mere 20,000-25,000 rpm. It was still an unfamiliar scale of things that we motoring historians took time to accept.

Like all its predecessors, the gasifier comprised a centrifugal compressor, powered by a single stage axial turbine. There was only one combustion chamber, which as usual drew heavily on Lucas's expertise, and a single stage power turbine. For the first time ever in a Rover turbo-car, a heat exchanger was installed, a bulky contra-flow matrix-type. Rotating types were mentioned in passing when the company's latest work was discussed but these, made of compressed ceramic powder, had not been a success; their day was yet to come.

The engine itself was above and behind the line of the 'back axle' which contained not only the step down gears, the differential, and the forward-and-reverse selection, but the provision for drive to the front wheels. Step-down gears between power turbine and transmission shaft gave a ratio of 6.3 to 1, there was a second step down gear of 1.2 to 1, and the final reduction through the differential unit. The overall step down was 28.92 to 1. The rest of the transmission comprised a propeller shaft up the centre of the chassis which, uniquely of course, took the drive from the rear to the front. A chassis mounted differential at the front had Dunlop disc brakes fixed to its flanges, as did the rear transaxle, along with a transmission handbrake. The freewheel necessary to equalise front and rear drive shaft speeds on corners was incorporated in the rear transaxle unit.

De Dion suspension itself was not new, but the fixed length drive shafts combined with a tube having a sliding joint were a Wilks-King invention. They were always sceptical of drive shafts with spines which tend to jam at embarrassing moments so a sliding tube joint was the alternative. In this application, the tube did nothing but keep the wheels upright and parallel to each other.

There were other pointers to the future, if only we had realised it. At the front, the top wishbone was angled back at its pivots to get most of the loading direct to the scuttle, and at the rear the fore-and-aft location was provided by Watts linkages. It would all surface seven years hence, on the brand-new P6 saloons.

Fuel consumption had improved dramatically, but as it was starting from the appalling figure of around 5 mpg that wasn't very difficult. With the heat exchanger fitted about 13 mpg was possible, and since the government hadn't got around to taxing paraffin the economics began to make sense. Even so, by comparison with a piston-engined 110 bhp machine, which might be expected to record 25-30 mpg on petrol, there was obviously still a long way to go.

T3, however, was not all about economics, but about practicalities. Other firms —

notably Chrysler in Detroit, Renault in France, and Fiat in Italy — were working on turbine engine cars, but they all looked like record cars, 'dream' cars, or outrageously impractical research machines. T3, apart from its four-wheel drive, which wasn't perhaps as essential as its designers first thought, looked like a very nice and very desirable rear-engined two-seater coupe. There were hundreds of people quite willing to place orders, which would have embarrassed the company horribly if they had!

Although T3 proved that turbine cars were practical, it also proved that they would be expensive. No amount of research or experimental work could broach the barrier of cost. Gas turbines revolved very quickly and got extremely hot. If speeds were reduced, and temperatures curbed, power output dropped alarmingly; if not, then the exotic materials and the incredibly detailed machining to match them put economic manufacture completely out of reach. A 100 bhp piston engine could be built by the company for less than £100 — but it cost more than that even to make one turbine disc.

T3, if only we had known it, was the highpoint in Rover's gas turbine activities. Even the arch enthusiasts like Spen King, who probably knew more about turbine engines than anyone else in the world's motor industry, began to realise that the dream *was* just a dream: 'Trying to do something which was only dubiously possible,' says King, 'got a bit wearing. T4 was very serious, but we weren't able to make it competitive in terms of cost and fuel consumption.'

Activity sank to a new 'low', most of the staff dispersed, and it took the new managing director, William Martin-Hurst, some time even to find and investigate his technically brave subsidiary. In the meantime, Spen King's insistent optimism had led to P6 being conceived with space for a gas turbine engine to be installed, in the hope that some would be offered before that base unit was out of date.

The last desperate fling was to build the fifth, and last, prototype — T4. This, at least, would be even more practical than T3, because it was to use a prototype P6 Rover 2000 base-unit body shell. Those of the Press 'in the know' were surprised to see Rover revealing their future intentions a good two years before the production cars came along, but the vast majority of people who inspected T4 never twigged the connection.

Yet again, it was a case of matching the latest in turbines to a conventional structure, though at least it had not already appeared in public. The body shell, in many respects, was exactly that which P6 would share, but in this special case was given a heavily modified version of the original shovel-nose frontal section, along with twin headlamps which actually disguised the air intakes to the engine.

As yet another variation on the installation theme, the engine was front mounted, ahead of the line of the wheels, and there was front-wheel drive through a simple forward and reverse transmission and an integral transaxle. An automatic two-speed gearbox was claimed to be under development for later fitment, but never made an appearance.

There were four-wheel Dunlop disc brakes and rear suspension was by swinging half axles and coil springs. Unlike the unsuccessful front-engined car of the 1950s, there was no insoluble problem over the disposal of exhaust gases from T4, which were neatly passed through ducts down what we would normally call the 'propeller shaft tunnel', and were then expelled through big velocity-reducing jet pipes near the tail.

The engine was yet another major new design, created in this case by Noel Penny.

Called the 2S/140, it reverted to the original 1948 layout of centrifugal compressor backed by centripetal compressor turbine, and only the power turbine was of the axial-bladed type. This was a successful attempt to reduce costs, as machining individual turbine blades was a major hazard, technically and financially, and certainly did nothing to reduce power or operating economics. A regenerative heat exchanger was fitted, and in spite of the 140 bhp output a normal fuel consumption range of 16 to 20 mpg was recorded.

The car was undoubtedly very fast. From rest to 60 mpg, after a 'brakes-on' full-throttle start, took only 8 seconds — something of which the later P6 3500S would have been proud, and the handling was most acceptable. Under the skin the engine was more complex than ever before, and still by no means cheap enough to be a production proposition.

Nobody outside the factory got his hands on T4 for many years — though T3 was given occasional outings by the enthusiast Press, so in 1974 I was very honoured to manage a drive in the car, when it had been dragged out of retirement preparatory to going on permanent exhibition. The subsequent day out, with T4, T3 *and* a turbine-powered Leyland truck, was an unrepeatable joy, passed down with great pleasure to *Thoroughbred and Classic Cars* readers in June 1975.

Starting drill is simple, but rather drawn out. You simply don't flick the starter switch, rev the engine, and drive away. One turn of the key actuates the special Lucas starter motor. This winds away for several seconds — it felt like about 10 seconds on this particular occasion — and a faint and distant whine rises in pitch and intensifies before 'light-up' occurs, and the engine settles down to 'idle' at around 35,000 rpm.

That is quite enough to send the car creeping off up the road if the brakes are not applied because there is about 4 bhp of residual horsepower at idle, though this is much less than with earlier prototypes. To get moving properly one merely engages forward gear and presses on the 'loud' pedal. The jet lag on T4 appeared to be about three seconds, reduced on the Le Mans car, apparently, to not more than 1.5 seconds, after which engine speed rises rapidly to more than 50,000 compressor turbine rpm, and the car fairly whooshes off up the road. Once under way the engine noise is left behind, and is acceptable even to close passers-by.

It was, without doubt, a magnificently civilised swansong, but it was almost the last attempt at private car gas turbine motoring which Rover made. When questioned, Rover's publicity chiefs suggested that T4 *could* be in production in three years *if* the market were ready for it, and that it *might* cost between £3,000 and £4,000 (P4 100 then cost £1,507), but that was really no more than whistling to keep their spirits up. T4 was shown at the New York Motor Show, but by then Spen King had already moved back into the main stream of development to take over the new vehicle projects office.

William Martin-Hurst's great passion for motor sport led him to approve the building of the Rover-BRM (described more fully in Chapter 9), but this was not so much an engineering advance as a great publicity and marketing coup. 2S/140, which had been on test since 1959, was the last of the true automotive turbines, and the Rover-BRM engine was developed from it.

After the Leyland take over of 1966/67, Rover (Gas Turbines) Ltd were soon redirected towards turbine powered lorries, which showed more signs of being practical users. Noel Penny's team knuckled down to design a new, more powerful, and considerably larger turbine, which could produce up to 400 bhp. The Corning Glass rotary heat exchangers first blooded in the Le Mans Rover-BRM were specified, and the first gas turbine trucks, with cabs styled by David Bache and Tony Poole at Rover, were on the road in 1968. These were launched at the 1968 Commercial Vehicle show, and seven prototypes were soon at work — some on loan to Leyland's most important fleet customers doing normal long-distance haulage. The first trucks actually used 2S/150R engines like those of the Le Mans car, but were all later converted to the new 400 bhp unit.

At about the same time, Rover were both flattered and delighted to get involved with British Railways, then at the formative design stage of their tilting-body Advanced Passenger Train (APT). 2S/350/R, as the mammoth new engine was coded, looked very interesting indeed, especially to the new team of British Rail engineers at Derby, many of whom had been recruited from the aero-space industry where they understood turbine engines and were not frightened of them. By the spring of 1969 they were ready to order a series of units from Leyland Gas Turbines Ltd (as the Solihull offshoot had now been named), and deliveries began in 1971.

As supplied to British Railways, the engines were set to deliver 300 bhp, or 224 kW for electrical supply purposes. In railway use, they were not directly connected to the track wheels for driving purposes, but merely served as prime mover power sources for the big generators. APT-E, which made its first tentative movements on open track in July 1972, had two power 'locomotives' — one pushing and one pulling — each with four 2S/350/R engines and a fifth engine to provide auxiliary power.

But even this exciting space age application was doomed to failure. The prototype duly achieved its target maximum speed of more than 150 mph, but there was no doubt that ten engines providing no more than 3,000 bhp was not enough, compared with the limitless power available from an overhead catenary for electric locomotives, and the fact that the Class 87 locos introduced in 1974 were already rated at 5,000 hp. By 1975 a few pre-production APTs had been ordered for use on the Euston-Glasgow main lines, but with conventional electric traction, and overhead pantograph current collection. The gas-turbine engine had lost yet another battle.

In the light of conditions after the Yom Kippur war of 1973, perhaps gas turbines for road vehicles have now lost all their battles. All design activity at British Leyland ceased some months ago, and no rival project appears to be under development. Even so, if Rover (and British Leyland) have been defeated, it was not because of technical incompetence. Whatever happens in future, Rover can be sure of one thing — they were world pioneers, and successful ones at that. T4, in particular, has never been matched by any other gas-turbine powered machine. Happily for posterity both T3 and T4 have survived, and both are in running condition.

Chapter 7

A Rover for the farmer

Board meeting minutes: September 4 1947

'The board considered the position, and also the numerous alternative product lines which had been under consideration since car manufacture had recommenced. Mr Wilks said that he was of the opinion that the all-purpose vehicle on the lines of the Willys-Overland Jeep was the most desirable . . . Considerable research had been carried out on this vehicle by our development department.

It was, therefore, agreed that this should be sanctioned for production.'

Make no mistake about this. The Land-Rover, always the 'ugly duckling' of Rover's post-war range, was the saviour of the company. Without the Land-Rover the company might not have survived. Because of it, Rover rapidly stopped being small, and became large. It was the machine which placed the Rover company firmly in the big time. Not that it was ever really planned that way. The Land-Rover was conceived as nothing more than a short-term stop-gap. In the event it stayed on, to become the stop-gap which broke all records.

The Land-Rover's birth was all due to a nearly empty factory, to a shortage of sheet steel in post-war austerity Britain, to some ex-WD machinery and their shortcomings, and because of the owner of an Anglesey estate. In 1947, the Land-Rover came about because of a succession of happy coincidences.

In the beginning, the Land-Rover really stems from the little M-Type project (described more fully in Appendix 1). The M-Type was a thoroughly modern little 700 cc car, thought up by Maurice Wilks and Robert Boyle just before the end of the war. It was aimed at expanding Rover's production and pushing the company's name into a new market sector, and would use as little sheet steel as possible.

It was brilliantly conceived, and competently executed. Work got underway quickly, and prototypes were running before the end of 1946. Apart from some vacillation over the final shape of the car (Maurice Wilks not having completely adjusted to post-war tastes in full width shapes), it was a perfectly viable machine. In 1947, however, several things conspired to kill it off. Apart from the exhortations to 'Export or Die', the government urgings to a one-model policy, and similar interference, there was the old problem of tooling costs. Everything in the M-Type, almost every part, was brand new. A lot of capital expenditure would have been needed to tool up for a new body, chassis, suspension and engine/transmission units.

It was too much. In more expansionist times the company might have been tempted to go ahead, but in the gloomy crisis atmosphere of 1947 Britain it had to be a non-starter. But cancellation would mean a big hole in Rover's medium term plans. Without the M-Type, or something to replace it, large areas of the big Solihull factory would stand empty. There was no way that sales of 3,000 or 4,000 'quality-first' Rover cars could sustain the business.

The question of the estate in Anglesey now enters the story. The owner was Maurice Wilks, Rover's technical chief, so the link is suddenly obvious. Wilks owned about 250 acres in North Wales, which included normal farmland, woods, and sand dunes. He couldn't spend much time there, particularly during and immediately after the war, but liked to get his hands well and truly dirty when in residence. Maurice Wilks wasn't just a 'gentleman farmer'.

Wilks' basic problem on this estate was that he wanted a machine to do everything for him — to pull a plough, to haul logs, to drive other machinery, to keep going on any surface, and to climb the steepest gradients. This, he reasoned, would have to be a four-wheel-drive or cross-country vehicle. First of all he bought an ex-WD half-track Ford truck, which had the lusty 3.6-litre V8 engine. This was bulky and rather too unwieldy. Next he replaced it with another WD vehicle, the ubiquitous Willys Jeep which the American forces had made so familiar in Britain since 1942. The Jeep was useful enough, but somehow it rankled Wilks that he had to use imported machinery to do his jobs.

At the same time, Spencer Wilks was faced with the gaping void of his Solihull factory. He and his brother had already laid their other plans for post-war Rover cars, which they were sure were going to sell in greater numbers than ever before. P3 would come on stream early in 1948, and the more advanced P4 would replace it for 1950. In the meantime, Spencer Wilks reasoned, he needed a stop-gap, a product that could be put on sale quickly. It would have to employ a readily available labour force, but must cost the absolute minimum in capital tooling. Whatever it was — and at that time he was not committed to any one scheme — he was quite happy to see it phased out in two or three years.

The brothers agreed to go their separate ways for a while in 1947, to think through their individual ideas on this 'mystery' product, then meet up again to compare notes. Fate, however, took a hand. On a visit to his brother's estate in Anglesey, so the story goes, Spencer Wilks asked his brother what he would do when the battered old Jeep finally gave out? 'Buy another one, I suppose,' said Maurice, *'There isn't anything else.'*

This quite suddenly crystalised their thinking. Both were aware of a worldwide shortage of agricultural vehicles, caused by the way farmers were continually raising their standards and taking to mechanisation. They had also noted how Ferguson's cheap and effective tractors had started to flood out from Standard's premises at Banner Lane in Coventry.

Rover, they decided, could plug a gap. They should, and would, build a 'better Jeep'. Their final decision was taken after they had thrashed the long-suffering vehicle up and down dale, through deep water, across the sand dunes, and through the rocky woodland around Maurice Wilks' house on the island. After that fateful weekend, Maurice arrived back in the design office at Solihull and started work. He personally christened the project 'Land-Rover' right from the start, and thought it would make a splendid stop-gap.

He was quite wrong. The Land-Rover, once on the market, was a rotten stop gap. Whether the Wilks brothers liked it or not (and there is evidence to suggest that Spencer Wilks, at least, never really understood the mystique and the appeal of the machine), the Land-Rover took on a definite personality of its own, and soon became a permanent feature. By 1950 there was no question of it being a stop-gap; it was there to stay.

Within a year the Land-Rover would be outselling Rover cars. To the company, it became something of a benevolent Frankenstein's monster. The Rover company might be its master, but effectively the Land-Rover was really running the company. And since then, of course, in spite of restricted capital expenditure and antiquated facilities, the Wilks-inspired four-wheel-drive machines have always been at the centre of the Solihull scene.

Once committed to making Land-Rovers, the main problem, of course, was one of time. Solihull was empty right there and then. The gap-filler would have to be ready at once, if not before. There was no time for the usual Rover attention to detail. The company was used to taking two or three years to get an idea safely and logically into production. Development went ahead very rapidly indeed, though it would be nearly 18 months (July 1948) before the first deliveries took place.

The first Land-Rover owed a lot to the Jeep. Designer Gordon Bashford, who laid out the basic concept, makes no secret of that. It was also his job to go off to an ex-WD surplus vehicle dump in the Cotswolds, buy a couple of roadworthy Jeeps, and bring them back to Solihull for study. 'It is no coincidence that the Jeep's wheelbase and basic dimensions were repeated in the Land-Rover, as I based my first 'package' on the Jeep,' said Bashford, 'and in the very first prototype we used a lot of Jeep material.'

The 'lot of Jeep material' included the complete chassis frame. This was done to save time, and speed up development. Even with all the urgency in the world, it took months to build the first prototypes. The crucial transmission parts took the longest to arrive, after which assembly of the first example took about six weeks.

The basis of the vehicle was to be a sturdy and simple box section chassis frame, but the inspired move which has endeared it to more than a million customers was the light-alloy bodywork; that, in fact, came about more as an expedient than as a feature. The fact that it was *the* greatest long-life feature of Land-Rovers was not really realised until later. Capital, or rather a lack of it, shaped the Land-Rover's body. The Wilks' brief to Robert Boyle, Tom Barton and the other Land-Rover engineers was that the tooling outlay should be kept to an absolute minimum. The use of sheet steel, because of the nationwide shortage of the stuff in 1947, was to be eliminated wherever possible.

I am assured by the old hands at Solihull that in the beginning no money at all was spent on body press tools. Panels that could not be formed by simple bending or folding were avoided altogether. To make the task of shaping the body by hand easy, it was decided to use aluminium sheet everywhere. Only a few gussets and strengthening brackets, then as now, were of galvanised steel or iron.

The body, at first, was extremely sketchy — without doors or trim, no hood as standard, and with a centrally mounted steering wheel coupled by a chain drive to a steering box on the appropriate side of the engine bay. Mechanically, car components were used wherever possible. The first example was built with a 1,389 cc Rover 10 power unit, but as this dated from the early 1930s as a design, and was due to be phased out within months, it could only have been temporary. All subsequent prototypes, and the first production run, used the 1,595 cc P3 type of i o e unit. The main components in the gearbox and the internals of the front and rear axles, too, were existing post-war car parts.

The four-wheel-drive transmission followed the basic Jeep layout, with a drive-splitter behind the main gearbox and two exposed propeller shafts. Special to the

Land-Rover, though, was a Rover car-type of freewheel, mainly incorporated to allow for the front wheels overrunning the rears. Four-wheel drive was permanently engaged. The chassis frame, with box section side members made of four shaped strips of sheet steel, was an Olaf Poppe invention taken up after much deliberation by Gordon Bashford in engineering.

At first, Maurice Wilks looked on the project in a very expansive light. The Land-Rover, he thought, could almost be an all-purpose tractor. Prototypes seen working on the farmland surrounding the Solihull factory pulled ploughs, harrows, harvesting machinery, towed trailers, carried livestock, powered saw benches and threshing machines. Success was almost assured by the enormous number of extra fittings that could be supplied. A Land-Rover could be tailored, mechanically, to a lot of jobs from the very beginning. Tom Barton recalls that when he was designing the transmission, Robert Boyle insisted that there should be provision for winches and power take-offs. That was what Land-Rover customers seemed to want. Although Rover's early intention to sell the machine without doors, side curtains, passenger seat, heater, spare tyre and starting handle, nor even to provide a hood, was dropped before deliveries began, they made sure that luxury was not superfluously provided. A power take-off certainly mattered more than smart colour schemes, a winch more than luxurious seating. The optional low range of gears was infinitely more useful than snazzy bodywork. Practical usage was all-important.

After the first prototypes, with completely new bodywork identified by the much rounder section front wings and the early thoughts on rear quarter panel design, had been built, the company next commissioned a series of 25 pre-production or 'pilot-build' Land-Rovers for serious proving work. Amazingly enough, several of these survive and Rover themselves own the first of these — R1. This historic machine was actually sold off by the factory to a Warwickshire farmer, and repurchased from him in the 1960s.

The new Land-Rover looked as if it would do everything Maurice Wilks hoped of it, and it was committed to production in September 1947. World-wide launch would be at the Amsterdam motor show in April 1948, and the price would be a staggeringly low £450 in Britain.

The Wilks brothers thought they might be able to sell up to 5,000 of them in a year (how quaint that sort of forecast looks in the hindsight of nearly 30 years), which was not entirely coincidental with the number of M-Types originally considered in 1945. Officials in Whitehall, with their tentacles controlling material allocations, thought otherwise. In December an allocation had been (unofficially) promised, but this was sufficient for a mere 1,000 machines a year! It was almost as ludicrous as the permit to build 1,000 private cars given in December 1944.

Though launched with some doubt and trepidation, the Land-Rover was an immediate sensation. Right away it was clear that as many as could be built could also be sold. The customers, too, were making up their own minds about its purpose. Of one thing they were sure — a Land-Rover was not a tractor. The four-wheel-drive might be invaluable to them, but not for dragging implements across ploughed fields. If they wanted a tractor they could queue up for a 'grey Fergie' (and Standard's Sir John Black was delighted about that), but they would treat their Land-Rovers as dual-purpose machines. Within months the Land-Rover tradition was established, and the sales potential was realised.

Announcement was at the end of April 1948, but first deliveries were delayed until July. Only 48 were released before the end of that financial year. In 1948/49, although 5,709 cars were produced, nearly twice as many as in the previous year and a fine achievement, this was immediately eclipsed by 8,000 Land-Rovers. A year later, and getting on for the time when the stop-gap might have been expected to tail off, Land-Rover production had rocketed to 16,085.

But all this is jumping ahead. Having announced the Land-Rover, the most urgent priority was actually to get it into production. The short, three month gap between launch and first deliveries allowed the company to take note of customer reaction — the most virulent of which was that they were not willing to take delivery of the machine until some of the 'extras' were made standard. To Rover's eternal credit, they bowed to this pressure, and even sold the first batch at the original stripped-out launch price of £450.

Building production lines in the partly empty factory buildings at Solihull took several months, while at the same time machining facilities for the special transmission parts, and for building the 'Meccano-type' chassis frame, had to be installed at Tyseley and Solihull. Right from the start the export demand was almost embarassingly high, and outlets had to be signed up with the minimum of investigation at times.

One reason for Spencer Wilks' willingness to talk mergers with possible business partners (see Chapter 11) was that in many cases they had better, more organised, and more knowledgeable overseas concessionaires.

At first there was only one type of Land-Rover. Powered by its P3-based engine, with an 80-inch wheelbase, and with the stubby load-carrying area optionally covered by a canvas roof, it nevertheless attracted big orders. Even so, in spite of the original intention to keep everything simple and logical, the pressure to adapt, to modify and to improve, became unstoppable. Within months, even though the original restrictions on material supply were still serious, the variants began to appear. Ironically enough, the first variant was the least successful of all — almost entirely because of its price. At the motor show in 1948 (the first post-war show at Earls Court) Rover showed a station wagon version of their Land-Rover. Mechanically it was unchanged, but the bodywork was largely new. The doors had winding windows, and there were four inward-facing seats at the rear. Panelling was in Birmabright alloy, and weather protection was complete.

The first station wagon, sadly, sold badly, and was withdrawn in 1951. It was killed, quite definitely, because in Britain it was subject to purchase tax, and had to sell for £959 — more than twice that of the basic vehicle. Next was an optional 'van' body, merely the first of the closed versions, which soon expanded to include vans with windows, proper station wagon-type of windows and access, and the provision of a Land-Rover with a truck-type of cab.

This brought with it two problems. One was that the customers invented more and yet more jobs for their Land-Rovers, and the other was that the distinction between an agricultural Land-Rover and a 'private car' Land-Rover became very blurred. At the end of the 1940s, not only did this involve the question of purchase tax, which was levied on private cars, but whether or not a Land-Rover should use 'red' commercial-use petrol, or the uncoloured private-use and more severely rationed variety.

There were several prosecutions in this country, and the Land-Rover's status took years to be properly sorted out. The additional purchase tax wrinkle was that whereas a station wagon 'car' had to pay tax, a 12-seater machine was called a 'bus' and escaped it altogether! There was also the question of open road speed limits. If the Land-Rover was to be defined as a commercial vehicle it would be limited to 30 mph *everywhere,* but if a private car it could legally be driven at normal speeds. Only as late as 1956 was a test case involving the police and a Land-Rover owner, Mr C. Kidson of Wareham in Dorset, settled. It went all the way to the Law Lords. Lord Chief Justice Goddard eventually ruled that:

'. . . a Land-Rover was not a commercial but a dual-purpose vehicle, within the meaning of the act . . . Mr Kidson was driving a modern type of Land-Rover which was more like a truck. It could carry passengers in the cab and goods in the back, but it was capable of being used as a four-wheel-drive vehicle, and this brought it within the definition of a dual-purpose vehicle . . .'

The Rover company, and many of its customers, breathed a collective sigh of relief. This also got it off the hook as regards purchase tax, except for the seven-seat and ten-seat station wagons, which were always classified as 'cars'. The 12-seater, though, was a 'bus' and continued to escape the taxman's net. Since the onset of VAT in the spring of 1973 all anomalies have been swept away except for the 'car' versions which attract the special car tax.

The customers who demanded more and more from their Land-Rovers had two major wishes — that the machine should continue to get stronger and faster, and that it should be capable of carrying more. Fortunately, as far as Tom Barton's design team was concerned, the two things could be settled at the same time. In the meantime, mechanical refinement saw the freewheel disappear in favour of an 'optional' four-wheel-drive feature. The reasoning, substantiated so often since then, was that isolating the front wheels on hard surfaces got rid of front/rear override problems, while with four-wheel drive engaged on slippery surfaces there would be so much wheelspin anyway that it would be lost. At the same time the headlamps came out into the open from their protective wire mesh, and the original and very modest facia was replaced by an equally utilitarian panel with bolder instruments.

From the beginning of 1952 the engine was bored out to 1,997 cc, which was unique to the Land-Rover. In 1953, however, a much-modified engine with the same cylinder dimensions was adopted for the P4 saloons, with differently spaced cylinder bores, light alloy head and SU carburation. In 1955, therefore, things were once more commonised when the P4-type block was adopted for Land-Rover, but with the usual cast-iron cylinder head.

A more important change was revealed in 1954, when the original wheelbase was extended by six inches, the stretch being behind the cab, and at the same time a new long-wheelbase 107-inch chassis was offered. Once and for all this settled the grumbles about load space, and the choice has remained ever since. Sales continued to mount. More than 20,000 in a year were built for the first time in 1953/54, and the 100,000th machine left Solihull in the autumn of 1954.

In 1956, and with as little fuss as they could decently make, the company announced that both wheelbases were being stretched by a couple of inches — to 88 and 109 inches respectively. It made no sense, and the company were not anxious to explain why, because the extra two inches were inserted between the toe board and the front axle; there was no bonus in load carrying capacity.

The reticence was easily explained eight months later. The extra elbow room had been needed to allow for a new engine — a diesel unit. The diesel was entirely different from the four-cylinder petrol engine, being of conventional overhead valve design, and displacing 2,052 cc. It could make no sense in the long-term, unless Rover were planning to do something about the petrol engine as well.

They were — but they were also planning to change the Land-Rover in many other ways. Competition known to be coming from BMC with the Austin Gipsy and a realisation that perhaps it was time to make the Land-Rover that little bit more habitable, caused Maurice Wilks to take an astonishing decision. He would let the styling department have a look at the shape!

Tony Poole, of styling, said not long ago that they were not asked to make vast changes, nor as designers did they want to do so. The Land-Rover, as knocked together in 1947/48, was so 'right' for its purpose that it would have been sacrilege to replace it by rounded and more sophisticated lines. Styling, therefore, was confined to putting in a 'modesty skirt' between the wheels to hide most of the chassis frame and the exhaust system, to barrel-shaping the wings and door profiles, and to tidying up the panel work in the interests of cheaper production.

Mechanically, the most widely publicised change was to the engine line-up, where a new overhead-valve petrol engine, mainly machined on the tooling expensively bought for the diesel unit, replaced the i o e 2-litre. Rover had hoped that this change could be applied smoothly right across the board when the revised body was announced. Murphy's Law, however, applied, and a remaining sanction of the old 2-litre units was worked out on the first Series II machines.

Sales continued to rise . . . The quarter-millionth Land-Rover was built in November 1959, by which time production was running at more than 800 units a week. Several production lines were running in parallel, and Solihull's cramped premises were beginning to burst at the seams. Several times the directors decided to expand, but government policy always tended to push their new factories out into the wilderness, many miles from the Midlands. The only alternative was to decide which sectors of manufacture could be moved out of Solihull, and then to look around for factories in the Birmingham area which might be for sale, and might be suitable.

First purchase was a factory in Perry Bar (1952) followed by Percy Road (1954), and this sufficed for several years. Transmission and chassis manufacture was moved out first. Later, in the 1960s, the arrival of Range Rover, and the planning which led up to it, meant that another group of buildings was annexed — including Tyburn Road (1965), Garrison Street (1965) and 'Tyseley 2' (1969) — so named because it was bought from the Co-operative Wholesale Society whose premises were literally next door to the original Rover Tyseley buildings. Thus, in the mid 1970s, there would be eight Rover factories in the Birmingham, along with the small plant at Clay Lane, Coventry which supplied special bodywork items. This legacy of government restriction ensures that the lorry traffic in and out of the gates at Solihull is continuous. Anything from complete chassis frames to axles, gearboxes to door panels, and myriads of components supplied by outside specialists, is being delivered throughout the day.

Series IIs became IIAs in 1961, with the major change being the commonisation of diesel and petrol engines even further. The new o h v petrol 'four' had always been of 2,286 cc; now, after five years, the diesel 'four' was also enlarged to the same figure.

With Land-Rover production completely taking over the original 'shadow factory' buildings in 1964 with the exception of one P5 3-litre line, production could be pushed up yet again. In 1963/64 sales exceeded 40,000 for the first time. Apart from the civil versions, Land-Rovers were now being made for the world's military and security organisations — and Rover were later led to claim that they had supplied machines to every country in the world except for Albania and North Vietnam.

The 500,000th machine left the production lines in April 1966, by which time the Road Rover project (see Appendix 1) had come and gone, and the exciting possibilities of Range Rover (described fully in Chapter 10) had been realised. In between designing cars as different as the gas turbine, and the Rover 2000s, Spen King and Gordon Bashford found time to dabble with odd new 4 × 4 vehicles. There was at least one lightweight 4 × 4 which any other concern would have been proud of, and soon after the merger with BMH there were thoughts of making a proper 4 × 4 out of the 'Ant' which owed much to the BMC 1100/1300 for its parentage.

One lightweight which did make it was the military 'half ton' 88-inch wheelbase machine. Mechanically it was almost entirely standard, but a rapidly demountable body meant that it could be stripped right down for transport underneath a Sea King helicopter, or inside a Hercules transport plane. This strange and stark version is now the 'standard' 88-inch Land-Rover, though the 109-inch versions, apart from their colour, are still much like the civil versions.

Later in the 1960s, starting in 1967, the final 'power option' of a 2.6-litre six-cylinder engine (similar to, but de-tuned from the 95/100/110 P4 saloon car engine) was squeezed in under the existing bonnet space. At the time of writing this 'six' is still sold, in small numbers on the longer-wheelbase, but there are persistent rumours that it might be replaced by a V8 Land-Rover in the near future.

The 'six' first got in to the scheme of things when it was decided to make a proper forward-control Land-Rover, with a much greater ground clearance and a big 25 cwt payload. The first version sold very cleverly used the existing 109-inch chassis frame, but with a much-modified cab raised and placed well forward on a new chassis sub-frame. The snag was that it was quite a lot heavier than the normal control machines, and was desperately underpowered with anything but the 2,286 cc petrol engine. Even though, four years later in 1966, when it was substantially re-engineered and offered with the 'six', which meant that the front axle had to be pushed forward one inch, and given a bigger, 30 cwt, payload, it did not sell well. Land-Rover customers, in spite of their leaning towards long-life and ruggedness, also demanded enough performance for their machines not to be embarrassing. Note that the 'barn door' aerodynamics of the Land-Rover, or the great and unavoidable losses in the transmission, helped a lot. Not even with the 'six' would a normal-bodied Land-Rover consistently reach 70 mph, and most versions struggled to even beat 60 mph. Similarly, fuel consumption has always been a problem. Six-cylinder versions may notch up about 15 mpg, and 'fours' about 20 mpg.

Series IIA became Series III in October 1971, a year after the sensational debut of the Range Rover, just after total sales had passed the three-quarter million mark. The all-synchromesh gearbox (not liked by the long-time enthusiasts for the older, very strong, box), the full width facia styling, and the new front grille were all recognition points. Land-Rovers had begun to go 'soft' a little earlier, when a set of well upholstered front seats became optional. In the Series III, this process was carried a bit further, with padded door frames, and provision for a radio to be fitted. An intermediate visual change, phased in during 1968, had been the moving of headlamps out from the centre panel to the front of the wings; this was done to satisfy legislative requirements in certain countries, but standardised 'across the board'.

In the meantime, however, one of the most specialised Land-Rovers ever designed was under wraps. Meant purely for the British Army to tow their secret 105 mm gun, it was a most intriguing mixture of Land-Rover and Range Rover thinking. The chassis, with a 101-inch wheelbase, was all new, as was the stark and utilitarian forward-control driving position. Under cover, though, was a military adaptation of the Range Rover's 3,528 cc Vee-8 engine, and the massive four-wheel-drive centre transmission which alone among Solihull products includes a centre differential.

However, the Range Rover's sophisticated self-levelling rear dampers, and the well located coil-sprung axles, were not used. Instead the Army chose utilitarian, strong and incredibly uncomfortable leaf springing.

One feature unique to the 101-inch, as it always called by Solihull engineers, is the permanently specified power take-off at the tail of the machine, which is tailored to convert into a universally jointed drive shaft, and to be linked up to a powered trailer (or, indeed, a powered gun). Rover have shown some astonishing film of the Land-Rover/trailer combination acting as a phenomenally tractable 6 × 6, in which the mud and the hillclimbing abilities border on the miraculous.

Yet, for all that, the feature is not now considered vital by the Army. The vehicle/trailer hook, which combines towing, steering, articulating and a driving function, is very expensive and pernickety to build.

In June 1976, after it had already been filmed for TV purposes at the Bagshot proving grounds, the millionth Land-Rover was 'officially' driven off a production line at Solihull. It was quite a momentous occasion attended by the media, and by the civic dignitaries of Solihull, Birmingham and Cardiff, where parts are all made.

Production now, in a full week not marred by stoppages, can be as high as 1,300 every week. Nevertheless, the record for a year's output stands at 56,663 (1970/71) when capacity was rather less than it is today. Strikes and other stoppages (mainly at parts suppliers' factories) account for the shortfall since then.

If you were to walk round the Land-Rover assembly lines at Solihull today, you would immediately decide that they were overcrowded and even antiquated. You would be right. The area is literally bursting at the seams, and there is no prospect of increased production until more production lines can be built. There may, however, be light at the end of the tunnel. With the new Rover 3500 family safely launched, and the P6 North Block now cleared of its obsolete P6 facilities, a wholesale move is planned for Solihull. For the first time, 4 × 4 production will move out of the buildings which originally watched radial aero engines being assembled, and leave more room for those lines which are left over.

At the time the millionth Land-Rover was built, British Leyland issued a release which told us, among other facts, that three-quarters of the first million had been exported, and that exports now account for 80 per cent of sales. It took 17 years to make the first half-million, but only 11 more to double the figure. Petrol-engined variants account for four in every five sales, and long-wheelbase 109-inch chassis for two in every three. Iran, Iraq and the United Arab states, naturally enough, figure strongly among the exporting 'top ten'.

The Land-Rover's worth can perhaps be summed up with this final fact. Britain's Motor Industry Research Association kept a tame one for many years that they used for crashing into other makers' new models in destruction tests. It never lost a battle!

Chapter 8

The young generation takes over

Board meeting minutes: October 24 1960
'Mr M. F. C. Wilks said that the development of the P6 car had reached a stage at which a decision to put it into production could be taken.

'After discussion it was agreed to put P6 into production, and to proceed with the capital expenditure programme outlined by Mr L. G. T. Farmer . . .'

Peter Wilks, in a 1969 'Autocar' interview about the Rover 2000
'The sales department at that time were saying "But look, it *must* have a six-cylinder engine, you can't consider a car with four." And then we told them that it was only going to have four seats, so they just gave up. They insisted that it wasn't on to sell a four-seat four-cylinder car for £1,250 at a rate of 550 a week. 250 a week, yes, but not 550 a week. Of course, ever since then we've been trying to make 800 a week . . .'

The atmosphere at Solihull, particularly in the design and development areas, changed insidiously throughout the 1950s. There was a growing realisation that although the motoring press were happy to rib the company about its 'Auntie' image and its stodgy products, they were also very impressed by the Land-Rovers and the turbine cars. Spence and Maurice Wilks, even though they were getting old, gradually changed their attitude to future models. The whole scenario began to look more exciting.

It was not that Rover's designers, directed by Maurice Wilks and led by Robert Boyle, could ever be accused of being traditionalists. Unfulfilled projects like the little M-type and gas turbine cars, and the variety of still-born engines, surely prove otherwise. The problem, for some years, was that the company was still too small to be brave. With an established reputation and a faithful clientele, Rover were in quite an enviable position. It was better at this stage to be safe than sorry.

Fortunately, the hastily conceived Land-Rover transformed the company's standing, and its prospects. From being a prestigious middle class business in 1948, selling only 3,000 cars a year, Rover were turning out more than 40,000 machines a year by 1955, two-thirds of which were Land-Rovers.

The traditionalists, if such a body of men existed at Solihull, were certainly the directors. The team had been unchanged since 1933, when the company had dragged its way out of a horrifying financial mess, and they all knew how technical whizz-kiddery had led them astray the last time.

Only Maurice Wilks, the designer and the forward thinker, had joined them to shake up the pattern. He, through his regular contacts with business acquaintances, and through regular sessions with Robert Boyle, Spen King and a few others, could see what was happening to the motor car as he knew it.

P5, as already shown, might have been the car to modernise Rover, if it had been built the way Robert Boyle wanted it. In the event the P5 which appeared in 1958 was altogether larger, more costly and more conventional than originally proposed. It broadened Rover's private-car range, but it also signalled the obsolescence of P4. A replacement for P4 was obviously the company's next priority, even though such a car was not needed in a hurry.

In the meantime, Spencer Wilks was planning his succession. Knowing that Howe Graham intended to retire in 1957, and knowing that his colleagues wanted to see him promoted to that position, he therefore appointed his brother as joint managing director in 1956. A year later, when Spencer Wilks duly took the chair, Maurice shared the managing director's responsibilities with George Farmer. As one of their old colleagues summed it up:

'George's expertise stopped short of engineering, and Maurice's stopped short of finance — it was an ideal arrangement.'

Shortly after this, both A. B. Smith (production and supplies) and Robert Boyle (engineering) became executive directors, but the problem of replacing Jess Worster, the works director, remained for some time. Worster was fast approaching retiring age, and would need a successor before too long. The man who filled that slot would have a very important influence on Rover's policy in the 1960s.

In the meantime, Maurice Wilks and Robert Boyle had started to think about a successor to P4. Their first sketches, as already detailed, took shape in 1953, even though that project eventually escalated into a much larger and more magisterial P5 in the end. Nevertheless, the true ancestor of P6, which startled the public with its many advanced features in 1963, had been more than a gleam in Robert Boyle's and Gordon Bashford's eyes at least ten years earlier. Engineering innovation takes a long time to mature, as we all know, and there is no doubt that base-units were already being discussed at Solihull at the beginning of the 1950s.

P6, as an identifiable project, first surfaced at Solihull in 1956. By that time P5's design was settled and production tooling had been ordered. The advanced design team, when not diverted by work on the exciting rear-engined T3 gas turbine car, could begin to look more closely at a car to replace P4, but they had no urgent deadlines to meet at that stage.

It was at this time when both Spen King, who was theoretically completely tied-up with gas turbine projects, and Peter Wilks, nephew of both Spencer and Maurice Wilks, began to figure more prominently in the company's future. They were, of course, first cousins, both being sons of Wilks' parents, and with Spencer and Maurice Wilks for uncles — and they had been close friends and business partners for years.

The young Wilks had been apprenticed to Alfred Herbert Ltd in Coventry, and joined Rover after five years' military service. After collaborating with Spen King and George Mackie in building the single-seat Rover Special racing car (P3 frame and front suspension, Rover 60 engine, Rover P1 10 hp axle . . .) for private use, Mackie and he left Rover to set up the Marauder sports car concern in 1950.

Marauders were based on P4 chassis and components, but were not a success, with only 15 cars built and sold in two years. Spen King, a shareholder in the enterprise, though he never left Rover to become involved, once said:

'The whole thing ran into a tricky situation because costs rose faster than the price we thought we could sell them for . . . !'

Wilks then spent two years with Gethins, the Rover dealership, as service manager, before returning to the fold in 1954. For the next two years, he was production manager of Rover (Gas Turbines) Ltd, and was obviously very close to his cousin, but in 1956, at the age of 36, he became Robert Boyle's assistant. In theory he should have been dealing with all non-P6 matters, to give Boyle more time to think ahead, but as any other enthusiastic engineer would have done he also found time to get involved with P6.

Another key figure in the concept of P6, not because of the innovative work he did, but because of the sheer sweat of alternative ideas he had to contend with, was engine designer Jack Swaine. Although his team were still occasionally revising their vee-6 engine layouts, they were more intimately connected with the stretching of the old P4 engine to become a much-modified 3-litre. With P6, Swaine had almost an impossible task at first, mainly because its sponsors could not decide what sort of engine they were going to need, nor even at which end of the car they were going to mount it! The fact that the sales department was adamant that a six-cylinder engine was needed (the P4 Rover 60, introduced in 1953, had been a sales flop), while Boyle was determined to stick at four cylinders, didn't help. That both Spencer and Maurice Wilks were attracted to the idea of a water-cooled flat-four (the Jowett Javelin, in spite of Jowett's commercial failure, had cast a long shadow) was an added complication. The only thing Swaine could be sure of was that no version of an existing P4 'six' was being considered, and a four-cylinder version of it was not going to be powerful enough.

The most historic written reference to P6 which remains at Solihull is a document simply headed 'Some notes of a meeting held in Mr W. R. Boyle's office on September 21 1956'. Apart from laying down the procedures for holding regular project meetings in future, this paper confirmed the basic layout for P6, which was to have a base-unit body shell, separate bolt-on body panels, and de Dion rear suspension.

By this stage Maurice Wilks was both too busy and too far out of his artistic depth where modern styling was concerned. David Bache, and the growing design department which now included the ebullient Tony Poole (ex-turbine department), was given a free hand to produce the appropriate shape. Or nearly so. 'Not that he didn't get in on the act,' says Bache, 'but he used to do it in a most diplomatic manner. He would ask rather tentatively whether *this* line couldn't be moved to *there*, and I would tell him why not, but in the end we would usually compromise.'

We now have to put the concept of P6, and the attitudes of the younger people who were urging its development, in context with the rest of the motor industry. The Suez canal crisis erupted in the summer of 1956, and the first Suez war followed it. There was a trade depression at about the same time, and the five months of petrol rationing which followed Suez didn't help a recovery one bit. However, at about this time the prospects for technically advanced new designs suddenly improved. The British were shaken out of their complacency by the first European imports, and reviving national prosperity gave a boost to visionary planning.

Rover, at Solihull, suffered quite badly from the sale hiccups of 1956/57 because more economical motoring was wanted for a time and Rover couldn't supply it, but once expansion got under way again in 1958 things began to look a lot brighter. This, of course, was no consolation to Rover's management, who were faced with the same set of problems as they had been in 1955. P6 looked certain to be smaller, cheaper and more saleable than P4 had become, which meant that it would be built and sold in larger numbers. But the P4 lines were alongside those building Land-Rovers, where extra capacity was always needed. Since the company was planning a Series II Land-Rover for 1958, and was still thinking of putting Road Rover into production, they wanted to take over all redundant P4 facilities as soon as possible.

This automatically meant that P6 would have to be assembled in a brand-new building, and in view of its forecast specification a lot more space would be needed. The directors knew exactly where they wanted to put a new building, more than 100,000 square feet was projected for an area to the north of the existing factory, but they were not at all sure they could get a planning certificate to erect it. There had, after all, been enough trouble a few years earlier when they had fought successfully for permission to build the test track near the site's eastern boundary. There was also a sneaking suspicion at that early stage that if P6 was a completely new car from end to end, then a great deal more capital for tooling and a great deal more factory space would have to be found.

The 100,000 square feet talked about in 1957 proved to be a serious underestimate. By 1959 this requirement had risen to more than 250,000 square feet, but there was the further complication of the ever-pressing requirements for Land-Rovers. Even though Road Rover had been shelved, demand for Land-Rovers continued to mount. Production stagnated at around 28,000 a year between 1954 and 1959, a very unsatisfactory state of affairs, and even after additional space had been located at Garrison Road, nearer the middle of Birmingham, there were still bottlenecks.

The solution came as a compromise. Even though the entire P6 project was held up for nine months while the arguments raged, the company, in negotiation with government planners, was adamant. They were quite willing to consider expansion in a far flung redevelopment area, to provide new jobs, but they insisted that for the long-term good of the company private car assembly must remain at Solihull.

At one stage Maurice Wilks and George Farmer agreed that P6 should be held back for a year and introduction delayed until 1965 so that Land-Rover production might perhaps be moved out of Solihull altogether. In another phase it was even suggested that P6 assembly, after all, should be remote from Solihull.

The breakthrough came in the autumn of 1960, when the government sanctioned the building of what we now know as the North Block, while at the same time the company agreed to build a new factory at Pengam, near Cardiff, where P6 gearbox production would be established, and other related operations transferred as soon as possible. Once decided upon, work went ahead as quickly as possible, with a release date for P6 agreed as October 1963. This, in fact, was at least two years later than Robert Boyle had originally estimated, though the delay had given his engineers more time to refine and improve the initial concept of the car. Styling, in particular, were able to change the car considerably (in fact, against their will in certain respects).

In the beginning P6 was a difficult car to classify. The engineering promised to be much more advanced than any previous Rover, while the styling engineers set out to try to eliminate as much as possible from the body. While the engineers were busily adding complex features like de Dion suspension, the stylists were arranging to delete the grille. While the engineers were insisting on a brand new engine, the stylists were hoping that a pillarless door layout would be accepted. With no kind of detailed brief coming down from management, because they wanted to see what their team could evolve, given a free enough hand, the P6 project took months to settle down.

Work got under way strongly in the autumn of 1957, but it would be at least a year before the general layout was agreed, and prototypes were on the road. Those prototypes, it must be said, bore little relation to the Rover 2000s which would eventually be released in 1963.

First of all it was vital to sort out a difference in philosophy. Rover's sales force were, by now, thoroughly accustomed to selling high-quality middle-class cars, where the biggest single selling point was the smooth and refined six-cylinder engine, with five-seater passenger space as a bonus.

Maurice Wilks was happy to see P6 evolving as a strict four-seater, but his sales department was not at all sure. They agreed that P6 should be a cheaper car, but it was very logical that they should fight hard against any feature important to them being deleted to save expense. The question of the four-cylinder engine was a distinct crisis of confidence. P4s with 60 engines were not exactly setting the cash registers ringing at Solihull, and they had grave doubts about prospects for the 80 model, already designed, and due to be announced in 1959.

Management planned to lay down enough capacity — in new tooling for engines and transmissions, and in assembly line space — to make 550 cars a week in the new factory block, but sales were not sure that they could sell that many. This, in fact, was one reason why five-cylinder and six-cylinder versions of P6 were proposed *before* the basic car was announced. Afterwards, when it became clear that the public loved the Rover 2000 just as much as its designers had hoped, such incremental models had to be abandoned.

Finalising the engine, even in its barest bones, was only one of the problems. The car itself oscillated from an occasional four-seater to a more-than-four-seater, before settling down in its familiar guise. The style of suspension was soon agreed — there would be wishbone i f s and a de Dion rear — but not how it would work. Gordon Bashford and Robert Boyle were going through their hydro-pneumatic phase, influenced by what Citroen were doing, but had to drop this eventually because of the lack of British expertise on the subject, and because of the cost implications. About the base-unit structure, however, there was never any doubt.

De Dion rear suspension was not unknown to the design team. Gordon Bashford was an interested follower of motor sport, where it was still in vogue (he had designed a complete 500 cc Formula 3 machine, the Mezzolitre, for Coventry enthusiast Rupert Instone), while Spen King and Peter Wilks had already learned about de Dion by building it into the developed 'Formula Two' version of their Rover Special single seater. The T3 gas turbine car, conceived by King and Gordon Bashford before P6 was invented, also had the same layout.

As alternatives, front-wheel-drive was seriously considered, along with the cheaper possibilities of swing axle independent rear suspension, but that was just too much of a major development headache to face along with all the others already guaranteed for P6. But isn't it interesting that precisely that layout was chosen for the last of the road-going gas turbine cars, T4, which used a prototype P6 Rover 2000 base-unit?

De Dion suspension with inboard disc brakes was chosen, with the added complication of fixed length drive shafts and a de Dion tube with a sliding joint. This meant that although the rear wheels were kept parallel to each other, and vertical to the road at all times, there were track changes to be accommodated — driveshafts with splines are notorious for locking up under load and cornering stress, as Triumph with their 2000s and Stags found out with some dismay.

Independent front suspension would have been simpler to arrange if it had not been for two factors; there was still the strong possibility of a gas turbine engine being offered as a high-price option at a later stage, and there was great attraction in taking some forces directly back into the very rigid scuttle pressings. These, collectively, ensured that the 'top wishbones' were turned round, pivoted from the scuttle instead of from a cross-member, and operated coil springs mounted above and in parallel with them, which also abutted to the same stiff area.

The axle, like the all-synchromesh four-speed gearbox, would be brand new and this was where the government-sponsored Cardiff factory played its part. It was also noticeable that to keep as much noise as possible out of the car the gear lever was mounted to the tunnel pressing with true 'remote' connection to the gearbox top. This feature dates from Rovers of the early 1930s.

Years later, after the car had been selling strongly for six years, Peter Wilks told an interviewer. 'We had great arguments in those days with Maurice Wilks about all sorts of things. He was against the overhead cam because he said it would be noisy, and another thing he was dead against was the de Dion back end, which he thought was a quite unjustified expense. We took the view, though, that for the sake of an extra £35 — which is about what it costs — it was well worth it just to be able to write de Dion in the specification of the car, even if it hadn't turned out to be any better. We did in fact succeed in creating an image of engineering innovation which had an impact which the car might otherwise not have had.'

This shows that while Maurice Wilks might have had all manner of doubts about his new project he was always ready to listen, to discuss, and perhaps to be convinced. Nothing, but nothing, was ever finalised for P6 before those involved had thrashed out their differences.

Even so, Jack Swaine was handed down a difficult problem regarding engines. He was told that it should be a four-cylinder unit, that it should produce at least 90 bhp as a 100 mph maximum speed was needed, and it should be between 1.7 and 2-litres. While it would have been nice, for reasons of rationalisation, to use much-modified existing units, there was quite clearly no chance of doing so. The sloping-head 2-litre P4 60 unit was both heavy, underpowered, and about to become obsolete, while the new Land-Rover P4 80 unit was too agricultural and heavy, and was not designed for power tuning. Yet another all-new unit, Rover's third since 1948, would have to be designed. Swaine's bosses were attracted to the idea of a single overhead camshaft layout and after a lot of preliminary sketching to consider breathing and particularly charge burning, the Heron head layout with the combustion chamber in the piston was chosen.

Almost incidentally this meant that a 'flat-head' cylinder head casting could be chosen, which tied in well with the company's decade of experience with similar units machined for all the P3s and P4s. Even the M-model, designed in 1945, would have shared the same feature.

In the meantime, David Bache and his team had been converting their pretty sketches into clay models. The first quarter-scale clay was almost dart-shaped, with a very pointed shark-like nose and with tail fins. These fins were pared off almost at once, and at the same time the characteristic screen/roof/side glass lines began to emerge. Quarter bumpers were suggested at first — the same pressing for each corner — and the radiator air intake was hidden away under the sloping nose, with rather frog-like headlamp positions. Full-size clays built in 1958 looked remarkably like the production P6s from the screen backwards, but all had the very sweeping, Citroen-like nose. Prototypes were built to that style, and tested in wind-tunnels and on the road, with exemplary results. One car, with a standard 90 bhp engine, lapped MIRA at 109 mph.

When the Wilks brothers periodically came down to the styling department to view progress on this and other models, they were provided with a pair of specially mounted P5 seats, known irreverently as the 'Wilks thrones'. They would rub their hands, look gleefully around, and ask each other 'Is it time to kill off Auntie yet?' Usually they viewed the latest offerings rather benignly. But not always. They could not accept the steeply sloping nose of the P6 schemes, and it was here that styling lost a battle. No matter what arguments were put to them, and not withstanding the outstanding practical results achieved, they refused to approve the nose. The sales division, they said, would have enough trouble selling four seats and four cylinders, without having to cope with (by their standards) bizarre shapes.

Thus it was that P6 gained a conventional grille, and lost 12 per cent on its drag coefficient, together with about six to seven mph on maximum speed. There are those at Solihull still prepared to say that it was a mistake; others were rather relieved.

To look after the production of this vast project, and to inject new blood into an ageing team, Spencer Wilks then looked round for a new production director. His appointment, if blessed by failure, could easily have been labelled 'nepotism', but as it was one of the most successful ever carried out at Solihull there was no danger of that. The new man, already with vast experience behind him, was William Martin-Hurst.

Martin-Hurst had been closely involved in the development of the thermostat business for more than a quarter of a century, and met Maurice Wilks in the normal course of business in the 1930s. His sister met and married Rover's technical chief, and the families obviously became close friends. He was first 'head-hunted' by Maurice Wilks in 1956, when already managing director of the British Thermostat company, but turned down his offers as the firm's development at Merthyr Tydfil was at a critical stage. Three years later, with P6 still at a formative stage, the offer was renewed, and Martin-Hurst accepted. He joined Rover, as executive director (production) in January 1960, but within ten months became deputy managing director to Maurice Wilks.

'One of the very first things I did,' relates William Martin-Hurst, 'was to disagree strongly with Maurice Wilks about the boot on P6. When you think of it, I'd done the same thing over P4! As I recall, there'd been some trouble on the pavé with a full petrol tank breaking up the back of the body, and to sort this out the tank had gone up into the boot, which made it a lot smaller.'

Martin-Hurst persuaded Wilks that the boot was now too small and too shallow, and in spite of having to get Pressed Steel to alter the tools (which cost tens of thousands of pounds) a 'big hole' was dug in the floor to enlarge the capacity.

'And then,' continues Martin-Hurst, 'I said "it's still hopelessly small, and that spare wheel is the trouble". There was *tremendous* resistance to that, especially when I suggested making an external mounting optional, but' (with a gleeful chuckle) 'I got my way, and that's been a success ever since.'

Getting the new P6s on the road was one thing, but keeping their identity secret was another. In one form or another, the cars would be out on test for the best part of five years before the car was publically launched. Those taunts made about prototypes having to take their MoT 'five-year-test' in 1963 were not altogether without foundation!

Project engineer Ted Gawronski achieved lasting fame by lending his initials — TLG — to the badges chosen to confuse the inquisitive. Prototypes were badged as Talagos, which made management a bit happier even if the Press were not fooled. Rover, incidentally, seem to like this little game with the spies. When Range Rover was under development, they played 'alphabet soup' with the parts bins, and came up with 'Velar' for the prototypes.

In the industry, among the insiders, there was plenty of light-hearted comment about P6 and the time it took to get it out on sale, but little serious criticism. P6, after all, was completely new with no major parts in common with P4 or P5. This involved production tooling from hundreds of suppliers, for parts as different as a body panel, a gearbox casting, or a plastic storage locker. It was going to be a massive new undertaking, and apart from the installation of the new machinery, the building of the factory, and the training of the workforce, most of whom had never worked for Rover before, there was a little matter of £15 millions to be raised. It was the biggest venture ever made by Rover, and certainly the biggest by any British car maker not already a member of the 'Big Five' car makers.

Small wonder, then, that Rover took five years. Only Ford, with the 105E Anglia, Vauxhall (with the Viva), and Rootes, with the Imp, had commissioned new cars in the recent past — Ford with excellent results, but Rootes with disastrous consequences to their future. Almost every other post-war car 'new' or not had important 'carry-over' components from an existing and well-proven range.

In the build-up to P6, there was a big publicity and promotions campaign to be mounted. Somehow, in advance of the launch of P6, the public had to be made to realise that great changes were afoot with Rover, and that the cars to be produced in future would be very different from those of the past.

With the accent on modern engineering, the exposure already gained by the gas turbine cars was put to good effect. There had been no new turbine car since 1956, when T3 was revealed, so the team, still controlled by Spen King, were asked to build a new car — T4. This, as already mentioned, took a prototype P6 body shell, was given a non-standard nose and tail panelling, a front-drive gas turbine/transmission power pack, and swing axle rear suspension. Revealed in the autumn of 1961, it was sent to the New York Show in April 1962, and was then given an accolade by the Le Mans 24-Hour race organisers, who asked that it should be demonstrated on the circuit before the race had begun.

In the meantime, in January 1962, Spencer Wilks completed his reshuffle of management. After 29 years of control at Coventry and Solihull, he retired from the chairmanship. His brother Maurice became chairman immediately, and William Martin-Hurst became managing director at the same time. Not long after this A. B. Smith became the company's general manager.

The first 'off-tools' P6 cars, now christened Rover 2000 officially, were built, very slowly and with painstaking care, in the spring and summer of 1963. The Cardiff factory was officially inaugurated by HRH Princess Margaret, with Lord Snowdon showing more than just polite interest in the engineering and layout of the car. The first 50 pre-production cars were consecutively registered 101 FLK to 150 FLK, which makes them collectors' pieces. Some were used by Solihull's engineering department, who thrashed them unmercifully to make sure that 'off-track' cars were the same as the prototypes they had already approved, some became Press demonstration models, and a few were given out to selected people for long-term trial.

The car's launch, timed for the beginning of October 1963, should have been a happy time for the company, which collectively had been looking forward to that day for some time. The fact that Triumph, who had started much later in 1961, were proposing to launch their '2000' just a week later made the event more piquant.

As far as management was concerned, it was all disastrously spoiled when they arrived for work on September 9. There they were greeted with the sombre and shattering news that Maurice Wilks had died very suddenly, but peacefully in his sleep, the night before. It was a serious blow to his family and to the company, more so than for almost any other concern for, in spite of admitting that no man, or no family, can make a business, it has to be said that the Wilks brothers had been everything to Rover for more than 30 years.

Maurice Wilks had genuinely been well-liked by the staff and workmen, and almost revered by his business and Press colleagues. One of them made a particularly telling remark about the perfectionist streak for which he was known. 'We were talking about refinement in motor cars, and he said, "I think it is such a pity that refinement is always so heavy!" '

In less than two years, therefore, the company had been deprived of the full-time services of both members of the Wilks family, for Spencer Wilks, though remaining on the board of directors, was now over 70 years old, and had moved to his retirement house on the Isle of Islay. It is a measure of the depth of management available that George Farmer immediately became chairman, and with William Martin-Hurst, ensured no lack in continuity or direction.

When the car was launched, its reception was ecstatic. The Press loved it, the dealers loved it, and the public (those difficult-to-define 'young executives') queued up to buy it. And well they might. It was launched at a total selling price of £1,265, only a matter of £28 more expensive than the P4 95 model, which it outpaced in all departments except that of sheer space, and compared well with the £1,641 asked for the Rover (P5) 3-litre Mark II. Triumph's own 2000, incidentally, a fine car but not nearly as advanced in some respects, had the six-cylinder engine which Rover designers thought they could do without, and cost £1,094 when it finally became available in January 1964.

Rover's sales force had the decency to bow their heads and admit that they had been wrong. Not only could they sell more than the 250 cars a week they had threatened, but probably more than the 550 a week of which the new North Block was initially capable. The last P6, incidentally, was built just before Christmas 1976, as these very words were being penned, and was the 327,208th to be made in the 14 years that the production lines were in operation.

In the meantime, Rover's engineering line-up had developed yet again. Robert Boyle came up to retirement age at the end of 1963, and his place as technical director was taken by Peter Wilks. Activity in the gas turbine department, meantime, had been restricted to little more than continuing engine development, and a dabble in motor racing. Spen King moved across into the mainstream of design engineering in 1961, to take over planning of all future models, while Noel Penny replaced him as the turbine chief.

The phenomenal success of P6, even in its original single-model form, took almost everybody by surprise (everyone, that is, except the new-car enthusiasts like Martin-Hurst and Peter Wilks), and immediately posed a problem. By all the tenets of practical production planning — in which, it must be admitted, Martin-Hurst had been involved at a criticial stage — production capacity for P6 and all its variants should have been greater than the estimated sales of the first 2-litre version, even with a good margin for optimism built in.

As a follow-up, overdrive versions, faster versions, and perhaps even re-engined versions, could all follow, so that after a decent interval the factory and the lines which fed it would be working full stretch. The snag was that by the spring of 1964 management found that P6 facilities were already at full stretch, and the Rover dealers were quoting waiting lists of ridiculous lengths to anxious 2000 customers.

Martin-Hurst had hoped to be able to approve production of a six-cylinder version of the car in due course, and engine machine tools were built with that very provision in mind, but by the time prototypes were ready at the end of 1963 it was quite clear that four-cylinder engine production was keeping Tyseley and Acocks Green fully occupied. This still-born 'six', and the even more intriguing 'five' which followed it, are described in more detail in Appendix 1.

In the beginning of its life, several interesting versions on the P6 theme were proposed. A 2000S might have appeared, with more power and more equipment; an overdrive version; a five-speed gearbox car; a 2000TC version and finally, of course, there was the vee-8 engined car.

But that is jumping ahead. For a couple of years, at least, the company was far too busy satisfying immediate demands to urge more complication. Triumph probably outsold Rover at first in the 'Battle of the 2000s', and there is no doubt that the strictly four-seat layout of Rover weighed against it for a while, but there was never any shortage of customers.

The complex but effective base-unit structure gave less trouble to build than had been feared. Even the gigantic drill/pierce/tap jig which seemed to carry out hundreds of operations at once to units newly arrived from Pressed Steel, was relatively trouble free. At Solihull, the sight of a Rover 2000 running around the place without skin panels in place soon became very familiar.

P4 died an honourable death in May 1964, after which even more of the company's efforts could be turned to the 2000's future. Ralph Nash's performing rally cars blooded the prototype twin-carburettor engines before the public got at them, and an automatic version of the ordinary 2000, not a great success, as it was much slower than the manual version, preceded it.

With the TC, Jack Swaine's team were able to correct the only basic failing of the original engine — that (like P4) the inlet manifold had been cast integrally with the cylinder head casting, and made performance tuning very difficult. He could argue, and did, that the engine was laid down and committed for tooling in 1960, even before Harry Weslake was asked to wave his airflowing wand over the similarly afflicted P5.

The 2000TC engine unlocked some of the efficiency for which overhead camshaft engines are noted, and made the car as rapid as it had always deserved to be. Now, for the first time, the Bache-styled lines, and that tremendously practical interior, could be matched to suitable performance. Road tests gave the 2000TC a top speed of 110 mph and acceleration to match.

But all this was rather incidental to the company's activities. While the 2000TC was being developed, the company had gone into the take-over market and, even more important to their future, William Martin-Hurst had been indulging in a bit of marine salesmanship in North America. Both, in their respective ways, were vital to the future of Rover.

Chapter 9

Carving a new image — racing and rallying

'Autocar', Le Mans race report, June 1963

'Even the tremendous Ferrari 'walk-over' victory did not overshadow the undoubted star performer on the circuit . . . the Rover-BRM turbine car driven by Graham Hill and Richie Ginther . . . The car was superbly impressive not only, as the song says, for what it did, but the way that it did it . . .'

Spen King and Peter Wilks get much credit for conceiving the new generation of Rover cars. But how should they begin to get the message across? How could they begin to convince people, strangers to the Rover car, that it was all going to be different?

Firms have spent millions of pounds, and fired regiments of public relations consultants in trying to do this sort of thing. Rover didn't need to go to that sort of trouble. They had a new managing director — William Martin-Hurst — with great enthusiasm and undoubted charisma. To him there was only one obvious method, and he was its biggest backer — Rover should go into motor sport!

It was a startling change of direction. There was no motor sporting tradition at Rover (we can discount the milk-and-water forays of the 1930s), and no competition expertise. Was there even any interest within the firm? William Martin-Hurst didn't care about that — *he* wanted to see Rover in motor sport, and *he* believed in the cars. Being managing director helped a lot, but with his personality the policy could probably have been bulldozed through in any case. There was a suspicious gleam in his eyes about actual motor racing, but that could wait — for a year or so.

How to emphasise strength, reliability, quality in construction, and performance? The answer was to pitch the company straight in to long-distance international rallying. In the beginning the company had only the big and rather cumbersome P5 3-litre cars to use, but they were to make a considerable impact on the scene.

The first 'works' Rovers were built for the East African Safari in April 1962, and the last for the Monte Carlo Rally in January 1966. It was a brief involvement, but their achievements make very interesting reading. It was, in the event, a triumph against all the odds. The established rallying circus treated Rover as a bit of a joke at first — but not for long. Would anyone previously have credited 'Auntie' with the ability to take class wins in the Safari? Of Roger Clark getting a Rover 2000 into the top six on a Monte Carlo rally? Or of a Rover gas turbine engine racing at Le Mans?

For his competition manager Martin-Hurst chose Ralph Nash — for all the wrong reasons. Nash knew nothing at first — absolutely nothing — about big-time rallying. But he *was* superintendent of the engineering workshops, could find expert mechanics to staff up a new department, and could run the department as an

Above *The Rover-BRM in 1965, complete with extra driving lamps, and the Caravelle-type of air intakes behind the cockpit. Jackie Stewart is at the wheel at Arnage. In spite of engine damage the car finished tenth overall.*

Right *The rebodied Rover-BRM in 1964 at the practice sessions held in April. On the way back from the circuit the car came adrift from its trailer and was badly damaged, and did not race that year.*

Below *The 1965 race engine, complete with regenerative heat exchangers and exhaust outlets which expel their air to the top of the tail, ready for installation. The transaxle is almost hidden under all that ducting.*

Above *P6 decoration — what might have been a 2000S with wire wheels and different badging. The sheet metal is absolutely standard.*

Left *William Martin-Hurst (left), Sir Alfred Owen (centre) — both looking very happy — talking to a short-haired Jackie Stewart and Graham Hill about the Rover-BRM in 1965.*

Below *This is how modern motor car packages evolve. The first wooden mock-up of P6's interior, with the 'shin-bins' already settled, and seating layout being studied.*

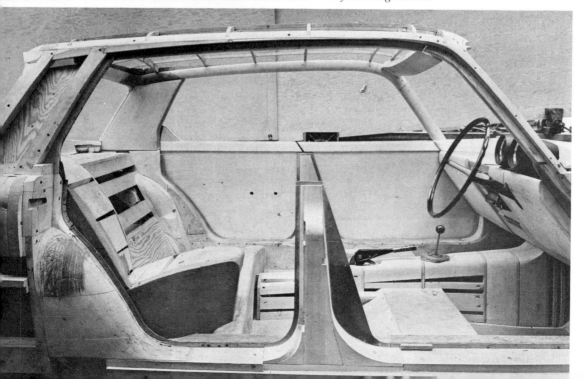

Above *Early thoughts on a shape for P6 — 1956/57. But the distinctive side window and windscreen contours are already developing.*

Right *Sneak picture of a 1958/59 P6, with the droop nose, on test at the Solihull test track, complete with wool tufts for airflow to be studied.*

Below *P6 in production form — actually the first production 3500 where the badging and the extra air intake under the bumper are recognition points.*

Above *Solihull from the sky — a picture taken at the end of the 1960s. The P6 'North Block' runs across the top of the picture, the original shadow factory buildings are in the centre of the shot, and the new design centre is between them. The SDI factory would be built on the far right, and Elmdon airport is off the top of the shot.*

Left *A. B. Smith — office boy to divisional chairman, who retired from the company in 1975.*

Below *P6 3500 at rest.*

Above *The drive which made Roger Clark and the Rover 2000 a star — sixth place in the 1965 Monte Carlo Rally.*

Right *Bernard Jackman, managing director of Rover immediately before the shake-up caused by the Ryder Report's implementation, whose speciality was in production engineering.*

Below *The lecture is by Peter Wilks, for Princess Anne's benefit. Sir George Farmer is on the left of the picture, with Bernard Jackman and Ralph Nash on the right.*

Above left *How many people realise that the new 3500's steering wheel is not circular? But here is the evidence, and it has caused no reaction from the customers. This is a view of the splendid mock-up used to develop the controls.*

Above right *Maurice Wilks (left) and Robert Boyle discussing chassis design on the Land-Rover.*

Below *Story without words — the car was a 2200TC, built in December 1976.*

THE LAST ROVER P6
BASE UNIT
327,208 UNITS BUILT
FROM
1962 — 1976

Above *Sumptuous trim and sensible fittings in the new 3500. Note that the seat belt webbing disappears into the door pillar.*

Below *A new 3500 body meets its mechanicals on the track at Solihull. Note the Watts linkage attached to the back axle case.*

Top *Well, does it stand up to Italian supercar styling? A side-by-side comparison with two Maserati models at Solihull in 1972. The line of lorries was so placed as to hide the cars from the Solihull main road!*

Above *Side view of SDI — the new 3500: The five-door layout was a big gamble at this level of the market, but has paid off handsomely.*

Below *The enormous factory built at Solihull to house manufacture of the new 3500 in 1976. The original shadow factory (top left) and the P6 'North Block' (top right) are dwarfed, and the test track (squeezed between the new factory and the sports field) had to be realigned. It was part of a massive £95 million investment.*

offshoot of engineering. Learning all about tactics, finding the right sort of drivers, and developing all the cunning which goes with active involvement in motor sport would follow.

When Rover's first competitions programme was announced at the end of 1961 there were plenty of scoffers. It wasn't as if the company had a very fast and specialised machine to use — all they were offering was the solid old P5 saloon. P5 might have been large and heavy, but this was its virtue. It was also extremely strong, and stood high off the ground. If a team of these cars were entered for the Safari, the Acropolis and the Liège-Sofia-Liège, who knew what might happen?

But how to succeed? It wasn't going to be easy especially as performance wasn't startling. Besides, BMC with their Mini-Coopers and Ford with their Cortinas were the leaders in that department. Worse, along with Triumph, Rootes and the others they had also snapped up the quick drivers. Ralph Nash would need to develop his own resources, cars, experience and preparation very quickly; his drivers would also need to be rugged, dependable and patient. He would tell his drivers what they could look forward to in a couple of years, but for the time being they would have to adopt different attitudes.

Dig deep enough in any car factory, and you find the most surprising skills on tap. The bosses like Spen King and Peter Wilks already knew about racing cars and they had, of course, built their own single-seater Rover Special to prove a point. A look at the latest turbine cars, particularly at T3, proves that they knew a thing or two about fast road cars as well. But, for once, it was not the bosses who could immediately help. Nash needed mechanics, and assembled a splendid team from within his own department. Foreman, tester, innovator and chief villain in almost everything that was going on was Toney Cox, himself a club rally driver of no mean ability. It didn't take long for Rover's mechanics to build their own reputations — as well as a set of very solid cars.

Ronnie Adams, ex-Monte winner of 1956, Bill Bengry, ex-RAC rally champion, Johnny Cuff and Ken James were all in that first team. It took just 24 hours, and the northern section of the Safari, to shut up the scoffers. At half distance, on returning to Nairobi, not only were the Rovers still running, but Ronnie Adams and *Autocar*'s Peter Riviere were holding fifth place. But it was asking too much for the cars to win anything on their first Safari — the Adams car hit a very large gulley at high speed and snapped a steering shaft like a carrot.

Even so, the cars were quite fit enough to be brought back from Africa, rebuilt, and used as practice and service machines on the Liège-Sofia-Liège. It was this monstrously rough and fast 96 hour thrash from Belgium to Bulgaria and back which finally proved that Rover were not joking, and that William Martin-Hurst's enthusiasm was not misplaced. Not only did two of the four brand-new cars finish the event (when only 18 of the 100 starters made it in all), but they finished first and third in the big saloon car class, with Ken James and Mike Hughes taking sixth place overall behind seasoned rallying machines like Mercedes-Benz, Citroen, Volvo and Austin-Healey 3000. In addition the other two P5s were eliminated by accidents, both due to driver error, and Bengry's car would have been up alongside James if he had not stopped for a time to help one of the other crashed team cars.

Three months later, the new team finished a splendid first season on the RAC Rally. BBC motoring correspondent Raymond Baxter joined James, Bengry and Cuff and all finished well. James was 11th overall, behind some of the fastest rough road car/driver combinations in the world; the team itself finished intact, third overall in that contest, behind BMC's Minis and Triumph's TR4s.

The difference, compared with the beginning of the year, was remarkable. The 3-litre was already a rally car to be proud of, and some observers were pointing to the big Mercedes-Benz as another unsuitable machine which had established a world-wide reputation; could Rover effect a similar transformation?

At the start of 1962 Ralph Nash had to search for his drivers. Now, after just one season, they were beginning to approach him. There was, after all, much to be said for a rally car which looked sure to reach the finish and reward a dependable driver with success. There were no big changes for 1963. The rally workshops were placed in the newly-built P6 North block — which was good psychology, and very intriguing for the team drivers. Every time they were tempted to have a moan about the big old P5s, Toney Cox could take them round the corner for a sneak pre-view of the pilot-built P6 2000s and say. 'Patience fellers, this is what we will be using *next* year!'

The P5s, like the big Mercedes cars, had instantly proved their point. Built, as every Rover engineer knew, like tanks, solid and rugged almost to a fault, with ample ground clearance and adequate handling, they were ideal for rough road handling. Perhaps their normal users might never have known it, but you could throw a P5 around with some abandon. To be fair, it did help to be strong — no eight-stone weakling ever shone in a rallying Rover.

In event after event, 1963 proved the point. Bill Bengry struggled home in the Safari that Easter — seventh (though last) of the 84 starters. Not, mark you, in a brand new car, but in the same P5 which he had already used in the 1962 Liège and RAC rallies. Once again Ken James took a class win on the Liège, this time finishing eighth overall, again in an 'old car'. The company then went ahead to add insult to injury for every other team. Realising that they couldn't win the event on perfor-mance, they decided to major on publicity. There would be five team cars — none of them new — and no service. Each car would carry its own spares, and every team driver would be expected to do his own repairs.

It worked. Great publicity was wrung from non-success. Five cars started and all five finished — even Toney Cox was allowed to compete under the works banner in a privately prepared machine. Ford and VW beat Rover to the team prize, and Volvo to the class win, but the publicity feedback was still good. The company made much of the trouble-free runs, and the drivers — in their radio-listening armchair luxury — were happy. It was a good gimmick, but it could only be expected to work once. It also confirmed a basic truth — that in the end motor sport is all about winning and losing, but not about finishing. Whatever the directors might have thought, it showed that the P5s were not getting any faster, or even any better, and Ralph Nash was going to need the nimble, smaller P6 to help him.

For 1964 there was certainly no problem in finding quick drivers. Brave young men like Vic Elford, who later made his name driving Porsches and Grand Prix cars, were tempted along for test drives in the new cars. Among the new signings were the vastly experienced Peter Riley, Logan Morrison, and Ann Hall.

While Toney Cox and his mechanics got down to the job of developing a new rally car (the 2000s were registered 1 CUE to 4 CUE for the curious), they also had to maintain the ageing P5 3-litres. For the Acropolis rally, held in May, no fewer than five P5s started, one of them loaned to Richard Martin-Hurst, the managing direc-tor's son, and co-driven by a promising young man called Roger Clark! Nobody knew much about Clark at that stage, not even Martin-Hurst himself, but they would soon find out.

Three of the entries finished in fine style, with Ken James the best performer with sixth overall. Ann Hall crashed her car, and Logan Morrison's shed a rear wheel and broke wheel studs too far from a service car to be rescued. The young Martin-Hurst finished ninth. The original deal was that he and Roger Clark would drive turn and turn about, but after just one demonstration of Clark's 'sideways' methods in a 3-litre, Martin-Hurst drove the car for the rest of the event!

The P5s had one final fling, in the last of the Lièges. It was the roughest and the fastest of all the Belgian road races, and perhaps Solihull took on too much when they prepared three P5s *and* three P6s. Not one car finished, though in fairness to the P5s two retirements were a result of accidents, and the other to a rock smashing through the water radiator. It was rather a sad exit to a fine effort.

The Rover 2000s, on the other hand, were already warming up. Four cars — two standard and two with prototype 2000TC engines installed — were entered for the classic French Alpine Rally. Ralph Nash had lost no time in signing up Roger Clark after his first outright win in the Scottish Rally in his own Cortina GT. The 2000TC 'prototypes', of course, had to run as Grand Touring Cars against the Porsches and Alfas, so nobody was expecting miracles from them.

The P6s started their rallying with mechanical troubles. Roger Clark's standard car broke its back axle, and Ann Hall's 2000TC ran all the bearings. Peter Riley's car, however, finished third in Group One behind the redoubtable Eric Carlsson's Saab and Verrier's Citroen DS19, and Ken James managed third in class behind two racing Porsche 904GTSs.

The Liège, as already mentioned, was a disaster for Rover. Ann Hall's P6 ran out of time when her co-driver missed an autobahn turn-off, Roger Clark's car blew its engine after repeatedly jumping out of gear, and Logan Morrison's machine simply ran out of petrol. The RAC Rally, too was a Rover disaster, with only Ann Hall's car finishing, and this wound up a rather unhappy year for Ralph Nash. 1965, on the other hand, was something else.

The year can be summed up very simply by two names — Monte Carlo and Roger Clark. The rally in 1965 was hit by the most appalling blizzard, which eliminated the vast majority of the entry before they even arrived in the principality. The mountain circuit, with numerous special stages, served to eliminate a lot more. At the end of the day, only 22 cars from the 237 which started were still running. One — just one — was a Rover, but it finished out in front of every other standard car in the event, and finished sixth overall behind Timo Makinen's winning Cooper S, Pat Moss-Carlsson's Saab, and three ferociously fast sports cars.

The weather was so bad that everybody had an excuse for retiring. As it happens, Logan Morrison's car blew its engine soon after the start, but both Ann Hall and Ken James went off the road in conditions of nil visibility and what felt like nil grip. Roger Clark, who loved to go rallying in bad weather — 'It separates the men from the boys — you soon find out who's brave and who isn't!' — swept serenely on, even though he had started at number 136 from London and reached the Alps at the height of the blizzard.

Only Makinen reached the principality without losing any time. Clark, with a very standard car had dropped 11 minutes, and lay seventh. On the final night, which included more than two hours of stages, the lad from Leicester gave best to one flying Porsche and as two Citroens fell out clawed his way up to sixth place. It was the most astonishing virtuoso performance for which Rover's publicity machine were quite unprepared. They were even less prepared for the sequel. Clark's car, along with several others, was shipped off to Sweden for a TV-spectacular of what we would now call 'rallycross'. Among others, Clark managed to defeat the Swedish hero Bengt Soderstrom on his home ground.

Ralph Nash, who was no slouch when it came to recognising real world class talent when he saw it, now knew that Roger Clark was a very precious commodity to his team. He also knew that he personally couldn't spend as much time organising the programme as he should, and decided to employ an assistant. His first choice — another rallying co-driver — did not work out. His second, to ask Clark's own co-driver Jim Porter to work for Rover, was brilliant.

Jim, in fact, did his first rally as a Rover employee a few weeks later, when he and Roger tackled the Acropolis Rally together. But, as Clark recalled in his best-selling book *Sideways . . . to Victory*, something went wrong. 'The pace notes were fine . . . but nobody had warned us that the local council would be digging up the road just before the rally arrived . . . It was just like driving on marbles, and as we spun off we clobbered the back axle on a signpost . . . What annoyed me was that my other team-mates were using the same notes, and they didn't go off, which meant either that they were driving better than me, or that I was going far too fast . . .'

The problem was that Roger was trying his very hardest to get performance out of what was not a quick rallying machine. As he said in the same chapter. 'I seemed to have more than my fair share of shunts in the Rover 2000 . . . the cars were so beautifully balanced that it was always very tempting to drive them absolutely on the limit, and occasionally beyond it . . . it was essential to row the car along with the gear lever and get it into the most incredible situations . . .'

Not that Clark's driving style impressed Spen King when he first witnessed it on the test track at Solihull. Spen cornered Roger when he came off the track, told him that *that* was the wrong way to drive a Rover 2000, and that he would take Roger out on to the track to show him the best method. They set off in fine style but, as Roger recalls. 'Almost the next thing that happened was that we went into one corner with no hope of getting round on a proper racing-drive line; the car charged straight off, and cleared up a row of marker poles . . . There wasn't a lot said after that, and nobody tried to discourage me any more.'

It wasn't Rover's week in the Acropolis for Andrew Cowan's car broke its de Dion tube, and Logan Morrison's machine was crashed. On the Alpine, fortunately, things bucked up considerably, with Andrew Cowan's 2000TC prototype winning its class and finishing third overall in the GT category behind an Alfa-Romeo and Donald Morley's Austin-Healey 3000, while Roger Clark's standard car missed a *Coupe des Alpes* by one single infuriating minute.

On the RAC Rally, which ended the season in November among a lot of snow, every one of the Rover cars was shunted — some several times — and Toney Cox must have been happy to contemplate the thought of removable skin panels for repairs afterwards! Roger Clark and Logan Morrison finished second and third in their class behind their deadly rivals, the Triumph 2000s from Coventry.

At the end of that year, Roger Clark left the team to join Ford, who had potential outright winners in the Lotus-Cortinas. Only the fact that the Monte Carlo Rally was to be held for strictly standard 'Group One' machines kept Rover interested in that event, even though they had lost Clark, Cowan and Peter Procter to other teams. That year, as almost every rallying enthusiast knows, was 'disqualification' year for BMC and Ford. A dispute about headlamps and dipping methods dragged on for months, and although the British were convinced they had interpreted the new rules correctly, the disqualifications stood. Not that this affected Rover at all, whose perfectly standard cars had not been altered to improve their lights. The disqualifications helped a bit, and when the dust had settled Geoff Mabbs and Jim Porter were seen to have taken tenth place overall. Along with Triumph, however, Rover were so incensed about the brouhaha caused on the Monte that they decided to disband their team forthwith. The cars, all brand new for the Monte, were never used in competition again, and the drivers were released to find other drives. The only real embarrassment was that Jim Porter, who had joined Rover only a year earlier, was now staring redundancy in the face, and couldn't drive with Roger Clark at Ford until he left the company! That little snag was not resolved until the following year.

Perhaps it was as well that Rover withdrew from international rallying. As the months went by they found that even the 'standard' cars entered by the opposition were much faster than those usually sold, and their standing went back, rather than forward. There seemed to be no commitment (and there was certainly no 'know-how') at Solihull to making the 2000, even in TC tune, go any quicker, or lose any weight. The drivers were beginning to mutter about the company's complacent attitude. It was all very well protesting that standard cars were being used, but if they were not winning . . .

But now we step back in time by more than three years. Once William Martin-Hurst had decided to commit the company to motor sport, he did not want to confine the effort to rallying. Motor racing, in one form or another, was even more prestigious. But how could Rover get involved, without spending a fortune on special 'one-off' cars? Once again it was the ebullient Martin-Hurst himself who found a way — not only would he get the Rover name into motor racing, but he would also give the gas turbine team a boost at the same time. Why not, he thought, marry the Rover gas turbine engine to a special racing chassis?

There was a great attraction to building a car for Le Mans. In 1962 the Automobile Club de l'Ouest had invited the company to send T4, the Rover 2000-based gas turbine prototype, to the circuit, and at the same time they made it clear that they were prepared to offer a special prize of 25,000NF (about £1,830) for the first turbine powered car to complete 3,600 km (2,237 miles) at Le Mans in 24 hours.

'We gave the gas turbine people a tremendous boost when we asked them to build T4, and then showed it round the motor shows,' says William Martin-Hurst, 'and you could just see their morale, their spirit, rising. So I asked Maurice Wilks why we shouldn't build a car for Le Mans, and everybody said, "Don't be bloody ridiculous!", but I got my way in the end.'

That was in 1962, and Martin-Hurst first approached John Cooper to see if he was prepared to build a chassis. Cooper refused (and there was a definite impression that he thought Rover were suggesting a rather wild scheme), but Martin-Hurst was not daunted and next approached Sir Alfred Owen, who was not only the owner of BRM, but had been following the fortunes of the turbine cars closely for years.

Faced with the possibility of establishing a world 'first', it took very little time for him to be convinced that Rubery Owen (or, effectively, BRM alone) and Rover should get together to make a special two-seater car. Rover's contribution would be confined to the engine, while BRM would look after the chassis and the transmission.

At first it seemed that BRM would have much the most involved part of the job, and if they had gone ahead to design a completely new chassis there would have been no possibility of the car being ready by mid-summer, let alone for the trials in April. Their solution, on which the whole basis of the deal was based, was simple (if crude) and very speedy. The Rover-BRM chassis and suspension would be nothing more complicated than a reworked Grand Prix structure!

BRM in 1962, of course, had had an extremely successful year, with Graham Hill winning the world championship in one of the mid-engined 1½-litre cars. For the Rover-BRM project, BRM quite simply took a redundant Grand Prix car to one side, cut the chassis frame about as appropriate, widened it in the cockpit area and very rapidly produced a 1963 sports-racing two-seater from a 1961/1962 GP single-seater. Suspension, brakes and many other details were all unaltered.

To David Bache's great chagrin, he was given no opportunity at that point to design a sleek body shell for the car. BRM, on the other hand, had their own ideas on what a two-seater should look like, and asked Motor Panels (another of the Rubery Owen subsidiaries) to make it for them. At the time we were told that the body had been conceived and built in a hurry — the best thing that can be said is that it looked like it! Beauty was not among its virtues; neither, apparently, was wind-proofing, for at the trials one of the drivers' biggest problems was that they were very cold due to air leaks in the body, especially with the absence of a water radiator in the nose.

BRM would not only tackle the transmission, but would also supply the drivers. Their two contracted Grand Prix drivers, Graham Hill and American Richie Ginther, were engaged for the Le Mans race, and because of the unique torque characteristics and 'throttle lag' which were still present in the turbine, they had to learn a completely different driving technique for this one race.

The brakes, of course, had a much harder job than they would have had on a Grand Prix car. Not only was the Rover-BRM quite a lot heavier than the 1½-litre BRM — though, at 1,350 lb it was a lot lighter than it looked — but it suffered from almost a complete lack of engine braking. This, at least, gave the very simple one-forward-one-reverse BRM gearbox an easy time, but the brake discs were thicker and larger in diameter than in the Grand Prix car.

Because of the nature of the Le Mans regulations a gas turbine powered car could not actually 'race' against the piston-engined cars. It could, however, be allowed to provide a 'demonstration', and to compete against the clock. The French made this doubly clear to the crowd by setting off the field at the traditional 4.00 pm, but holding the Rover-BRM until 30 seconds later.

Both Rover at Solihull, BRM at Bourne and Motor Panels in Coventry, moved very quickly, and the car was ready in time to practice at the Sarthe circuit in April. The slightly modified Type 2S/150 two-shaft engine had already been subjected to a full 24-hour test bed cycle, which included acceleration, braking, and idling — all to make it completely representative of Le Mans conditions.

The car was frankly ugly, especially when compared with the grace of the race-winning Ferraris — having been shaped purely for function and practicability. The gas turbine engine intakes were behind the doors and just ahead of the rear wheel arches, and the exhaust was through an outlet in the tail. The screen looked like an afterthought (and was!), and the whole ensemble was ungainly. But its performance was staggering. Right from the start it achieved 111.24 mph around the Le Mans lap, which, if sustained, would beat the prize winning requirements by a very large margin. Even without a multi-ratio gearbox the acceleration was impressive enough (the overall ratio drop between power turbine and road wheels was 23.1 to 1), and it was also remarkably quiet. There was something uncanny about the thin high-pitched whine from the engine, which turned over at a maximum of 65,000 rpm (gasifier) and 40,000 rpm (power turbine) and it was incredibly quiet compared with the shriek of 12 highly-tuned Ferrari cylinders, or the gruff bark of a Porsche flat-four.

By race day in June the body had been modified slightly, with a rather more raked windscreen, and had a raised exhaust outlet behind the seats. Competing as '00' — a number, incidentally, painted on the sides by Tony Poole of the styling department in what he describes as a very alcoholic condition — the car astounded everybody but its sponsors by circulating like clockwork for the full 24 hours, averaging 107.84 mph and finishing in what would have been eighth place overall if it had been competing against the other cars on the circuit.

The seven cars to beat the Rover-BRM were six Ferraris and a 4.7-litre AC Cobra. The Rover-BRM, which would officially be rated as a 2-litre car in 1965, 'won' that class from the Barth/Linge works Porsche with its GP-based flat-eight cylinder engine.

The bad news was that the Rover-BRM had been granted special dispensation to run with a very large 46 gallon fuel tank. This explains why there is such a huge difference between the 'dry' weight and the fully-fuelled 1,725 lb quoted by the organisers — the paraffin weighed no less than 350 lb. Fuel consumption with gas turbines was still a problem (the 1963 car ran without a heat exchanger), and during the race the car averaged only 7 mpg. Even the race winning Ferrari, which had a 350 bhp 3-litre engine, a 175 mph maximum speed, and could lap Le Mans half-a-minute quicker than the Rover-BRM, averaged nearly 10 mpg on expensive high-octane fuel.

Nevertheless, it was an astounding maiden performance, which in terms of world-wide publicity must have paid for itself many times over. Better still, for future years the Le Mans organisers were able to agree on a formula, connected with the turbine's air intake, which would allow turbine engines to race against piston engines. Even though this calculation made the Rover a '1,992 cc' engine, and they had only 150 bhp to compare with at least 200 bhp from the Porsches, the challenge of full-blooded racing in 1964 was irresistible.

The big change for 1964 was to the car's shape. There were several high-level 'discussions' (some people at Solihull remember them as flaming rows!) about this, where David Bache's designers expressed their opinion very strongly about the BRM-conceived shape, and demanded to be allowed to do another one. The fact that the original 1963 body was not aerodynamically smooth clinched the matter.

The new shape, inspired by David Bache but tackled in all detail by Bill Towns, then working for Rover, was both sleek and slippery. In 1964 it had no obvious upstanding turbine intakes, and this detracted from the power output and the engine bay cooling. Thus, for 1965, the 'Caravelle-type' intakes on each side of the cabin were adopted with great success. The new-shape car practised in the rain at Le Mans in April 1964 with its original engine, but for the race a new unit with a heat exchanger was promised. Then, shortly before the great day, the car's entry was withdrawn, ostensibly because the new engine was not yet race-ready. A good story, even a plausible one but not, alas, the whole truth. The other disaster which struck the team on their way back from Le Mans was that the race car came adrift from its trailer, fell off it at speed, and was very badly damaged! The combination of remaining engine problems *and* the difficulty of making major repairs to the car, for which spares simply did not exist, meant that it had to be withdrawn. This story, as now revealed, has never been admitted to before, and the trailer incident never previously mentioned.

This gave the two companies plenty of time to prepare for 1965, and for the latest engine to be thoroughly tested. BRM would be running the car once again, with turbine experts like Mark Barnard from Solihull in attendance, and BRM-contracted drivers Graham Hill and the up-and-coming Jackie Stewart. Both, incidentally, hated Le Mans and its race, but applied themselves very seriously to the job in hand. The driving techniques required were completely different from any other car in their experience and in particular the need to start accelerating the engine while the car was still in the braking area *before* a corner. Because of the 'jet lag' this method was needed to ensure a competitive lap time and to make sure the car was 'balanced' as it actually tackled the corners. It meant, too, that in that state the car could only have been used at Le Mans. The difficulties of driving like this on circuits such as the Nurburgring are obvious, and explain why the car never raced anywhere but at Le Mans.

For the first and only time on Rover-designed gas turbine engines, the 1965 Le Mans unit was fitted with twin regenerative heat exchangers. These were large ceramic discs made by Corning Glass of the United States in the form of glass honeycomb, driven by a cross shaft from gearing connected to the gasifier unit, and mounted athwartships. The gearing was such that the discs rotated at no more than 15 rpm, a speed reduction of around 4,000 to 1! They were placed so that they were exposed, in turn to the hot exhaust gases and then to the cold air intake stream. This meant that heat going to waste in the exhaust was transferred to the ceramic discs, which then rotated and shed much of that heat to the incoming air in a painless and continuous process. The big discs and the ducting which went with them helped to produce a very bulky, old-fashioned looking unit, but it was certainly efficient. In the race the car would record 13.5 mpg, compared with 7 mpg for the 1963 car.

For 1965 the team were looking for consistent lap speeds of more than 110 mph even though the engine was slightly less powerful in its new guise, but the fates decreed otherwise. Very early on in the event, after the customary bad start caused by the time it takes to fire-up a turbine engine, the car whined its way into the pits for Graham Hill to hold an anxious conference about performance. The car was suddenly slower than expected, and the exhaust 'jet-pipe' temperature was much too high. At first this was thought to be due to the very hot prevailing weather conditions, and the engine governor was reset to limit fuel delivery (which would, unavoidably, limit the power output), and the car was sent out to lap consistently but not impressively at about 4 minutes 55 seconds, no quicker than the 1.1-litre Triumph Spitfires could achieve.

After night and the ambient temperature had fallen, the jet-pipe temperature still remained high, and the fuel delivery had to be screwed down yet again. That done, and with no more than routine attention to tyres and brakes, the car completed the course, averaging 98.8 mph and covering 2,371 miles.

By finishing tenth overall and third in class behind two Porsches, the car was also 'best British', but it was not as impressive a showing as in 1963. The car had covered a considerably shorter distance than in 1963, and even when the engine was fit it had been lapping no faster. Paddy Hopkirk's very standard looking works MGB was close behind in 11th place. It was, nevertheless, the very first time that a gas turbine car had competed in, and finished a motor race, and the Rover-BRM would always be remembered for that.

Not until the engine was stripped for post-race inspection did the reason for its overheating become clear. All the evidence was that at some point in those early laps, a 'foreign body' of some sort (which was never found) had been ingested into the unit. This item — a nut, a bolt, who knows? — had been thrashed through the centrifugal compressor, where it destroyed one vane tip and damaged two others, and had lodged in the ceramic disc of a heat exchanger where it gouged out a mark. Disruption of the compressor's aerodynamics undoubtedly caused the overheating, and it is interesting to realise that without the presence of the ceramic discs that 'foreign body' would certainly have found its way into the turbine blades and destroyed the unit. Rover, then, have more than one reason for which to thank Corning Glass on this occasion. When the motoring cognoscenti learned of the damage they were even more impressed, and ready to agree that the Rover-BRM might be a complete motor sporting breakthrough. In its final form, in performances, looks, and — somehow — in 'style' it was a credit to both organisations.

But that was that. At Solihull the enthusiasm for gas turbine units was already on the wane as it became clear that economic private car operation was still not feasible. With nothing to be gained by a return visit to Le Mans — except a higher placing in 1966 (the car might, with luck, have been eighth instead of tenth in 1965) — Martin-Hurst decided to call a halt to the Rover-BRM. Perhaps if the rest of the competition programme (which was never, incidentally, concerned with the Le Mans project) had carried on, then the turbine car might have appeared again. In the event it was retired but happily not discarded. It is now a nicely preserved display car, still owned by British Leyland, and regularly shown either at their own Donington collection or at the Coventry motoring museum.

Rover's competition programme, in context with the company's 100 years of history, was short, but it left a lasting impression on its public. Before 1962 the public thought of all Rovers as 'Aunties'. After 1966 that reputation had been destroyed completely. Martin-Hurst's objective had been achieved, and his company had elbowed its way sturdily into the forefront of motor industry engineering. What has happened in the years which followed only serves to confirm this. Martin-Hurst was content, and from 1964, in any case, he had other fish to fry. A chance visit to North America in 1964 was to produce the most dramatic sequel.

Chapter 10

Modern times — vee-8s and Range Rovers

Board meeting minutes: July 30 1964

'The managing director reported that we had been in negotiation with General Motors Overseas Operations with a view to obtaining a licence for the manufacture and sale of the Buick 215 cubic inch vee-8 aluminium engine, which in his view was an engine that was highly suitable for incorporating in the company's products . . .'

William Martin-Hurst (managing director from 1962 to 1969) in a recent discussion

'I remember the decision to go ahead with the vee-8, I remember it very well, because it was an uphill struggle all the way. George Farmer said, "Do you *really* think we can sell enough of these?", and I said, "Of course, and not only that, we won't have to make a new 'six', and I'm sure we can commonise the base units." If I'd been wrong, I'm sure I could have been out on my ear . . .'

Now it was time for the next big step forward. The world of motoring was moving fast, and Rover would have to keep up with it. Everything they had done in the 1960s had been right for them. The turbine cars had shown that there was brilliant design talent at Solihull; the Rover 2000 had proved just how smartly they could jump out of the past into the future, and the competition programme had shown, even to the sceptics, that there was more to a Rover than dignity and quality.

Perhaps the next step would never have been achieved without William Martin-Hurst, who had that certain gleam in his eyes, and that cheeky regard for the Rover tradition which Maurice Wilks and George Farmer wore like a mantle. More than this, Martin-Hurst was an enthusiast, a man who bounced round the factory making a thorough nuisance of himself, but who liked to see new things happening. He was exactly the right man to be occupying the chief executive's chair at this time.

The problem developing as the Rover 2000 was launched was straightforward enough. In the overall scheme of things the Rover 2000 and its component parts could not readily be adapted for other uses. Nothing it contained was of great value to the Land-Rover, and it was completely different from the P5 3-litre. Almost overnight it had transformed the company's prospects and expanded its horizons, but in engineering it was all very self-contained. In the future, though, the P5 would need to be improved, or replaced, and there was always a need to up-date the Land-Rover. Financial prudence suggested that the P5 could not be replaced by an entirely new motor car, but would need radical revision.

A new engine, or family of engines, was the kernel of this. Whatever was eventually settled upon would have to be usable for P5s, P6s *and* Land-Rovers. The search for that engine, and the studies that led up to it, began to dominate the thinking of both Martin-Hurst and Peter Wilks. What form it would take was not at all clear, but what it would replace was obvious. The famous old i o e slant-head 'six' would have to be retired. Its replacement would have to be more powerful, versatile, modern and preferably a lot smaller and lighter. Not that there was anything new about Rover engineers designing new power units. As described in more detail in Appendix 1, they had been looking at vee-6 designs during the 1940s and 1950s, and now turned their attention to new in-line units. The problem there was one of weight and length; a big but efficient lump could be tolerated in the magisterial P5, but simply would not work in up-market versions of P6. Between 1963 and 1965 Jack Swaine's designers built six-cylinder *and* five-cylinder relatives of the overhead-cam Rover 2000 'four' (see Appendix 1), but neither was considered appropriate.

Although this was not an immediate problem (in the Rover 2000, certainly, the 114 bhp twin-carburettor engine, with its more efficient head and breathing arrangements, would soon add a new dimension to that range), the old 'straight-six' could not be further improved. The stretch from 2.6-litre to 3-litre, and Weslake's attention to the breathing, had been the final one. Its layout, after all, dated it in concept from the late 1930s, and in execution from 1946.

The solution, unexpected and miraculously appropriate, arrived with all the magic of a good fairy story. William Martin-Hurst takes all the credit for finding the vee-8 and much of it for pushing ahead with production. It was unexpected because he found it while trying to sell something else. A meeting to promote diesels and gas turbine units led to the vee-8 instead. Nothing, not even in fiction, could have been more romantic. Martin-Hurst recalls with great glee, how it happened. 'I was on a visit to Mercury Marine in North America to talk Carl Keikhaefer into buying Rover gas turbines for his pleasure boats. When he and his chief engineer, Charlie Strang, had studied all the details, documents and balance sheets relating to Rover, Strang suddenly said, "I see you have a 2¼-litre diesel", which of course was the Land-Rover diesel. He then told me how they were developing an inboard-outboard scheme for Chinese fishermen, and that they were using expensive Mercedes diesels. So I supplied him with a couple of Land-Rover diesel engines, which he fitted into boats down at his private lake in Florida.'

That led to further visits, until one day. 'I was in his experimental workshops in Fond du Lac, in Wisconsin, talking about this and that, when I saw that lovely little light alloy vee-8 engine sitting on the floor. I said, "Carl, what on earth is that?", and he told me it was for a racing boat, and that he'd originally winched it out of a Buick Skylark car. I asked him whether it would be available, and I was astounded when he told me that General Motors had just taken it out of production!'

Martin-Hurst then ran his rule over it, discovered that it was just an inch or so longer than the Rover 2000 'four', though much wider and, he guessed correctly, a little heavier. (His guess was a good one — the weight penalty was a mere 12 lb!). Having already been out in one of the GM 'compacts' with that engine fitted, he realised that it was a gutsy and responsive unit. Looking back over the years, he is still sure that from that moment he was certain this engine would do for Rover. How, and in what way, he did not know, but that was what he was paid for — it was up to him to find out. His worry was that if GM had made it obsolete, there must be something wrong with it. Or was there?

He need not have worried. The engine itself was fine, but no longer fitted into the overall scheme of things at General Motors. If anything, it was too good, and certainly too expensive, for GM's future needs. Work on the engine had started way back in 1950, and the first experimental light alloy Buick vee-8 had run on a test bed in 1952. Developed because Buick wanted a light and powerful engine for 'compact' cars, it was forced through to production in 1960 because alternative technology in the form of thin-wall iron castings had not then been developed. But by 1963, thin-wall cylinder blocks were well understood around Detroit, and with GM swinging the 'commonisation' axe the light alloy vee-8 was an obvious candidate for the dustbin. The fact that North American buyers were growing out of their liking for the small 'compact cars' also had much to do with it. Therefore, after 750,000 aluminium engines had been built and fitted to the Buick Special/Pontiac Tempest and Old-smobile F85 Cutlass family, they were replaced by an enlarged cast-iron relative.

The problem, of course, was to find out who would be able to talk to him about the engine. Keikhaefer told him to go and see Ed Rollart at GM, but as this was also New York Motor Show time the American was very difficult to locate. Martin-Hurst eventually finished up having a working breakfast with him at the Essex hotel, found that Rollart was not the man with authority, and was sent off to see Phillip Copelin at GM International. Martin-Hurst was pleased by this, for until 1961 Copelin had been running Vauxhall in Britain, and the two had met more than once.

The meeting with Copelin was affable enough, and Martin-Hurst made it clear that he, on behalf of Rover, was interested in testing Buick engines with a view to licensed production in Great Britain. Copelin found all this 'very interesting', but requested time to consult his colleagues. After three months, Rover had heard nothing. Fearing the worst, Martin-Hurst flew back to New York, met up with Copelin, and was greeted with amazement. 'You see, General Motors had not treated my request seriously. They simply wouldn't *believe* that we were really interested! Anyway, my second visit made it clear that we were in deadly earnest, and then we got down to serious negotiation.'

This was in the winter of 1963/64, but in the meantime Martin-Hurst had not been idle. Before leaving Mercury Marine after discovering the Buick engine, he had persuaded Keikaefer to crate the unit, and have it shipped back to Britain where, on arrival in the engineering department, it caused a considerable stir. Peter Wilks, though about to become technical director on Robert Boyle's retirement, knew nothing about Martin-Hurst's manoeuvrings, but probably knew a lot more about the engine's design than anyone else at Solihull. When Martin-Hurst arrived home, button-holed Peter Wilks, and told him of his plans, he was aghast. Exciting it might be, but it couldn't have happened at a worse time. The Rover 2000 had just safely been launched, the 2000TC was well on the way, and the first of the 'straight-six' P7s was on the road. Spen King and Gordon Bashford were already thinking about a 'straight-five' for the car.

'Peter took one look at the engine,' recalls Martin-Hurst, 'and said, "Now look, this is absurd, it may be a good engine but we're not going to put it in a P6 because you'll never get it in — and anyway we're all far too busy." I reckon I was the only true believer at that time, and anyway I was managing director and it *was* my idea.'

Martin-Hurst, however, persisted. Ralph Nash, superintendent of the experimental workshops, also had control of the competition department and the mechanics, led by Toney Cox, were 'between events' because of the considerable gap between the RAC Rally in November and the Acropolis Rally in May. Wilks' reaction at first was to say, 'For God's sake don't ask them to do it, they might get big ideas'. But the idea made so much sense that it was tackled in that manner.

Without fuss, and with the very minimum of engineering design, that ex-powerboat engine was shoe-horned into a Rover 2000. The next job was to convince other directors that the idea made sense. Martin-Hurst took the car down to a board meeting in London, waylaid ex-chairman Spencer Wilks on the way back and said, 'Try this car, I've got a little surprise for you!' Wilks drove the car and was so amazed he pulled into the next motorway service area and gasped, 'William, what *have* we got here, this is the very first Rover I have ever driven which isn't underpowered!'

As an intitial demonstration that was enough, and Martin-Hurst was then given *carte blanche* to go back to Phillip Copelin in New York to negotiate terms. Rover's initial problem had been that while GM thought they were not serious about taking up a licence they were not able to glean much information. Once it became clear that a deal would eventually be done, in Martin-Hurst's words 'the floodgates were opened'. Not only were all the GM drawings and service records made available, but as part of the deal the company took over 39 new Detroit-built engines for a negligible sum.

By now Peter Wilks and Spen King were completely convinced about the light-weight vee-8. While their senior colleagues were talking terms with the mighty GM, the 'terrible twins' were busily scrapping all the 'fives' and 'sixes' which had been squeezed into the P6 base units. Spen King and Gordon Bashford were already sketching away at a variety of ways of using the vee-8s.

Though the first conversion had been into a P6 Rover 2000, that wasn't the top priority by any means. The big P5 3-litre, now starting its seventh sales year, was beginning to look its age, and nothing that David Bache's styling office could do was likely to sustain it for long. Bache had looked enviously at the Mercedes-Benz 600 announced in 1963, and considered a 'Grosse Rover' conversion on the same pre-stigious lines, but he wasn't going to be helped by any engine power boosts and the idea was dropped. The last of the P4 cars was made on May 27 1964. This left the 'straight-six' i o e unit out on a limb. Production only for the P5 began to look uneconomic, and a scheme to fit the engines to Land-Rovers was by no means settled. Development of the new vee-8 in advance of securing GM's agreement would therefore go ahead on two fronts — first for fitting to the P5, and second for the P6. That was enough for Solihull's engineers to digest and further and more exciting schemes would have to wait.

It was about this time, and because of this P5 updating decision, that all ideas of replacing P5 by a new model were discarded. Peter Wilks, with the five-year experience of the Rover 2000 project behind him, realised that only one or other of the existing private car lines could be completely re-engineered at once. What this meant to Rover, however, is described later, in Chapter 12.

Taking on the ex-Buick vee-8 was an enormous project for Rover, and important by anyone's standards. Getting a new engine into the showrooms, never simple even in the 1930s and 1940s, was now a lengthy and costly affair. To take on a well-proven design and modify it to British requirements of tooling and quantities, is ambitious enough. That said, to pick up a completely strange engine in 1964, gain a licence to manufacture it in January 1965, and have it in production by the autumn of 1967, is no mean feat. The merger with Alvis came too early to affect its progress, and the merger with Leyland too late.

One thing became clear to Martin-Hurst and Peter Wilks right from the start. The Buick engine was a fine design, but they couldn't possibly make it in the same form in Britain. There was also a lot about the engine which they didn't understand. This might have been the umpteenth vee-8 designed at General Motors, but it was the very first at Solihull. That problem was sorted out in short order when Rover literally 'took over' Joe Turley from Buick, where he had been in charge of engine design, but was within 18 months of retirement. A bit of fast and persuasive talking on Rover's behalf led to Turley and his wife being installed in a Solihull flat, Turley being paid a handsome American-sized salary, and asked to be a general adviser on the project. When he arrived, and got used to the 'Limey' way of life and work, he was very puzzled by Rover engineers' insistence on better breathing and a higher rev range. The Buick ran out of breath at around 4,700 rpm, but Rover were looking for at least 5,200 rpm and preferably even 5,500 rpm.

'Why do you want all those revs?' asked Turley, 'we never needed them at Buick. People just don't drive like that.' The only way to convince him otherwise in speed-limit-free Britain was to put him in a test car alongside one of Rover's more enter-prising drivers, rush him up and down country at more than 100 mph in a Buick-equipped P5, and wait for his reaction. He was quite shattered by the experience and completely convinced!

Rover were also puzzled about discrepancies between actual engines, and the drawings they had received. Turley was able to point out that changes with which the designers concurred had often been made in GM foundries and machine shops but had never been formalised by official modifications. That gave Rover a new insight into the much-admired GM's methods. Even so, Turley was not always happy. He once approached Martin-Hurst and said he didn't think he was earning his salary.

'How many people have you talked to this week?', his managing director asked.

'About half a dozen, I reckon.'

'And what did they want to know?'

'Well, they wanted to know why the crankshaft webs had a smaller radius than we showed on GM drawings. I told them that after we made about 50,000 engines we started to get crank problems, and we discovered that by reducing the web radius we got round that.'

'We don't know anything about vee-8s yet. What do you think that sort of informa-tion is worth to Rover? You can't put a price on it.'

End of conversation, and end of Turley's worry. He could see the point.

Details of the changes Rover made to the ex-Buick design have been published many times before. Apart from SU carburettors instead of the Buick's Rochester, and Lucas instead of AC-Delco ignition, most of the effort went into 'production engineering'. The Americans, for instance, had gone in for gravity die casting of the cylinder block, with the iron liners held in place by mandrels during the casting process. For this, incidentally, GM had been using a redundant automatic transmis-sion die casting machine, and the whole thing had been done with the block on its end. Rover, for their part, chose to have sand-cast blocks, with press-fit liners. These, along with the relatively simple gravity die-cast cylinder heads, and the pressure die-cast front timing covers, would all be supplied by Birmingham Aluminium from Smethwick.

The result was a delightfully refined, light and compact 3,528 cc engine which very easily produced more than 160 bhp at 5,000 rpm. Nor was it anything like fully developed; GM, after all, had only used it for three years, in a motor city where engine lives are measured regularly in decades. Rover knew, as did the more know-ledgeable among the motoring press, that examples of the GM-built engines had already been enlarged to 4.4-litres in North America, and that tuners like Traco had been extracting a very reliable 350 bhp from them. Even with the 160 bhp engine, which was much more lusty than any previous Rover unit, the company had a power plant that might be useful to them for at least 20 years.

Even before it went on sale the publicity began to mount up. Jack Brabham used Repco single-overhead camshaft engines to win his third Grand Prix world championship in 1966 and these units, in the beginning, were developed from the light-weight Buicks. It proved, yet again, that the cylinder block's basic structure could deal with higher stresses than Rover were intending to impose. There was, however, one remaining problem. The company might now have a splendid engine, but they found themselves without a manual gearbox which could deal with more than 200 lb foot of torque. In the case of the P5 car, this was no great embarrassment, because sales were convinced that most people would want an automatic version in any case, but P6 prospects were rather daunting. From 1968 when the Buick-based engine was first offered in the P6 base-unit, to 1971 and the 3500S, there was a hiatus when no manual transmission was offered.

In the meantime, too, Rover had been involved in mergers, more fully noted in Chapter 11. The purchase of Alvis, in 1965, came at exactly the right time as far as the vee-8 engine was concerned. Alvis, with their recent aero engine history, were well-stocked with precision machinery and the people to work them. Rover, for their part, could see many vee-8 items which could ideally be made by such methods.

The more significant merger, with Leyland-Triumph at the end of 1966, was potentially more worrying, especially as far as new products were concerned. The motor industry's grapevine had already told Peter Wilks that his opposite number at Triumph, Harry Webster, was pressing ahead with a new overhead cam vee-8 engine. After the merger, however, he found that, in 2½-litre form and with about 120 bhp, it was not a direct competitor. But neither was yet in production. Was there really scope for both units in Rover-Triumph's future? And if not, which should be dropped? It seems incredible now, in the hindsight of British Leyland's financial history, that both were approved, and that both (at the time of writing) are still in production. The vee-8, with a little installation difficulty, would have been ideal for Triumph's Stag. Rover's vee-8, too, was well on the way to the completion of £3 million worth of production tooling at the beginning of 1967, while none then existed for the Stag's vee-8.

With final assembly located at the Acocks Green factory, the first production-line engines were ready in the summer of 1967, and the cars to use them were coming along nicely. The last of the P5 3-litre cars, with its 'straight-six' engine, was built before Solihull's summer holiday close down in August, and the first of the P5B cars (B for Buick, naturally enough) rolled out in September. Apart from being very much faster than before (*Autocar,* in their road test, recorded 108 mph instead of a 3-litre's 102 mph maximum, and 0-to-90 mph acceleration in 31.5 seconds instead of 54.9 seconds), the 3.5-litre car was nearly 270 lb lighter than its predecessor. Not only did the vee-8 put in the power, but it also took out the weight.

More notable was the trend in fuel consumption. Although the new vee-8 version of the car was much more powerful than before (160 bhp against 121 bhp peak power output), it was also more efficient. *Autocar's* testers had recorded a greedy 15.6 mpg for the 'straight-six'. For the vee-8, whose test mileage included a run to and from Sweden, they achieved a very creditable 19.2 mpg.

The public liked the new cars too. Rover's ever-cautious sales division, trained so prudently and assiduously over the years by Spencer Wilks, had originally thought that 85 cars a week would satisfy their market. Within a week of the Earls Court motor show, they smartly doubled that figure. Nonetheless, the P5B was merely a holding operation. Even with its brightly modern engine it was not expected to be a wild success. Its great bulk, its dignity, and its rather ponderous road manners, would see to that. Maurice Wilks, if he had been around to observe, would still have been proud of it.

The important project, as far as volume sales and prestige was concerned, was the insertion of the vee-8 into the Rover 2000 structure. P6, in Solihull language, would become P6B, and *that* transformation was expected to be startling.

The sheer impact of this transplant was rather blunted by the lack of a suitable manual gearbox. If ever a modern sports saloon cried out for a good long-legged five-speed transmission, the P6B was it. Unhappily for Rover they did not have a five-speed box — they didn't even have a suitable four-speed box! That fitted to the Rover 2000 was purpose-built for the 2-litre car, was manufactured in Cardiff, and was quite unsuited to grappling with the vee-8's torque. Neither was the 3-litre's box man enough for the job as it normally came in unit with a Laycock overdrive and would not easily have squeezed under the 2000's floor pan. In a move quite uncharacteristic of the company, a German ZF five-speed gearbox was considered, and tried, but this was not refined enough for them. As soon as the Leyland-Rover merger had been formalised, early in 1967, a Triumph 2000 box was also tried but this, too, did not have the reserves to deal with vee-8 torque.

The answer, in the short term, was to go into production with an automatic transmission car only, put a brave face on it, and declare that the customers preferred it that way. It didn't convince everybody. There was a frustrated queue of sporting-minded and young-at-heart Rover customers who could hardly contain their impatience. In the event they had to wait more than three years for 'their' car.

After much experimentation and a great deal of finger-crossing the company announced the manual transmission car, the 3500S, in October 1971. The box chosen was a thoroughly reworked and specially adapted derivative of the Rover 2000 unit, but with such refinements as taper-roller bearings to withstand end thrust, shot-peened gear wheels, an entirely new finned casing, larger sump capacity and an oil pump driven from the back of the layshaft to provide positive lubrication to gears and bearings.

A bonus, made possible because the new gearbox was physically smaller than the Borg Warner automatic, was that the exhaust system could be realigned and maximum power slightly increased. The results were startling. While the 3500 automatic had been good for at least 115 mph, and would record about 19 to 20 mpg, the manual-transmission cars would rush up to nearly 125 mph in great style, sprint from rest to 100 mph in less than half a minute, and still be able to keep their fuel consumption about 23 to 25 mpg.

Since the essential forced changes to the 2000's base-unit had been relatively few (the biggest investment went into the new gearbox, the new axle unit, and the drive train to suit), William Martin-Hurst's assertion that the base units could be commonised was proved feasible. More than this, the 3500 was such a refined car that it made nonsense of some of the rorty and unreliable 'transplant specials' which the specialist tuners had been selling. Until the energy crisis and the rise in petrol prices bit deep into Europe's prosperity in 1974, the Rover 3500S was a very hot property indeed. No self-respecting British police force was complete without one. As fast as a Jaguar, much less expensive, and just as nimble in a crisis, a 3500S made an ideal

Above *The SD1 mock-up as finally approved in 1972. This is actually a 'clay'.*
Below *The massive and brutally impressive P8 car — seen here as a clay model in 1968.*
Bottom *On the way towards the final 3500, the 'Type A' body style of 1971 by David Bache's team.*

Above *A forerunner of the new 3500 — this was a Michelotti-styled P10 proposal from 1971.*

Left *Series I Land-Rover chassis showing the original very discreet instrument panel.*

Below *The original Land-Rover prototype of 1947, with centrally-placed steering wheel, and extremely rudimentary bodywork without doors or any sort of weather protection.*

Above *The forward-control Land-Rover, based on a normal chassis, but with an extra front subframe. Much of the cab, too, was normal Land-Rover.*

Right *Road Rover in its final form, with a Rover P4 90 chassis, and a Land-Rover engine. Its styling was heavily influenced with Chevrolet estate car thinking of the early 1950s.*

Below *First and millionth Land-Rovers, 28 years apart. HUE 166 is actually R1, the very first of the pilot-build cars, and has been owned by the company for many years.*

Above *The unique 'kneeling Land-Rover', developed to transport the Rover-BRM to Le Mans in 1965. This used front-wheel-drive only, and a much modified forward-control cab.*

Left *Rover's Scarab in 1931 — a very minimal type of motoring indeed.*

Below *Range Rover, as designed by Spen King in 1967.*

Above *The unique 101-inch Land-Rover, with its Range Rover vee-8 engine and central gearbox in a special chassis for the British forces. Here it is towing the Rubery Owen driven trailer — a very effective 6 x 6 formula.*

Right *M-Type prototype number one, with the interim body style approved by Maurice Wilks. There were four seats, but only just!*

Below *Range Rover as retouched by David Bache's department. The original work is a great credit to Spen King because the basic proportions were all retained.*

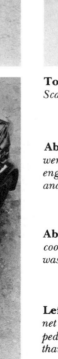

Top *The only Rover tractor, built in 1931, with a Scarab engine ahead of the fuel tank and seat.*

Above *Solid proof, pictured in 1976, that Rover were serious about their 'in-line' five-cylinder engine. This was the three-carburettor version, and fitted snugly into a P6's engine bay.*

Above left *Scarab's rear-mounted vee-twin air-cooled 1-litre engine. Rear suspension, of course, was independent.*

Left *Scarab with the lid off, showing that the bonnet concealed nothing except the footwells and the pedals. You couldn't get much closer to an accident than that!*

Above 'Gladys' was a smart fast-back two-door body style on the P6 chassis, and was at one time intended to become the Alvis GTS. David Bache now owns the car.

Right Another Rover that 'might have been' — the badge says 'Rover 20hp', but front and rear details are very strange. This was an early post-war scheme which came to nothing.

Below Leyland's gas turbine lorries owed much to Rover. Not only did Solihull provide the engines, but David Bache's department styled the cab and interior.

Left *P6BS from above — one hatch covers the engine, while the other gives access to a very useful stowage 'boot'. In prototype form the carburettors were visible under a perspex cover.*

Below *The sharp-edged P6BS as conceived by Spen King in 1966, and* **bottom** *the smoothed-out P9 which evolved from it in 1968/69. Wouldn't we all have liked to buy one costing several hundred pounds less than a Jaguar E-Type?*

chase car.

It was, of course, ideal for the company's image. Though their new masters, Leyland, had refused permission either for the Bache-styled two-door fastback version ('Gladys', as she was always known in styling), or for Spen King's brilliant mid-engined coupé (see Appendix 1) to go into production, Rover was now well-known as a sporting-minded and virile company.

Both Spen King and Peter Wilks were desolate at the thought of losing the P6BS, but they thought they could get some sports car 'action' into the fold without enormous effort. Even as the P6BS prototype was being built, Peter Wilks paid a visit to his friend Peter Morgan at Malvern. If Rover made their new (and still secret) vee-8 engine available to Morgan, would Morgan be interested in joining forces with them? Would Peter Morgan, in effect, be willing to trade his future independence for an assured supply of components and financial support?

It was an intriguing offer, but not for Peter Morgan an unfamiliar one. Morgan, tiny, vigorous, and alone since the beginning of the century, were quite used to receiving suitors. Peter's father 'HFS', and Peter himself, were both used to rejecting them in an urbane and civilised manner. But Rover's offer was one with a difference, and both Wilks and Morgan knew it. The Malvern suports cars relied on Ford and Triumph for their engines. Continued Ford supply was guaranteed, but what about Triumph? Rumour had it that the TR4A was the last of the four-cylinder line of sports cars at Coventry; the Morgan Plus Four used TR4A engines, so if the car disappeared could the engines be far behind?

In short, Peter Morgan loved the idea of the vee-8 engine, especially as it was no heavier than the lusty old Triumph 'four-banger', but he didn't like the idea of a merger. Happily, discussions were held in such a friendly atmosphere that Rover smoothly withdrew their offer while saying that engines could be made available anyway. By 1967, with a vee-8 already shoe-horned into a development Morgan, Leyland had come on to the scene, and things now got complicated.

Leyland had been interested in putting Rover's new engine into their Stag. General Motors, though, were not. They were quite happy to see a Rover saloon car, and even the small production Morgan, fitted with their redundant unit, but if a Triumph sports car was likely to provide competition to their Corvettes they were not as compliant. This meant delay to Morgan's hopes, but Harry Webster's suggestion that Morgan might try the Stag engine instead made matters even more complex, politically. However, everything was soon sorted out amicably. George Turnbull of Rover-Triumph visited Malvern, blasted-off for a high speed tour of the countryside, came back with his hair well windblown and with a silly grin on his face, and agreed that Rover should supply engines for the new Plus-Eight sports car, but 'you mustn't take too many!' That didn't worry Peter Morgan too much, anyway, because peak production in a good week at Malvern was only ten cars, and a proportion of them would be Ford-engined.

In the meantime, back at Solihull, Spen King's 'New Vehicle Projects' team had been busy. It was difficult to keep their enthusiasm in check most of the time, but on this occasion they had surpassed themselves. With the Rover 2000 safely in production, the mid-engined coupé being built, and all thoughts of another private car design put back for a while, they had had some time to spare. Peter Wilks and Spen King therefore turned to the company's other arm — cross-country vehicles.

Throughout the 1950s the company had experimented with the two-wheel-drive Road Rover project (see Appendix 1). Other projects, and particularly the Rover

2000 itself, had eventually pushed Road Rover aside. The concept of a bigger, faster, and more refined Land-Rover was abandoned — but not forgotten.

Spen King always meant to get back to this idea when he could find time, and in 1966 he got his chance. There were all manner of portents. The latest in Jeep Waggoneers were by no means stark and agricultural, but they were still good cross-country vehicles. The Land-Rover's competition intensified every year, and each model was better-equipped than the last. Even though the Land-Rover continued to sell well, its trim and finish standards were criticised more and more frequently.

Nagging away at the back of their minds, Spen King and Gordon Bashford were convinced that the world was now ready to start buying a lot of 'luxury' Land-Rovers. On the other hand, they were quite sure that the only way to achieve their aims was to start afresh, and not even consider the Land-Rover's leaf-sprung chassis. In any case, their new concept would have a different emphasis. Whereas the Land-Rover was a cross-country vehicle that could go by road, the new design would be a road 'car' which could go over rough terrain if needed.

It was a rare pleasure for Gordon Bashford to be allowed to start his package design with a clean sheet of paper. However, before the project became serious and urgent Bashford says 'We started off in the early 1960s by considering the car with the old six-cylinder P5 3-litre engine. We called it the 100-inch Station Wagon because when I had finished sketching up the first package the wheelbase turned out to be 99.9 inches, so I said we should round it up, and call the car after that dimension. That was one of the few things we didn't change from first to last. We had no serious competitor in view at that time, because I don't think there was an existing machine which did what we were trying to do.'

Suspension design, to give a good ride *and* acceptable cross-country performance, took time. Both King and Bashford wanted to use low (coil) spring rates, long wheel travel, and good damping. With a possible payload of more than 1,500 lb that was difficult. Ride levelling of the rear suspension was thought to be essential.

'That wasn't going to be easy,' says Bashford, 'but Spen King and I visited the Frankfurt motor show where — lo and behold — we saw the Boge Hydromat levelling strut on display. It was ideal for what we wanted. It wasn't a damper, and it didn't need extra power — it powered itself, pumping itself up to a pre-set level as the car started off.'

The 'missing link' which, in 1965/66, turned the 100-inch Station Wagon into a gloriously promising machine, was the vee-8 engine. Powered by the old P5 'straight-six', the car would have been good, but not outstanding. Worse, there would have been excessive weight in the nose which the lightweight vee-8 did not impose.

With mechanical design settled, there was then the question of the body style. A three-door estate car shape was obviously wanted, but who would do the styling job? Normally, of course, this would have been David Bache's department responsibility, but in 1966/67 he had other things on his mind. P8, the multi-purpose saloon car which was intended to replace all existing Rover private cars at the end of the decade, was filling his team's drawing boards and modelling studios.

Spen King, therefore, decided to do the job himself! He had, after all, already been responsible for the mid-engined T3 turbine body style, and for the individually-shaped mid-engined P6BS coupé, still not complete in Rover's Solihull jig shop. There are those at Solihull prepared to swear that King is intuitively an even better stylist than he is an engineer, and that is saying a great deal!

Factory pictures show just how closely the King-Bashford prototype shape resembles that of the production cars. When handed over to styling in 1967, it was so impressive that although much attention was given to making the body easy to produce, no change was made to the overall shape.

Apart from the vee-8 engine, which was considerably modified and de-tuned in its new application, the transmission was new. As had been the case with vee-8 applications in the Rover private cars, there was no prospect of the Land-Rover's transmission being used. Tom Barton's specialist team, in conjunction with the King/Bashford partnership, came up with something bigger, more massive, and entirely new. The Range Rover's transmission philosophy was radically different from that of the Land-Rover. Indeed, on sober reflection, for a predominantly 'road' four-wheel-drive machine, it all looked a bit topsy-turvy. Certainly, by comparison with Land-Rover, the Range Rover's layout showed an engineering and marketing somersault.

Principally, the Range Rover would have permanent four-wheel-drive (the Land-Rover's front wheels could be disengaged if required), and to take care of transmission wind-up it would have a third central differential with a limited-slip differential mechanism. (The limited-slip feature has now been deleted). Coil springs instead of leaf springs, four-wheel disc brakes instead of drums, the already described self-levelling rear suspension, and a very nicely trimmed interior (always a Bache speciality) all showed the vast difference in concept.

When finished, in August 1967, the very first 100-inch Station Wagon caused a bit of a sensation. Compared with the Land-Rover, it was so nicely built, and so obviously 'right', that it made an enormous impression. Leyland, Rover's new masters, were impressed, demanded production as soon as possible, and made it quite clear that the capital investment would be available. Development and tooling then went ahead even faster than usual, and the first Range Rover met its public in June 1970.

Perhaps it was all a bit too rushed, as there was evidence in the trim and furnishing areas that more deliberate work could have resulted in a more plushy specification. Certainly, when announced (in the same month, incidentally, as Triumph's Stag) there were no back-up stocks to sell immediately. Deliveries began slowly, and the Range Rover waiting lists soon assumed the proportions for which they were notorious by 1976. It was the Land-Rover story all over again. Demand exceeded supply right from the start, and still does. In the activist days of 1976, Range Rover production workers even went so far as to plead with management to invest more in the production lines, so that they could make more of the export-winning machines. This hasn't happened yet, and the single production line at Solihull can build no more than 250 Range Rovers every week. More than 50,000 examples had been sold by the end of 1976, and it seemed as if dealers and distributors were even prepared to pay over the odds for one of these £6,000 vehicles.

But we have already jumped ahead too far. Rover's union with Alvis has already been mentioned, and the fact that Leyland-Triumph arrived on the scene 18 months later than that. How and why it happened is a fascinating story in itself, and would have an over-riding effect on the marque's future. December 1966 and January 1967 were months of great significance to the company. It was, in fact, a complete watershed in their affairs.

Chapter 11

Mergers and manoeuvres — Alvis, Triumph and Leyland

Board meeting minutes: December 12 1966

'The chairman reported formally that as a result of a recent approach from the Leyland Motor Corporation, informal discussions had been taking place between the two companies on the possibility of a merger, as a result of which a verbal offer had been communicated . . . . '

If this chapter had been written in the 1950s it would have been short and sweet. There would have been no actual mergers to discuss. True, there had been all manner of talks, as there is concerning any healthy and expanding concern, but nothing had ever matured. Even in 1931/32, when Rover's losses were mounting, and the future looked grim, they did not run for cover. Even so, without Spencer Wilks and Howe Graham to guide the company's turn-around, there might not have been an alternative.

By 1934 the financial crisis had passed, and in 1936 the company was quite strong enough to be looking for other firms to take over themselves. Rover certainly had the opportunities, but always passed them over. Spencer Wilks, as we have seen, had a master plan for the company, and was all set to mould its 'image' into a new shape. At that time he envisaged a compact, profitable, medium-sized and respected concern, which would only make as many of the type of cars *he* preferred as *he* decided to have made. They would be advertised and sold in a discreet and orderly manner, and built at a civilised pace.

Rover, to this remarkable visionary, was unique. It was a 'cause' to be followed faithfully. To link up with any other firm would have diluted the vintage he was cultivating. Even his later involvement with the aircraft industry was a chore to be accepted in the national interest.

In those days, building and selling motor cars was different. Not always easier, just different. In the 1930s it was quite possible to build less than 10,000 good cars in a year *and* to make good profits, even if that meant having only about four per cent of the market. 20 years later, ten times that rate of sales was desirable. By the 1960s it was essential. Rover achieved all this, and survived beautifully.

Up to the 1920s, the Rover company stood completely alone. As car makers they recorded their first loss in 1908 and their first serious loss in 1925, after which the financial problems redoubled. The shareholders' revolt early in 1928 led to several new directors being appointed, less rather than more control over the balance sheets, and a slide towards the perils of management by a receiver. Perhaps it wasn't so strange, therefore, that at the end of 1929 an outside firm of financial advisers urged the company to join forces with the Standard and Lanchester concerns in a new and theoretically stronger combine. Colonel Searle went along with this vision for a time, not least because Standard's new factory at Canley had acres and acres of possibilities for future expansion, but within months this scheme was dropped. There were, it appears, no contacts between the directors of each firm, and one suspects that the financial wheeling and dealing was all a bit above their heads.

By 1930 Spencer Wilks was the company's general manager, but even so by 1932 its fortunes were at a very low ebb indeed. Things were desperate for a while, but obviously not without hope, for Wilks found time to hold informal merger talks with Siegfried Bettman and Colonel Claude Holbrook of the Triumph company! So though Rover-Triumph first came into existence in the 1970s talks had been held 40 years earlier!

Such a merger made little practical sense at the time, for Triumph, unbeknown to Wilks, were also planning to make precisely the same sort of middle class, medium-performance cars as Wilks had in mind for Rover. Triumph's own factories, too, were small, dispersed, and none-too-modern. Rover would certainly have been very much the senior partners in such a combine. As with the formation of British Leyland many years later (from BMC and the Leyland Group) it might have appeared like a merger, but one company was obviously to be the master. Triumph could not accept this (after all, it was originally 69-year-old Bettman's own company), and even though the Triumph chief was offered the chairmanship, with Holbrook and Wilks as joint managing directors, the deal foundered. The new company name would probably have been Rover-Triumph Motors Ltd — and how's that for a historical precedent?

For the next 20 years, Rover kept themselves to themselves, and were sturdily independent. Moving out of their original factory to concentrate on the Helen Street facility, launching a new range of quality middle class cars, and getting involved with the Air Ministry over the 'shadow factory' scheme, was quite enough, though there was an approach from Singer (in Canterbury Street, Coventry) who wanted more capital for expansion, and needed more space as well.

Singer (whose Coventry factory is now used by Chrysler UK for making plastics components) were situated not far from Helen Street, and were trying to keep up with Austin and Morris and keep down to their prices, but didn't have the sales volume to support them. The only attraction to another firm was their sporting cars, and Wilks had no need of those.

During the Second World War there was little time for financial manoeuvring, even though Rover were once asked to take over a Birmingham gear-manufacturing company and didn't, and in spite of idle claims in the Press that they might be considering a marriage with Rolls-Royce. It was a credit to the way the Wilks brothers had transformed Rover's image that this sort of talk should arise at all. Commercially the two companies would have benefited very little. An obvious link to make the rumours credible was the handover to Rolls-Royce of their pioneering jet engine work, and Rover's acceptance of manufacturing responsibilities for the Rolls-Royce Meteor vee-12.

But if this was reason for a tie-up, wouldn't links with Bristol or Armstrong-Siddeley (because Rover's 'shadow factories' were making parts for their aero engines too) have been just as logical? The directors were tempted to ignore all such stories in a detached manner, even though Rover's standing in the Stock Market had risen as a result, but decided to put out a denial in June 1944. That was the end of that, and no further links with Rolls-Royce were ever 'invented'.

By 1946, Spencer and Maurice Wilks could be justly proud of their achievements with Rover, but they were not foolish idealists. They could read all the signs. Every post-war economic pointer spelt out a simple truth — that Bigger was Better. Or, if not that — Bigger is Safer. Better, that is, for profits and for survival, if not for continuity and individuality. If their future as an independent concern should begin to look impossible, Rover would be prepared to look for a partner.

There was nothing new, even then, about the urge to merge; this was already fashionable in the 1930s. Rootes had made a combine of Hillman, Humber, Commer, Sunbeam and Talbot (Spencer Wilks had left Hillman when he saw this coming on). The BSA Group did it with BSA, Daimler and Lanchester. Even Rolls-Royce annexed Bentley. The biggest and most successful of the groups was controlled by Lord Nuffield, with Morris, MG, Wolseley and Riley already under his wing by 1939. But there were still plenty of independent car makers who showed no signs of wanting togetherness in 1946. Surprisingly enough (or was it?), several were Coventry-based.

The Second World War had changed everything. Social patterns had altered, different classes had new priorities for their money, prices had soared, and the hated purchase tax bore down hard on the more expensive cars. None of it helped Rover's future prospects. Export priorities, what appeared to be a shortage of everything from steel to coal, and petrol to rubber, the government's attempted 'one model' policy, the infamous 'Covenant' scheme of car purchase in Britain, and many other restrictions, all weighed down on the beleaguered car makers.

Prices, too, had rocketed. In 1937 Spencer Wilks spent £60,000 with Pressed Steel for a new 10 hp car body shell. In 1948 the P4 body dies cost £230,000 from the same source. Both these cars had separate chassis frames. The P5 3-litre car of 1958, a monocoque shell, set Rover back a cool million pounds. Not only was the price of tooling up for a new all-steel body style rocketing, but the options open for sourcing a quantity-built unit body were falling rapidly. In the 1930s many firms, Rover among them, could erect their own body shells and several pressings specialists could supply them with panels. After the war, these firms were gradually taken over by one or other of the 'Big Six' car makers.

When Ford snapped up Briggs Motor Bodies in the 1950s, and the emergent BMC captured both Fisher & Ludlow (1950s) and Pressed Steel (1965), it began to look depressing. An independent company would either have to take its bodies from a possible competitor, and give away styling and development secrets, or would have to do something on its own. Worse — could they even be sure of supplies in five or ten years time?

One by one the smaller companies came together, stopped making cars, or disappeared from the scene altogether. Rover survived because they could rely on the Land-Rover for volume and profits. In every year from 1949 onwards the Land-Rover outsold Rover passenger cars by a big margin. More important that this was that the bodies were made by Rover themselves. Certainly the 'shadow factories' had helped enormously. Rover's Helen Street plant in Coventry had been plastered by bombs in 1940, and even when repaired would not have been adequate for post-war plans. The big aero engine factories at Solihull and Acocks Green, de-requisitioned and converted in 1945/46, were leased from the Government on a long-term basis, and released precious capital which could be channelled into new models.

At first, then, Rover were content. With the Land-Rover launched in 1948, and the P4 'Auntie' a year later, production rose rapidly. The future was promising, except that everything depended on the suppliers. If you were large, like Ford, you built almost everything for yourself. Tiny concerns like Aston Martin and Jensen tried to do the same. Rover, caught in the middle, had to shop around.

Up to 1939, production was often leisurely enough for Rover bodies to have ash frames and handbeaten body panels. As production rose, they still shaped their own wood, but bought pressed-steel panelling from outside suppliers. Above a certain rate this, also, became uneconomic — a pressed-steel spot-welded body shell became essential. Rover teetered over that final border line with the 1939-model Rover '10', and after the birth of the P4 in 1949 they never again assembled their own passenger car bodies. Instead they relied completely on the Pressed Steel Co — and in doing so they probably sealed their eventual fate.

By the early 1950s, certainly, Spencer Wilks had come round to the idea of taking a partner just so long as it was his choice, and the result was to the company's advantage. That choice, in any case, had narrowed somewhat to Alvis, Jaguar, Singer or Standard-Triumph. Others were either too small, too large, or too financially rocky. A link with Armstrong-Siddeley, for instance, might have made some sense, if only the car manufacturing side had been separate from aero engine work. It was when he settled down to considerations of model 'fit', of non-automotive activity, and of such vital aspects as export networks, that Wilks saw his only possible partner.

Alvis, at that time, could be eliminated because it was exporting very little and making only a few cars, and was rather reliant on military orders for its aero engines. Singer were making very boring cars, and looked likely to collapse financially at any moment. Jaguar, very healthy equals to Rover and still in the Lyons family's hands, were direct competitors. In the end, therefore, there was no choice — if there was to be a link, it would have to be with Standard-Triumph. There were even family connections. Spencer Wilks had married one of William Hillman's daughters, and so had Standard's Sir John Black; the first approaches ought to have been easy. They were not. The plain fact was that Sir John was operating Standard-Triumph as something of a dictator. He came as near to being universally feared, and disliked, as any other boss at this time. In spite of those family ties, the urbane and civilised Wilks could not contemplate being in the same business as his brother-in-law. He also realised who would want to be the dominant executive.

In practice, though, Standard-Triumph had everything that Rover needed in a partner. They built tractors (for Ferguson) — Rover built Land-Rovers. They had a mass-produced small saloon car at the very cheapest end of the market — Rover had nothing, nor contemplated anything. They were developing a fast new sports car (the TR2) aimed specifically at the United States — Rover had nothing with which to attract the Americans. Best of all, they had a thriving export chain of distributors — Rover were still learning. Not only this, but Standard-Triumph, at Canley, had spare capacity, and room to expand further. Rover, at Solihull, with their Land-Rover boom showing no signs of dying back, were cramped and crowded. In 1953 they had turned out 9,000 cars and nearly 20,000 Land-Rovers. Already they were thinking about an additional private car line (which became the P5), but could not easily find the space in which to assemble it.

Spencer Wilks did not have to wait for long. In January 1954 Sir John Black was ousted from Standard in a boardroom revolution, and the 37-year-old Alick Dick took his place. Incidentally, Alick Dick's uncle had also married one of William Hillman's daughters. Was it unexpected, then, that within days of Dick's new appointment, he was telephoned by Wilks, who had merger discussions in mind?

Standard-Triumph had any number of attractions for Rover, but some of the most noteworthy were the petrol and diesel engines used in the Standard-built Ferguson tractors. Although it was selling as strongly as ever, the Land-Rover didn't yet have a diesel engine option, and was in need of that sort of boost. Rover had not begun diesel engine design themselves, so the Canley-built units might be most useful. It wasn't until talks at high level had been going on for some weeks that engineers at Solihull discovered that the Vanguard-based Ferguson engines could not easily be adapted to the Land-Rover . . .

If you walked through the main entrance to Solihull's management office block today, and scanned the company name plates on the wall outside, you might worry for a moment over one of them. Who, or what, is Allied Motors Ltd? The name of the proposed combine was just one of the problems which began to appear almost as soon as discussions were under way in February 1954. Big firms, after all, are run by big men, all with a measure of pride.

The proposed merger, in terms of capital employed, would have resulted in Standard-Triumph shareholders having more than half the stock, so naturally enough Alick Dick and his directors thought they should also have a majority. They were, on the other hand, ready to cede the chair to Spencer Wilks.

Wilks, for his part, insisted that there should be equal representation and that he should be chief executive. Rover's business record was far superior to that of Standard, and he was determined that Rover should be the dominant partner.

Negotiations might have broken off even earlier than they did if Wilks had not learned of two things. Firstly he heard that Willys-Overland of the United States (famous , of course, for their four-wheel-drive Jeeps) were seriously looking round for a European manufacturing base, and that they had already been talking to Standard-Triumph. Secondly, though he did not treat this quite so seriously, was the news that Standard were thinking of making four-wheel-drive vehicles of their own design.

All sorts of names for the holding company (it was proposed to leave each existing company autonomous for a while) were put forward. United Motor Corporation, Consolidated Motors, and finally United Motors were considered; the last name would probably have been adopted.

But the more the two sides talked, the less likely they looked to agree. Personal disagreements, and Rover's nagging suspicion that Standard's financial performance could be a burden, weighed heavily against agreement. Rover's profit return on capital was steadily increasing, after all, while Standard's, in spite of the tractor deal with Ferguson, was falling fast.

It was finally agreed to drop the thoughts of a complete merger, though for a while Allied Motors Ltd was formed as a joint private company so that a team could design new engines suitable both for the tractors and the Land-Rovers. It was to no avail. By July 1954 it was all off, and co-operation ceased. Rover bought Standard's half of Allied Motors for a mere £500 in 1955.

Five years later, in 1959, Wilks and Alick Dick got together again. Things were somewhat different now that Standard-Triumph had finally been released from their tractor manufacturing agreement. Ferguson had become Massey-Harris-Ferguson, and as recently as 1958 there had been proposals for M-H-F to make takeover bids for Standard-Triumph. Life was getting complicated! The fact that Harry Ferguson himself had once talked to Rover about mergers just made the merry-go-round even more difficult to unravel.

Standard, in those five years, had materially been altered. The TR sports cars were worldwide successes, the Standard 8/10 range had made its mark, and production had soared from 73,000 to 86,000 a year. The multi-version Triumph Herald, mainly bodied 'in house', was about to be launched. The attraction to Rover was two-fold. First there was realisation that Standard-Triumph, for all its difficulties, had managed to tool up for an entirely new body without recourse to an established concern. They had been forced to as both Fisher & Ludlow and Pressed Steel had turned the job down. Secondly, and this was very important, Alick Dick had come out of the termination of tractor manufacture (and the withdrawal from Banner Lane in Coventry) with about £12 million in cash.

A further attraction, which only became obvious after talks began, was that both Rover and Standard-Triumph were developing the same type of new 2-litre model. Solihull's product, of course, was the P6 project, still not finalised in style or mechanical specification. Standard's was the Vanguard III's replacement, coded the 'Zebu', which was to include a new six-cylinder engine, and, as styled at that time, a reverse-slope rear window. It made no sense for two nearly identical projects to go forward in competition if the companies agreed to get together.

What began as amicable merger discussions, soon descended into bickering and financial haggles. Merchant bankers and company accountants wanted to get the very best for their clients, and the two sides could not agree. At one stage Rover even threatened to make it a takeover bid, but they would have had to raise additional capital from their shareholders to be certain of having the cash, and drew back from that plan. Once again, and by the end of May 1959, the talks collapsed. Standard-Triumph were left to soldier on alone (and suffered because of it). Rover, and Spencer Wilks, discreetly drew back to consider their future.

The fascinating equation of 'Land-Rover plus Tractor equals More Profit' dominated their thinking for some time. Harry Ferguson, as already mentioned, also realised this in 1952, and in spite of the fact that his tractors were then being made by Standard he was still ready to talk mergers. Once Spencer Wilks had discovered the difficulties of dealing with the volatile old Irishman, there could be little progress on that score. Clearly, though, there was something rather appealing about a link with tractors, for in 1957 Rover were tempted again. On this occasion they were approached by the Huddersfield-based David Brown Corporation, who were interested in selling off the whole of their tractor and agricultural machinery division. A few years earlier one or two of Rover's Land-Rover design team had been tempted away to David Brown's, and it became clear, as talks progressed, that they had designed, and now abandoned, a 4 x 4 'Land-Rover' of their own.

Although this offer had some attraction, mainly in that some much needed production capacity would be gained, the company could not get away from the feeling that David Brown's were proposing to sell them a division that was not making any profits. Although contacts dragged on for years, they never became serious, and were finally killed off altogether when the Rover 2000 project filled everybody's time.

By the early 1960s, as we have seen, the Wilks brothers had steered the Rover company to the very edge of the 'Big League'. They had committed the new Rover 2000 to production with its attendant gearbox/axle plant at Pengam and the new North Block at Solihull, and in 1964 a total of nearly 60,000 vehicles were delivered. Nevertheless, with demand for Land-Rovers already ahead of supply, there was still critical shortage of space at Solihull. The Rover 2000, originally thought likely to sell at 300 - 400 cars a week, was already attracting orders at twice that rate. Therefore when, quite suddenly, John Parkes of Alvis approached Rover's chairman George Farmer, and suggested an amalgamation, he was received with great interest.

On this occasion, of course, there was no question of bickering about equal partnerships, as Rover were much larger than Alvis. The prestigious Coventry concern, with its splendid factory on the Holyhead Road, was quite simply offering itself as a takeover candidate. This would not be a marriage of models, or necessarily of philosophies, but it would certainly be a merging of skills. Alvis, of course, had been an important manufacturer of sports and sporting cars between the wars, but since the early 1950s they had been selling only one basic model — the classically-engineered 3-litre — and it was rapidly running out of development and customers. Their principal product was the versatile six-wheel-drive military machines — Saracens, Saladins and Salamanders.

The offer could not have come at a better time. Rover, having just announced publically that they were to start making the ex-Buick vee-8 engine, could use every square foot of factory space offered to them. Unlike every previous affair, this was an extremely civilised and affable business. Alvis, though vulnerable due to the drop in sales of their Leonides radial piston aero engines, and their dependence on government orders for the military six-wheelers, were by no means unprofitable. The offer by Rover — to buy every Alvis share with one of their own — was made public at the end of June 1965, and within a few days a majority of the shareholders had accepted. The offer was declared unconditional on July 22, and John Parkes became a director of Rover.

Almost at once, the roof fell in. Just days after the Alvis-Rover merger had been finalised came a shock announcement — BMC proposed to take over Pressed Steel! Directly, and functionally, this would not affect Rover, but the implications were enormous. Each and every one of Rover's private car body shells were made by Pressed Steel, and they had been looking in that direction for supplies of P8, when finalised. What would happen next?

Rover, naturally, were worried both about future body shell supplies, and about the fact that they would have to face up to delivering styling secrets into a competitor's hands. BMC, for their part, were at great pains to insist that 'they intended the existing goodwill and business relationships that Pressed Steel enjoy with their own customers to continue'. At the time the Rover 2000 shells came from PSC's Swindon factory, while the older P5 shells were built at Linwood. Linwood was an even bigger problem to them, for in due course that PSC factory was sold off to the Rootes group, whose Imp bodies formed the lion's share of its output. The offer by BMC was made unconditional in September, once a government threat to refer the merger to the Monopolies Commission had been withdrawn. To be fair to BMH, as the company was renamed with the annexation of Jaguar, they preserved very good relations at Pressed Steel with outside customers, but it was nevertheless noticeable how quickly these firms began to make alternative arrangements for their future.

Rover, for a time, could not, and did not. It was one — but not the most pressing — of their problems. That was almost certainly the question of new capital. By 1966, as already explained, the Land-Rover had been running for 18 years, the P5 3-litre car for eight years, and the Rover 2000 for three. In the pipeline, as projects and even as prototypes, were further expansions of Land-Rover production, the mid-engined sports coupé programme, the new and very promising 100 inch Station Wagon, *and* thoughts of a P8 to replace both P5 and P6. The vee-8 development and tooling programme was still at an early stage.

By July, too, they had further cause to worry. BMC, having digested Pressed Steel next proposed to, and were accepted by Jaguar (or rather by Sir William Lyons). At a stroke this brought an important customer of Pressed Steel into the corporate fold. Standard-Triumph, for their part, had flown for protection to Leyland some years ago, and might be expected to be making their own future arrangements. Suddenly, and not at all to their management's satisfaction, the Rover company was alone, exposed, and vulnerable. An approach from Leyland, therefore, at the end of 1966, was not the insult that the Wilks brothers would once have considered it. Leyland, as most of those in the business realised, were quite determined to match BMH's size, and were determined to do this by acquisition. Having been foiled in their thoughts of joining forces with Jaguar, for a real prestige name is what they desired, they turned to Rover instead.

It was not only the prestige of the Rover car, of course, which attracted Leyland. The Land-Rover, its range still expanding, was an ideal 'fit' to the vast number of Leyland trucks being made at Leyland and AEC's Southall factory; furthermore, they sold, and were popular, in the same parts of the world, and did the same sorts of jobs. As with the Alvis merger, at Rover there was very little need for discussion or argument over the Leyland approach. It made so much sense in every way that the directors unanimously agreed to recommend it to the shareholders. The formalities were swiftly completed; the public first heard of the approach on December 12 1966, there were no important dissenting voices and everything was officially tied up by March 1967. Thus it was that Rover and Triumph finally got together, nearly 35 years after the original Wilks-Bettman discussions.

With that merger complete, Spencer Wilks, now 75 years of age, must have felt that his mission at Rover was complete, and decided to retire from the board of directors. He had been a non-executive member of the board since 1962, when succeeded as chairman by his brother Maurice, but all-in-all had served the company for a total of 38 years. Sir Donald Stokes, very aware of the place Spencer Wilks held in the hearts of all true followers of the Rover tradition, therefore suggested that he should become the company's life president, a purely honorary post which he held until his death four years later, aged 79.

Without the trauma and aggravation of further management upheavals, Rover were now quite sure what their future developments should be. Sir George Farmer, in his first overall policy statement to his Leyland masters, made it clear that the 100 inch Station Wagon — which we now know as Range Rover — was the first priority, followed by the P6BS mid-engined coupé, and with a proposed successor to the existing cars (coded P8) following them up.

It was a good plan, and it would have fitted well with what Triumph were already planning for themselves. Unfortunately for both, Sir Donald Stokes was already looking one stage further. After an autumn and Christmas of mounting speculation about Leyland's next move had remained blandly unanswered, he played his ace, and got the British government to back it.

Wednesday, January 17 1968, was the fateful day — the day which was to see industrial moves affecting the motor industry for decades to come. Leyland, not without a lot of negotiation, merged with BMH. The implications were enormous.

Chapter 12

British Leyland and SD1 — the end of the beginning?

Before 1967, the Rover was a proud and independent marque. After 1968, and certainly after 1972, it became subservient to the corporate plans of British Leyland. Rover managers, when looking back, admit that the merger period brought all kinds of uncertainty to Solihull. The problem, they say, is not that the rules of the game had changed, but that they kept on changing. For months and years, it seemed, they were not sure of their place in the group.

British Leyland was founded amid a tidal wave of goodwill, and in some haste. The original BMC group, whose operations were about to plunge into the red, were delighted to find a strong partner. Prestige companies like Rover, and Jaguar on the BMC side of the deal, were not so sure. Not that they had any say in the matter. The merger, Britain's biggest yet, was set up by Sir Donald Stokes, Sir George Harriman, and the British government. The wishes of subsidiary companies did not have to be considered. It was a vast and rambling group which emerged from the dust of the takeover. The most important priority for British Leyland should have been drastic rationalisation and even surgery. In the event, it was tackled very slowly. Then, as now, the problems of the volume car divisions (which at the time meant BMC) overshadowed everything else.

From May 1968, after several months of speculation, negotiation, and dissension among directors, the British Leyland Motor Corporation began to operate. Rover and Solihull found that they were 'Specialist Cars', in a loose and not-yet-defined partnership with Jaguar and Triumph. In terms of prestige products, they were second only to Jaguar, and in profitability they were probably second to none. Bringing Leyland and BMC together caused a considerable upheaval. Among other things, it made the new Alvis-Rover-Triumph product plan obsolete almost before it had been written down and agreed upon. It was deeply worrying, especially to those people at Solihull who believed implicitly in the Rover tradition.

Leyland's first approaches to Rover, towards the end of 1966, had been personal and very informal. Lord Black, Leyland's chairman, had talked first of all to George Farmer, and of course there was a strong friendship between Spencer Wilks and Sir Henry Spurrier. It was quickly agreed that if a Leyland-Rover merger went ahead, then Triumph activities would eventually be restricted to making cars and sports cars up to around the 2-litre size, while Rover and Alvis would concentrate on the bigger machinery. The single and very obvious 'clash' was that the Rover 2000 and Triumph 2000 cars were directly, even deadly, rivals. That would have to be sorted out in due course, but with both selling very well and with new developments planned at Solihull and at Coventry there was no immediate problem. The prestige and standing of the Alvis name would also be given to one or possibly two new models — a fastback version of the Rover 2000 car which Rover would style, and a very exciting mid-engined sports coupé powered by the new 3½-litre vee-8 engine. (Both of these cars are described in detail in Appendix 1.)

From May 1968, this sort of strategy had to be abandoned. The corporate view suddenly had to be considered. When the formation of British Leyland was still being canvassed, in the early months of 1968, it was publicly stated that new-model programmes for the next five years were being prepared — and when the marriage was consummated we were all told that this programme had been agreed. Fine words, brave words even, but as far as Rover (and their Triumph relations) were concerned, it simply wasn't true. Rover managers knew what they wanted to do, and even what they had started to do, but it was not at all certain that the schemes would come to fruition.

The vee-8 engine, thankfully, was well and truly launched. The big P5B 'flagship' had been in production since the late summer of 1967, and the P6B, looking almost indistinguishable from the Rover 2000, made its public bow in April 1968. That was the good news. The bad news was that the company also released details of the mid-engined sports coupé, with the sad commentary that it would not now be going into production. No one outside Rover knew that the story was not as simple as that, and there were still a few gleams in engineering eyes back at the ranch, but even a smoothed-out P9 project never appeared. It was the first sign of inter-company conflict. P9 was one casualty, and the later big saloon was another. In the name of future rationalisation, which made good commercial sense, and because of inter-company rivalry, which didn't, projects had to be cancelled. Not only Rover, but Triumph and Jaguar also suffered.

This sort of thing brought a new and less secure climate to Solihull. In previous years, even after the takeover of Alvis, the future could be planned without a sideways glance. Now it was very different. What Rover might want to do, might also affect Triumph and Jaguar. Not only Canley and Browns Lane would be involved, but British Leyland headquarters in London would have to be consulted. The Land-Rover, thankfully, sailed serenely on, as it had no rivals in British Leyland; the Austin Gipsy, never a fast seller or a profit maker, had been dropped in the winter of 1967/68. 'Big brother' to the Land-Rover, the new Range Rover, was rushed ahead for a 1970 launch. The trials and tribulations were all centred around Rover's private cars, and the next generation. What had looked like an obvious development in the mid-1960s, now looked fraught with problems. Rover's trauma within British Leyland at the end of the 1960s centred around one project. Its code name, engraved on the hearts of the long-suffering directors, was P8.

Peter Wilks and Spen King had already started thinking about a new generation of Rover cars in 1963, before the all-new Rover 2000 was revealed to the public. There was nothing unusual in that, nor did it mean that they were abandoning a new baby before it could fend for itself. As far as design was concerned, the Rover 2000 had been settled by 1960/61, and engineering involvement was now in the proving and approving of cars built 'off-tools' in 1962/63.

Peter Wilks was about to become technical director, and he had put Spen King in charge of all new projects. In other companies we would probably call King's section an 'advanced engineering' area; once his ideas had been finalised and approved they would be handed over to Dick Oxley's mainstream engineering departments.

Wilks and King had enjoyed their years with the Rover 2000, but as intelligent and far-thinking engineers they had identified two trends which worried them enormously. Finding the capital for another new car was going to be very expensive — even at mid-1960s prices something like £10 million would be needed — and it would also take a good deal of time. Although they dearly wanted to produce successors for the big P5 and for the P6 2000 (and no one at director level had said this was not feasible), it began to look as if they simply did not have the manpower at Solihull to do it. They were therefore faced with a dilemma. Should they recommend a replacement to P5, which would be a massive and very fast flagship, and hope that the Rover 2000 was going to be such a success that it needed no updating for at least seven or eight years? Or should they let the good old P5 die gracefully, and push ahead with a replacement for the P6, which could be ready before the original car began to bore its public?

It should be added that at this time there was not even a glimmer on the horizon of the vee-8 engine from General Motors, so any consideration of new models involved thinking about power plants as well. There are documents with 1963 dates which make mention of vee-8 units, but these were no more than pipe dreams at the time. Brian Sylvester and Mike Lewis, at Spen King's request, were already forging ahead with paper ideas on this and other related subjects. By the end of 1964 Spen King was able to circulate a five-page brochure about new models, where the coding P8 was officially applied. P6, of course, was the Rover 2000 project, and P7s were the series of research cars, all based on P6s and some with very weird engine configurations, which were then being built.

Here are a few extracts from that brochure: '. . . the Rover company is only capable of developing one basic car at a time . . . a cycle time of approximately five years is required for a vehicle of new conception . . . it would be possible to engineer a P6 size as well as a P5 size . . . but it follows that each size of vehicle could only be renewed at ten-year intervals . . .'

Then came a brilliant thesis: 'The company could be placed in the position of having a first-class prestige car, if P5 was replaced first, accompanied by an outmoded and dated smaller model . . . If the company adopted the policy of concentrating on one single basic model of car, the disadvantage of the ten-year replacement cycle would then disappear . . .

King then went on to point out that Mercedes-Benz were adept at producing strings of different models from a single basic design, and recommended that Rover should adopt precisely that approach. It was not as radical as some observers have suggested. After all, the P1s of the 1930s subscribed to this method, even if 1930s economics allowed them many more obvious variations, and between 1949 and 1958 only a single basic P4 model had covered a very wide range. It was, however, very cold-blooded and very analytical.

Rover's management, with the Rover 2000 already a great success in terms of sales and profit-earning, were now very expansion conscious. They liked the idea of selling a wide range of Rovers, and their dealers were not likely to disagree with that. But for any large business the facts of life usually involve money. Big sums had been raised to capitalise the Rover 2000, and more would be needed for P8. They agreed with Spen King, and told him to plan ahead on that basis. But not yet. With Land-Rover changes, vee-8 engines, corporate activity (the Alvis takeover, for instance), and a build-up of the P6 family to plan, a new P8 would have to wait.

From 1964 to 1967, then, P8 was merely a paper project. Gordon Bashford drew up the first sketches in 1964 (front-wheel drive was considered seriously, but rejected), and refined them at intervals, but never had time to apply himself wholeheartedly to the project. Both he and Spen King had other fish to fry — first the mid-engined P6BS coupé, and then the 100 inch Station Wagon which turned into the Range Rover. Every time Bashford returned to the P8 schemes, however, he was asked to make certain of one thing — that the car should first of all replace P5 (or P5B as it had now become, with the ex-Buick vee-8 engine), and be ready to take over from P6 at a later date. Among his impossible objectives was a requirement for the new car to be as roomy *inside* as the old P5, but to be very little larger *outside* than the much-smaller P6. By 1965, too, he was able to plan the inclusion of the newly-acquired vee-8 engine, while allowing for four- and five-cylinder in-line engines to be slotted in as well.

Although the directors had agreed to consider a P8 project for introduction 'after 1970' as early as 1965, they did not push for its early development. Even in 1967, when Sir Donald Stokes and John Barber were briefed about the Solihull company's future programme, the P6BS and Range Rover projects took precedence. Stokes and Barber, however, were very attracted by the idea of a new big car, especially as it would not clash with anything George Turnbull was already planning for Triumph in Coventry. More important still, and this was at a time when Jaguar was firmly on the other side of the corporate fence, they liked to think that a big new Rover could damage Jaguar's prestige quite seriously.

Leyland, therefore, decided that they wanted a big, fast and ultra-modern saloon car, one which would represent the very best of British car engineering. Stokes, never a modest man in business, wanted to beat Jaguar and Mercedes at their own game, in quality, in construction and in performance.

This decision did not come at once. At the styling stage, the car's size first blossomed, then shrank, and finally blossomed again, before David Bache finally gained approval for a massively impressive car rather larger than P6 and even a little bit more roomy than P5. The other decision which matured in 1968 was that, for the time being at least, all the lower-cost options and alternatives were dropped; only the 3½-litre vee-8 car would go into production at first. In spite of Spen King's analysis of 1964, P8 looked like becoming a powerful five to six-seater with a 130 mph maximum speed. In that form Rover's sales force thought they could sell about 500 P8s a week (rather less than the number of P6s already being made), and the fact that it would have to compete with Jaguar was not thought to be a daunting prospect. Management looked for a public release during 1971.

Peter Wilks was happy to approve P8 with a considerable degree of complexity in its engineering. He was sure that Solihull could deal with this. They had, after all, got the P6's introduction triumphantly right and in any case, the reasoning went, P8 could not compete with modern Jaguars or vee-8-engined Mercedes by being simple. No matter what had been thought in 1963 and 1964, P8 would not be a straight replacement for any existing Rover — it would be a splendid 'flagship' to the Leyland range. This, of course, was still 'pre-British Leyland'. Once Jaguar, with their about-to-be-launched XJ6 models, and a vee-12 unit promised within a couple of years, became colleagues instead of rivals, things would be different.

Once approved, the programme went ahead at a great pace — unprecedentedly fast by Rover standards. Full-size styling clay model approval was not given until the autumn of 1968, and the first true prototypes would not be on the road before the beginning of 1970. Tooling, in particular of body panels, had to start at once, even before the first prototypes were built, and 'off-tools' bodies were demanded for the spring of 1971. Release to Press and public was to be in time for the 1971 Earls Court motor show.

P8, as finally approved in David Bache's styling studios, was a big and brutally impressive four-door saloon car. It is only fair to point out that it was by no means universally liked at Solihull, but there is no doubt that it exuded power, status and, somehow, the presence of money. It was, in every way, the car a successful businessman might be persuaded to buy, but it was by no means the delicately shaped creation of which Jaguar's Sir William Lyons might have approved.

Detailing was conventional apart from the built-in front bumper which surrounded the grille and headlamps. Early schemes for gullwing doors had been abandoned because of the cost and mechanical complication, and there were no serious thoughts of making any estate car variants. By Rover standards, construction was conventional enough, which meant the use of a P6-like base unit on to which skin panels would bolt, though it had been simplified somewhat.

Like any other project, during development it grew. The hoped-for 8 foot 10 inch wheelbase was eventually allowed to stretch to 9 foot 0.5 inches, just five inches up on the Rover 2000. The body, in spite of the faired-in bumpers, was only just shorter than that of the big P5 3½-litre car which was, by now, on sale. A completed prototype would weigh about 3,230 lb, and that was a massive 270 lb saving over the old P5 car.

If there was little to excite interest in the style, there was plenty under the skin. The vee-8 engine itself, in 3.5-litre form, would be uprated somewhat, but it was still hoped that the long-stroke 4.4-litre unit (used finally in Leyland's Australian-made P76) would be ready in time. As with the existing cars, a Borg Warner automatic transmission would have to be standard until a stronger manual box could be developed. Chassis innovations included power-assisted rack and pinion steering, double wishbone front suspension, ride-levelled de Dion rear suspension, and full-power high-pressure disc braking. The existing 'round-the-corner' P6 front suspension could safely be ignored as the gas turbine engine had been discarded, and the sliding-joint P6 de Dion tube was also simplified. Full-power braking, from Automotive Products, is something still not adopted by any British concern except Rolls-Royce, and in Europe it is only found in Citroens and Mercedes-Benz products. Whether or not such a system is essential to a fast and expensive car is a matter of conjecture — Jaguar, even on the 150 mph XJ-S coupés, have not found they need it — but it was all meant to add to the P8's aura of exclusive and prestigious transport.

As a piece of thoughtful design, planning and construction, the new car was a credit to everyone at Solihull. There was tight cost control and, after the complexities of the Range Rovers and the gas turbine cars, there was nothing to dismay the production planners. Space was found, somehow, to lay down production lines in the North Block at Solihull, next to the P6 lines, and capital spending went ahead with a vengeance. In spite of the marshalling of all possible resources behind the project, however, the launch date had to be put back. By the end of 1970 it became clear that a 1972 release was the best that could be expected. By 1970, too, the project was in danger, acute danger, not because it was turning out to be a bad car, but because Leyland's central management were beginning to worry about its other implications. The public, who still knew nothing about the project, were let into the secret in a dramatic and disheartening manner — in March 1971 the *Birmingham Post* announced, in headlines, that it had been cancelled!

Every firm, of course, cancels projects from time to time — but not usually at such a late stage. In the case of P8, it became clear from Press reports, leaked information, and some very skilful deductions on the part of the investigators, that something like £5 million would have to be written off. More than £3 million had already gone, and the rest was earmarked for cancellation charges from component suppliers. Pressed-Steel Fisher, now a part of the group and already being absorbed by Austin-Morris, were well on the way to completing the complex body tools.

How did it happen? How could a management which said 'yes' in 1968 start saying 'maybe not' in 1970, and — abruptly — 'no' in 1971? There were two main factors — one highly pertinent to the P8 itself, and one to British Leyland's overall financial position.

Comparing model with model, there is no doubt that P8 was becoming embarrassingly like a Jaguar. It was very fast, well equipped, would be well developed and luxuriously behaved — and it would be a lot cheaper than anything Browns Lane could turn out. Jaguar needed to sell every one of the XJ6s they could make, for they had no other volume-selling car on which to fall back. Rover, surely, could manage very well without yet another new model? Even though the Rover, with 'only' 3½-litres, was smaller than all but one Jaguar, Sir William's team thought it was too much like direct competition. In spite of the fact that Rover were competing against twin-overhead-camshaft engineering and 4.2-litres, it looked as if P8 would be able to outpace an XJ6. Furthermore, with their 5.3-litre vee-12 due to arrive in 1972, the same year as the new Rover, internal competition was something they could do without.

This, of course, was important, but the overall position vis-à-vis Triumph, and particularly Austin-Morris was also critical. Re-equipping Cowley to build Marinas in the modern manner had proved to be enormously expensive. The new corporation was not making the profits it had expected, and a £25 million rights issue was proposed at the beginning of 1972 to provide extra capital.

In 1970, the year in which Berkeley Square House had to start asking all manner of searching questions of the constituent companies, British Leyland's fortunes had taken a tumble. Sales exceeded £1,000 million for the first time, but pre-tax profits plunged from £40.4 million to only £3.9 million. Part of the total capital expenditure — £66.7 million — had to be financed by drawing on reserves. Even though the forecasts for 1971 and 1972 looked better (the actual results achieved matched up to expectations, in fact — with pre-tax profits of £32.4 and £31.9 million respectively) every forward programme had to be carefully scrutinized. After Cowley it would be Longbridge which would begin to devour the cash. The Allegro front-wheel-drive car, due in the spring of 1973, was now on the stocks.

Faced with this sort of problem British Leyland felt that they had to cancel the P8. It was a difficult and very expensive decision, and according to ex-managing director Bernard Jackman it also broke several loyal hearts. It might still have been possible to rescue P8 if one other important factor had not arisen — both Triumph and Rover could see that their respective 2000 models could not live for ever, and Triumph were already clamouring to be allowed to go ahead with a new car.

Gordon Bashford, who has lived through the birth and death of more Rover models than most people, remembers that he was shattered by the news. 'Of course, it didn't happen just like that, not all in a moment. Rumours had been flying about for some weeks. But, somehow, we were so committed that we didn't think it could possibly happen to us!'

Interestingly enough, over at the Chrysler UK (formerly Rootes) factory in Coventry, another team of engineers had just gone through similar unbelievable withdrawal symptoms. Compared with the 1930s, or even the 1950s, the projects were much bigger and more complex than ever before.

The new 3500, or the SD1 as it has always been known at Solihull, now comes into my story for the very first time. For while it is true that SD1 was by no means the 'son of P8', it was a fledgling which could not take wings until the P8 project had died off. That, of course, was just another of Leyland's troubles.

Sir Donald Stokes and John Barber, in 1968, had decided on a P8 'flagship', which automatically meant that *another* Rover-designed machine would be needed to replace the P6 and P6B models in the 1970s. At the same time they knew of, and made no attempt to quash, the Triumph thoughts on a re-designed Triumph 2000/2.5PI. Although it made absolutely no sense to let both Rover and Triumph design new cars for the 1970s which would compete with each other — in fact it was probably the most obvious model 'clash' within British Leyland — Stokes and Barber allowed the project chiefs to think on precisely those lines.

Gordon Bashford remembers clearly that as soon as his project work on P8 had been handed over to Dick Oxley's engineers, he was encouraged to turn his attention to a new and smaller car, P10. His biggest regret, he recalls, is that P9 became another of the missing numbers — this, the productionised version of the mid-engined sports coupé, having been discarded by the new management.

By this time, too, Spen King had disappeared, temporarily as it transpired, from the Solihull scene. He explains why with these words. 'One day I was called into George Farmer's office, to find Donald Stokes already there. It was just after the British Leyland merger had been announced, and I was told that Harry Webster was moving to Longbridge, and would I be interested in his old job? I was dumbfounded!'

Donald Stokes, as it happened, gave him all of five minutes to make up his mind, then told him he had better get started at Coventry. From that day on, Gordon Bashford became Peter Wilks' deputy, and began to work on successors to P8 on his own. 'At first P10 was purely a Rover project, and our only brief was to think of a successor for the P6,' Bashford says, 'and in the winter of 1968/69, when we started work, we were attracted to the idea of making the new car front-wheel-drive. It would have been about the same size as P6, or probably a bit bigger.'

P10, as it happens, made very little progress. In 1970, before the cold breath of spending cuts fell on Solihull from group headquarters, Triumph had already been told that they could not design their own successor to the Triumph 2000. Corporate sanity had prevailed, and Spen King and Peter Wilks were told to co-operate over future plans, even though the companies were still functionally separate. At that point, only a matter of weeks before P8 was painfully and publicly cancelled, P10 was cancelled, and RT1 was born. The change was purely administrative. The car's layout would not be changed in essence, but it would now be a joint Rover and Triumph model.

'But!,' chuckled Gordon Bashford, 'now the rules had all been changed. Now we were expected to produce the best at a much lower cost. It was probably at this point that we finally decided to make the car technically much simpler. Among the changes was a decision to revert to a solid rear axle.'

RT1, though, lived only for a matter of weeks. In April 1971, for no very good reason except that top management decreed it, RT1 became SD1, and the concept of the car which has now become Rover's latest best-seller was born. RT1, incidentally, for collectors of company hieroglyphics, means, very simply, Rover-Triumph Project Number One, while SD1 means Specialist Division Number One. More important, though, than the name the car was to have was the way it was to be designed, and the basic form it was to take. It is too easy in writing a book like this to get bogged down in double wishbones and overhead camshaft engines, while losing track of all the commercial implications.

At first, in the spring of 1971, when SD1 officially came into existence, there was a great deal of autonomy remaining within British Leyland. This was one of the features of the new group which the money-first, people-afterwards commentators in the newspapers were complaining about. According to them, the first priority should have gone to carving the corporation about, closing entire factories willy-nilly, and (presumably) throwing many thousands of skilled men out of work.

Lord Stokes (Sir Donald had been given a life peerage in January 1969) knew all about this, with its theoretical advantages and practical problems. He also knew that it made much sense to bring Rover and Triumph very much closer together, as he had been planning since the first merger discussions were held towards the end of 1966. But with people and personalities to consider, not forgetting the enormous problems facing him at Austin-Morris, the process had to take time.

The first public rumours of an internal merging between Rover and Triumph, which would represent another step on the way to elimination of individual marques, surfaced over Christmas 1971, were speedily denied, but were then officially confirmed in March 1972. Sir George Farmer, chairman of Rover since 1963, would be in overall control, though A. B. Smith would continue as managing director of Rover. At the same time, Jaguar were given their freedom once again; since the British Leyland merger in 1968 they had been reluctant partners of Triumph and Rover, but had kept themselves functionally and technically almost completely aloof.

British Leyland hoped to have the integration of Rover and Triumph complete by 1974. In fact the job was not finished until the spring of 1975, just in time to be thoroughly messed about again by the implications of financial collapse and the Ryder Report's recommendations. In the event, it took longest of all for engineering work to be completely shaken down, and the irony is that the process had started, informally, months before a Rover-Triumph rationalisation was publicly announced. Spen King was the new engineering supremo (Peter Wilks had retired, in failing health, in July 1971), and immediately began to weld the talents of the Solihull and Canley design offices together.

Triumph would still have much on their plates for the mid-1970s (TR7 and its developing family are the only publicly announced evidence which may be mentioned), but they would be able to supply SD1 with a new five-speed manual gearbox, and with a new range of engines to add to the vee-8 of which Solihull were so very proud.

Nick Carver arrived from Berkeley Square House, to look after product planning of this and future Rover-Triumph models, and the project very quickly began to gather impetus. The first priority was to define what SD1 actually was meant to do, and this was very easy. With P8 recently killed, and the company with a clear brief as to its future, SD1, quite literally, had to be all things to all men. At Rover, it would replace, as it now has, all existing models. The big, old, but graceful 3½-litre saloon would be allowed to die off (which it did in May 1973), and the P6 family would be replaced by a family of SD1 cars. (The last of the famous P6 cars, a 2200, has now been delivered.) Eventually it would also have to replace the Triumph 2000/2500 cars, though these would carry on in production for a time at Canley after the first SD1s were built and sold.

David Bache's styling department, of course, were years ahead of the game. Bache himself had spent hours doodling around the requirements of a P10 or an RT1, and before the end of the 1960s was almost sure that the next Rover should be a versatile five-door five-seater model. By the standards of the late 1970s that may not sound very clever to us as there are, after all, several large five-door cars on the market, but in 1969 it was very brave thinking. The market was already coming to terms with the five-door car at lower price levels, but it had yet to be proved that status and good looks could be equated with five doors and utility. Bache became convinced that it could when the biggest five-door cars on the market were still just the Renault 16 and the Austin Maxi, both with a mere 1,500 cc. The jump, in specification and credibility, between those cars and a sleek 3½-litre machine, was enormous.

Fortunately for Rover and for the customer, Bache's reputation and track record was impeccable. There are those working at Solihull prepared to swear that they could do the job better themselves, but there is a bigger band of devotees who would back even a three-wheeler with an engine on the roof if he had said it was necessary. British Leyland bosses, too, believed in him and in his staff; Rover had recently been asked to tackle the styling of a new Leyland cab for the gas turbine trucks, and made a very fine job of it. Another project, almost contemporary with SD1, was the Leyland National bus, now familiar in cities and on motorways alike.

The company, however, had lost a lot of time. The three years spent on P8, in effect, was a blank spot in their development, so the SD1 would have to be pushed through with the minimum of delay. It says much for individual skills, and for the resilience of a disappointed management team, that SD1's styling was not finally approved until February 1972, and that pre-production from 'off-tools' body shells began in April 1975.

In the same period, too, a new factory had been suggested, considered, planned, approved and built. Without the new plant there would have been no SD1, but the reverse equally applies. Rover, and Solihull, for all its misgivings about corporate control from afar, was flattered by the capital investment to be steered its way. The new block, now affectionately known as the 'SD1 plant', represented the biggest chunk of investment committed by British Leyland, and beat the sums spent at Cowley for the Marina and at Longbridge for the Allegro.

However, before the first sod was turned, there was much opposition to be met. The citizens of middle class Solihull might have been happy to see Rover producing so many new jobs on their doorsteps, but they were not at all happy about the way it was being achieved. In short, they were delighted to hear of new development, but they wanted to protect their own countryside. When the first schemes to build a vast two-storey factory on Rover-owned green fields to the east of the existing buildings were shown, there was uproar. To counter this, before and after the formal application was made, every other possible way of shoe-horning new production lines into the existing Solihull buildings was considered. P5B would have been dropped by 1973, but as it occupied only one production line in a corner of the Land-Rover building the space liberated would be quite inadequate. In any case, the continuous expansion of Land-Rover sales meant that *that* space would tend to disappear overnight!

The archives have file after file of schemes, some of which would have obliterated the parking and storage space which Rover still needs so badly. The problem, apart from that of local opinion, was that government policy over new industrial development had to be changed by diplomatic pressure. The main reason for the purchase of all those Land-Rover 'satellite' factories in the 1950s and 1960s had been that it was the only way for Rover to gain extra capacity in the Midlands.

By 1970, after several much-publicised rows between industry and the authorities, and the disturbing development of high unemployment statistics in the area (more jobs were moving out than could be created by factory modernisations), the political wind was beginning to change. British Leyland found that they might be allowed to build their vast new plant, if they could resolve all the local conflicts.

But they had their own problems — the SD1 block would carve its way through the Solihull test track for one thing, and there were even objections from nearby Elmdon airport that in certain conditions the new building might be dangerous to aircraft in the approach pattern. The fact that the estimates of which, how many, and what type of cars should be built there *after* SD1 was launched complicated things enormously.

A public meeting in Solihull to resolve differences between Rover and local residents was chaired by A. B. Smith ('I rate that as one of my finer achievements — reconciling the views of a lot of people who disagreed strongly'), and resulted in the classic British type of compromise. The factory would be sited where Rover wanted it, but would be reduced from a double to a single storey building (therefore lopping off 28 feet from its height), and would be doubled in width.

With a planned capacity of no less than 3,000 cars every week — much higher than Rover, or even Rover-Triumph, have yet achieved — the new block was certainly planned with the future in mind. It was immense, and therefore nearly all the statistics connected with it are jumbo-sized. In total it cost British Leyland £27 million, a considerable bargain in view of the implications it has on Solihull's future, and it is the biggest single new development by a British car manufacturer for more than 40 years. The Ford Dagenham complex, built at the beginning of the 1930s, was bigger, but Rootes' factory at Linwood — of early 1960s vintage — was not. It covers 64 acres, has a floor area of more than half a million square feet, a huge assembly hall 1,900 feet long and 500 feet wide, and the excavation and landscaping involved moving 10 million tons of earth . . . quite clearly SD1 cannot fill it on its own.

The car itself, which was to cost British Leyland a total investment of £95 million, admittedly including the new factory, and new facilities for the gearbox (Pengam, Cardiff) and body construction (Castle Bromwich), went ahead in great secrecy, and at great speed.

David Bache's theme style was approved by July 1971, but the final detailed style was not signed off until February 1972. Detail body engineering began at once, and expensive press tools were ordered months in advance of the original hand-built prototype being finished in the winter of 1972/73. To confuse the opposition and magazine 'spies', several P8 prototypes were used for systems and components testing. The sleek prototypes themselves were usually run on the roads with a crude canvas type 'tilt' which disguised the body profile.

The style approved by management was startlingly advanced, and completely different from any previous Rover. It was delicate where P8 had been massive, sleek where P8 had been brutal, and looked very much smaller even though it was the same length to fractions of an inch. One feature suggested by Rover, and subsequently 'stolen' by Austin-Morris was the non-circular steering wheel. In Rover's case the profile is so carefully shaped that most observers do not notice — but when Austin-Morris came to do the same thing their version was angular and crude. The Allegro 'quartic' wheel was speedily abandoned; the SD1 wheel shows no signs of being disliked.

Of course there were the usual brainless commentaries when the car was announced that it was a blatant copy of Citroen's CX, or that it was a contract-job bought in from Pininfarina. Such people clearly have no idea of the time scale of styling, planning and production. SD1 was purely and exclusively Rover. It was being tooled-up a long time in advance of the big Citroen's release, and there was never any question of Pininfarina being involved.

Fashions in European car styling tend to be universal, and this no doubt explains the likenesses. Lancia's Gamma, which appeared in the spring of 1976, was so similar at the prototype stage that it caused some embarrassment. Automotive Products of Leamington Spa (whose technical director is Harry Webster, ex-British Leyland and Triumph) were asked to develop the installation of their latest automatic transmission for the Gamma. Then, as Harry Webster relates, 'Lancia sent over a Gamma prototype, painted black, of course, for us to use. We put in our transmission, and started doing road work. It wasn't long before people were accusing us of running a new Rover without disguise, and accusing us of being indiscreet. You see, the Gamma started life with a styling crease down its flanks just like that of SD1, but went into production with plain sides, and our prototype had the crease. The resemblance was uncanny!'

Different stylists disagree, evidently. Lancia thought they didn't need the long crease, and deleted it. David Bache thought that his car couldn't be sold with plain sides, and added one.

Nose-on, certainly, SD1 was dramatic enough, and bore more than a passing resemblance to the Ferrari Daytona. Bache admits that he is influenced by all manner of cars in his working life, but says the Daytona was not a model for SD1. 'But if people want to call a Rover a four-door Ferrari that has to be good for sales and the image. I'm not complaining,' was his comment.

Bache even went so far as to arrange a static viewing at Solihull in 1972, where the finalised 'see-through' glassfibre styling model was lined up alongside a couple of Maseratis, a big Mercedes and a Jensen Interceptor to see if it passed muster. A picture of that occasion is in this book, and the reason for lorries being lined up in the background is that the viewing was situated rather close to the public road along Lode Lane!

Technically, too, SD1 was interesting — not because of its advanced features, but because of the lack of them. It was, not to put too fine a point on it, a complete engineering somersault compared with the P6. Out went the base-unit structure, out went the de Dion rear suspension, and out went the complex front suspension. In came almost everything now considered 'standard' in the business — a conventional five-door unit-construction body shell, a well located beam axle, and Mac-Pherson strut front suspension.

The power-assisted steering, the five-speed gearbox, and the Boge self-levelling damper struts, and the optional run-flat Denovo tyres were what we expected, and the familiar 3½-litre vee-8 engine was updated and uprated to give the new car a 125 mph maximum speed. The gearing is so high, in fact, that the maximum speed is always achieved at about the powerpeak in *fourth* gear. Fifth, with 28.6 mph per 1,000 rpm, is very definitely a cruising gear.

John Carpenter, Rover's marketing director when the car was conceived, showed me a very detailed market survey made of the Rover and its competitors when SD1 was being designed, and was adamant that the customer is not necessarily as impressed by advanced and complicated engineering features as the motoring press seems to be. Even so, when summarised, the new car's only 'ordinary' feature is the live axle, which thanks to the long wheel movements provided, the self-levelling dampers which ensure the same range of movement whatever the load, and hundreds of hours of niggling development by Solihull's engineers, gives an altogether exemplary ride.

The new car, of course, had to have a name, but as it was really a direct replacement for the original vee-8-engined cars that presented few problems. The 3½-litre (P5B to the code-name freaks) had gone in 1973, and the smaller but faster 3500 ran out at the end of 1975. It was therefore logical to call it '3500' like the predecessor, and make the naming of smaller, lesser-engined, versions easy as well.

Originally, the car should have been available in all its forms at the same time, and for many optimistic months a release date of October 1975 was planned. Rover's engine was good and ready, but the new units being hatched out at Triumph held things back for a time. In the event, the launch even of the vee-8 car slipped to June 1976, with the rest of the family planned for 1977.

But this gets us a little bit ahead of events. While Rover were busily selling every Land-Rover and Range Rover they could make, and frantically completing the country's biggest new car and factory complex to be started in modern times, the parent company was in trouble. British Leyland, which had recovered from the depths of 1970 to record a pre-tax profit of £51.3 million in 1973, had lurched towards the red again. Beset by the problems of inflation, by the massive rise in oil prices, and by the continuing problems of the Austin-Morris division, they made only £2.3 million in 1974. There was worse to come. The company found that the losses were building up (other giants like VW and Fiat were similarly afflicted), and that a cash crisis stared them in the face. With depressed share prices at precisely the wrong time (the stock market was in its manic depressive state at the end of 1974), a rights issue was out of the question.

Lord Stokes and his board were faced with only two choices — they could either face the prospect of going very publicly and agonisingly bankrupt, or they could turn to the British government for help. In the event it was Hobson's choice — a few days before Christmas, and just over a year after the 'energy crisis' had erupted in the Yom Kippur war, Lord Stokes went cap-in-hand to Whitehall.

Official reaction was to bale out the company for the time being — with something like 200,000 jobs at risk there was no real alternative — and to set up a team of investigators to enquire into all aspects of British Leyland's predicament. To chair it, and to influence it with his own trenchant views on British industry, they appointed Lord Ryder (ex-IPC and ex-Reed International). 'Ryder's raiders' — as one newspaper called them — would be able to visit every factory and ask any question. For the first time since the 1870s, there was nothing that Rover's management could do to influence its own future.

Chapter 13

Ryder and rationalisation — the future?

At the beginning of 1975, the atmosphere at Solihull was gloomy. Not since the dark days of 1931 and 1932 had things looked so desperate for the Rover concern. This time, too, things were different. In 1931 the company could only blame itself for the financial crisis which hit the Coventry-based business. In 1975 Rover, or — more accurately — Rover-Triumph, was a profitable part of British Leyland's activities. It was the volume car sections which were draining other parts of the empire of their cash and prospects.

Two years hence, just 100 years after John Starley and William Sutton set up their modest little cycle-making factory, Rover as a marque is safe. Its independence, however, is gone for ever. You could say, and you would be right, that Rover's independence was lost when they joined forces with Alvis in 1965. It was the end of the beginning when Leyland took control in 1967, the beginning of the end when the Rover-Triumph amalgamation was revealed in 1972, and the absolute end after the Ryder Report was implemented.

Lord Ryder's government team were economists, and were not to be swayed by sentiment, traditions, or history. Survival of British Leyland, or as much of it as could be rescued, was their task. Individual makes and models would not be sacrosanct in the face of necessary amalgamations.

The Ryder Report, published in the spring of 1975, recommended that the Government should inject huge and regular amounts of capital into British Leyland, and at the same time take a controlling share in the business. That done, they then recommended that the revived corporation should be split into four divisions — one of which would be called Leyland Cars.

That was all well and good, but in the small print came further suggestions. With the single exception of Jaguar (and at Solihull there are people who simply do not understand why the Allesley concern should be privileged), all other Leyland car makers should speedily and ruthlessly be joined into a homogenous whole. There was no immediate talk about scrapping marque names (although group managing director John Barber, who was to lose his job in the reshuffle, thought that all the cars should eventually be Leylands), but there was an immediate prospect of a loss of identity. Solihull, far from being The Rover Company, would merely be one of the Leyland Cars 'Large Cars' plants.

But Solihull was honoured. Not only had it been given the biggest single capital investment project in recent years, but it was now to become the centre of the entire Leyland Cars design, development and styling function.

One day, somewhere (and this is a question of money) the whole of the product planning function will be moved to a new purpose-built facility, and the company will also get a modern proving ground like Ford of Britain, who have a splendid combined facility near the Southend arterial road in Essex, which is the envy of the rest of the motor industry.

In the meantime, though, this was a great prize for Solihull. Spen King, turbine engine boffin who had shown himself to be one of the greatest innovative designers in the world's car-making business, would be in overall charge of Leyland Cars design and development, while the much-publicised David Bache would take responsibility for styling throughout the division. John Lloyd, Spen King's successor at Rover-Triumph, would look after the whole of current vehicle engineering, with Longbridge's Charles Griffin at his shoulder to run the advanced side of things.

Bernard Jackman, chief executive since 1973, left the company that he loved, and A. B. Smith (chairman) decided it was time to retire after 50 years' service. John Carpenter, sales director since 1965, left the company overnight, and issued a statement to the effect that he was 'shattered'; but not for long — he now occupies a similar and very prestigious position with Rolls-Royce. Chris Peyton, who had directed finance for some time, also retired, and within weeks the top level turnover was complete.

The government, as major (95 per cent) shareholders in the reborn British Leyland Limited, accepted the Ryder Report completely, and asked that it should immediately be made effective. That was fair enough, but what riled many established employees was that its ideas were hailed as new and fresh. They were not. In almost every case Lord Stokes' long-term planners had postulated future strategy, held up in their case by lack of finance to carry it out.

Since 1975, 'The Rover' at Solihull has ceased to exist. British Leyland would have us think of it as just another of their many plants. No longer is there a chief executive, but two plant directors — one to look after the Land-Rover/Range Rover side of things, and the other to control the private car function.

So what is the Rover name's prospects? The answer to that one, fortunately, is known and is encouraging. Leyland Cars' publically stated strategy is to reduce the number of different saloon car body shells to five basic lines; even this number is as high as the enormous General Motors combine in the United States would consider enough. In Leyland's case, three of the shells will be sired by the old Austin-Morris division, and one will be unique to Jaguar. The fourth will always be a Rover.

Times are such that the prospects of a multi-model range Rover marque occurring again are slim. The name, of course, appears on all the variations of SD1 already announced, even if the manual gearbox and the six-cylinder engines were designed by Triumph in Coventry, and on the Range Rover, which can only get more popular, and the ever-popular Land-Rover.

The vast new factory, completed in 1975 in time for SD1 pre-production to begin, is still by no means full. Leyland Cars have already announced that Triumph Dolomite production will be moved out of Coventry, and slotted in at Solihull, There may be more to come in that line about which the company's lips are still sealed.

The Rover 2000/3500 — the P6, as it was always known at Solihull — has already gone. The last of the four-cylinder versions, the 2200s, were built in the winter of 1976/77. Not even the engine will live on in any other Leyland Cars model.

As far as the new range of Rovers — the SD1s — is concerned, we can be happy to know that the European press has hailed them as world leaders in their class. By modern standards, too, their evolution is only just beginning. Splendid and desirable as they are in 1977, they will probably be even more so in the 1980s.

Appendices

1   Blind alleys and oddballs — the Rovers that got away

Board meeting minutes: September 25 1931
'. . . resolved that the 7 hp car should be exhibited at Olympia with a list price of £89, and that the matter of putting the car into production should be considered at a later date . . .'

Board meeting minutes: January 18 1945
'Mr S. B. Wilks strongly advised that we should aim to expand our output, and that to achieve this we should not look primarily to our pre-war models, but that we should add to our range by the introduction of a 6 hp model . . .'

Board meeting minutes: April 15 1953
'After discussion it was agreed that Mr Wilks' proposal that the Road Rover be put into production be approved . . .'

Board meeting minutes: January 30 1964
'It was reported that engineering was investigating the merits of a five-cylinder 2½-litre engine, with a view to possible use in P6 . . .'

Board meeting minutes: November 10 1967
'It was reported that the management had formulated its proposed product policy for the years 1968 to 1970 inclusive . . . The Plan included the introduction of the 100-inch Station Wagon in 1970, and a P8 car early in 1971 . . .'

In fact the public never got its hands on the tiny Scarabs or 6 hp M-Types, nor on the bulky Road Rover, or on any of the fast and luxurious P8 saloons. Neither did they get a chance to try out quirky designs like the five-cylinder Rover 2000. Yet all these, and more, were thought to be good and serious ideas for their time. Each one was built as a prototype; each was cancelled. Why? Who bungled? Did anyone bungle? Is the car-making business ever as simple as all that?

Rover, of course, have nothing of which to be ashamed. Their only habitual failing has probably been one of being ultra-cautious. Every car firm, after all, has its list of cancelled projects. Every product planner in the industry could turn out a drawer full of 'might-have-beens', and each engineering chief has design skeletons in his cupboards. Those companies which always decide to sell the first car they think of are very rare. Either they are brilliant — or they quickly go broke. Even Rolls-Royce have been known to change their minds. Rover often did, but it hasn't harmed their reputation one bit.

Over the years, all manner of projects have been started up and then cast aside. In almost every case the cancellation was due to caution over the financial forecasts, not due to deficiencies in the designs. It is also true that some of the cancellations have been on a grand scale, and that some of the machinery involved has been mouth-wateringly attractive. There are people still working at Solihull who mourn each and every one.

The company, to its eternal credit, makes no attempt to hide the false starts. Indeed, when British Leyland decided to open a collection of its historic vehicles at Donington Park, Solihull was able to supply a P8 prototype and the unique P6BS mid-engined sports coupé for occasional display. Historians wish that other companies were always so forthcoming. Even the five-cylinder engine and parts of the M-Type engine are preserved, but all trace of the rear-engined Scarabs has gone.

Among the stars, and it certainly is a good list from which to choose, the P8 saloon was the most expensive cancellation after something like £5 million had already been spent by 1970. Sidelining the splendid mid-engined P9 coupé broke the most hearts, but burying the rear-engined Scarab undoubtedly saved the company from a swift bankruptcy in 1931. But what about the M-Types, the P7 saloons of the 1960s, the Road Rovers, the fast-back Rover-Alvis, or the long-running saga of Jack Swaine's vee-6 engines?

Probably the most out-of-character of all Rovers was the cheap and crude Scarab. Not that Rover management ever really knew it by that name. From September 1929, when board approval was given to start design work, to September 1931, when a decision was made to freeze all tooling activity, it was unromantically known as the 7 hp light car. Scarab was a name dreamed up, at short notice, by the publicity staff.

Dictionaries tell us that scarabs are 'sacred beetles' — which is, at least, one way of defining a car once thought to be vital to Rover's future! In ancient Egypt scarabs were credited with marvellous powers; as far as Rover were concerned, struggling as they were against financial problems, the powers didn't rub off on their fortunes.

The car was originally conceived by Colonel Frank Searle, soon after he became managing director, and was dropped just after he left the firm abruptly. It was really the only important technological change pushed through in this uneasy period of Rover's history. But if Colonel Searle was responsible for the Scarab, it was also a big factor in his demise.

Scarab was authorised because Rover's new management wanted to expand. W. D. Sudbury as chairman and Colonel Searle as managing director wanted to break out of Rover's established routine and challenge the leaders. Remember that in 1928 Rover had made 3,766 cars; Morris, on the other hand had built 55,480, and Britain's total production was 165,352 cars in all. Morris's share, of course, was abnormally high — probably twice as high as Austin's share, for instance.

To do this they had to spread the range, and had to sell a lot of *very* cheap cars. Morris, and of course, Ford, had already proved that the expansion possibilities in price regions below those tapped by Rover were enormous. At the end of 1929, therefore, Searle and Robert Boyle began the design of a revolutionary small car, and were shortly joined by Maurice Wilks in his first Rover assignment. To do the job in secrecy, and to get away from humdrum factory affairs, they holed up in Searle's home at Braunston Hall, Braunston on the A45 not far from Rugby. In the design they certainly took no notice of existing Rover trends and traditions.

Apart from its declared price targets — the figure of £85 *retail* price recurs consistently in company discussions about the car — it was an astonishingly unorthodox machine. To get down to that price it had to be very crude, very basically equipped, and completely without any Rover precedent. It *must* have been Searle's brainchild — existing Rover engineers were incapable of giving birth to such way out ideas and the 1930s team led by Maurice Wilks would have shuddered at the very idea. It had no connection with the air-cooled Rover 8 of the early 1920s. The Scarab's engine, though air-cooled, was completely different in every respect, and the rest of the chassis was new to the point of being futuristic in thinking.

Detail design and layout is now well-known. What is not well known is whether it was truly a Frank Searle brainwave, or something refined from a car he had already seen. But at the end of the 1920s the British 'cycle-car' boom was over, and none had used the same, even vaguely related, rear-engined layout. The fact that Searle and Rover were granted a British Patent (No 375877) for the rear suspension, engine and transmission layout is significant.

There were four sparsely furnished seats within a short, 84-inch wheelbase. A very simple ladder-type chassis frame supported all-independent suspension and a rear engine. Not only was the engine at the back of the car (something almost unheard of in Britain — only the very expensive Burney Streamline emulated this), but it was a 60 degree, twin-cylinder, air-cooled 839 cc unit. There was much motor cycle influence in the engine's design, which was to be cooled by a simple two-bladed fan.

Front suspension was by coil springs on a sliding pillar (clearly influenced by Morgan thinking), but the coil spring swing-axle rear end had a new fangled support member pivot above the axle casing to give zero roll stiffness (So what was so new about Triumph's Mk IV Spitfire in the 1970s after all?). Body styling was very simple, with ash frame construction and sheet steel cladding. There was a dummy radiator at the front of the car so that the traditionalists would not be too affronted.

By the time the first car ran, at the end of 1930, the problems were becoming clear. The car was noisy, the engine was rough (a vee-twin with a 60 degree included angle and a long stroke could hardly be anything else) and it overheated, but basically the biggest problem was that the little car, somehow, wasn't a Rover. The board was so worried about the rear-engine layout that in March 1931 they asked Major B. H. Thomas to lay out a new scheme, with the engine in the nose, and with front wheel drive . . .

The Scarab was first leaked to the dealers in August 1931, shown (at a distance, behind barriers) to them at a Henlys Ltd lunch in September, and was promised for exhibition at Olympia in October. Not only was its design an opening-day talking point, but its price — £89 — caused a sensation. No car, before or since, has ever been listed in Britain at less than £100, and this was enough to make almost every observer sceptical about its chances.

The Rover directors were no longer among the sceptics — they had already acted. Even before the Olympia show, they had decided not to go ahead with the Scarab! In spite of previous historian's comments, there is really no mystery behind this. By 1931, like others around them, the company was in desperate financial trouble, and there was no money to be spared for new tooling programmes. £10,000 had been spent in getting design started, and a further £5,000 was allocated for certain preliminary tooling. To get the car properly tooled up for sale, even in its crude state, would absorb another £50,000.

The car was shown at Olympia merely to gauge public reaction. If this had been ecstatic, the big step to tooling might have been taken. Response was not favourable, and the project was swiftly abandoned after half-a-dozen prototypes had been built. A production rate of 30,000 cars a year had airily been talked of, but a conservative estimate of 10,000 Scarabs a year was more seriously discussed within the company. Incidentally, a further Searle-sponsored offshoot of the Scarab, which took shape at Braunston Hall in 1931, was a tiny tractor design, with the vee-twin air-cooled engine mounted in the nose. Only one was made, and this was scrapped at the end of 1931.

The Scarab's death was sudden and inglorious, and it would be overstating the case to say that the public noticed its demise. It was advertised by Rover once, in their *Autocar* and *Motor* motor show displays, but even three weeks later, when the Scottish show was at its height, all references to the car had gone. It was never mentioned again.

There has only been one more recent attempt to market a tiny Rover — this being the much more sophisticated little M-Type of the 1940s. Conceived for the same reasons as the Scarab — to take Rover out of one sales and production stratum and insert it convincingly into another — the M-Type was the Wilks brothers' first ideas on their Second World War destiny. Like the Scarab, it had a two-year life. Maurice and Spencer Wilks developed their ideas early in 1945, even before the end of the war, and had a prototype running in 1946, but had to cut out the programme during 1947. This time, however, the problem was not one of money, or even of the design's worth, but one of priorities. There might have been some doubts at the back of the Wilks' minds about the wisdom of making down-market Rovers, but in the end it was all a question of where and how the scarce sheet steel supplies available to the company should be used. It has already been shown how the whole concept of the Land-Rover evolved from this dilemma.

Spencer Wilks' original idea, in 1945, was that the post-war Solihull factory might be able to make 15,000 pre-war type Rovers a year at first, plus another 5,000 M-Types. In the car starved atmosphere which existed all round the world in the 1940s, and having confirmed that the M-Type's design was sound, there is no doubt that this low estimate would have been embarrassing. How many times, indeed, had Spencer erred on the side of caution in this way?

Compared with the layout of the Scarab, very little about the M-Type was unconventional. It centred around a tiny 77-inch wheelbase, was only 13 feet 4 inches long, and was given a new and very compact little 699 cc four-cylinder engine with the latest type of Rover sloping-head i o e valve gear. Bore and stroke were 57 mm by 68.5 mm, and the power output was a very creditable 28 bhp (gross) at 5,000 rpm. Only Reliant's own little post-war engine has been a smaller water-cooled British design.

To get round the known steel shortages, the car had a platform-type of chassis entirely fabricated from light alloy pressings, with a big boxy scuttle to give rigidity allied to minimum bulk. Front suspension was by coil springs and wishbones, an Armstrong lever-type damper also doubling as the upper wishbone — Austin A30 fashion, while the live rear axle was suspended by coil springs and located by radius arms and a Panhard rod. Need it be said that Gordon Bashford was responsible for the general layout and packaging?

Styling, at first, as carried out to Maurice Wilks' wishes by Harry Loker, incorporated a full width nose with recessed headlamps (the theme was later to be carried forward to the P4s which were designed later), and both open and coupé four-seaters were envisaged. The conservatism of the Wilks brothers then reasserted itself. At the same time as they decided to make the post-war P3s look like the pre-war P1s, they calculated that Rover's public (even a new, miniature car, Rover public) was not ready for such modern treatment on the M-Types. The three prototypes built, therefore, had cobby little two-door coupé shells, constructed almost entirely from light alloy pressed sheet, with the front and rear wings were still obviously separate, vestigial running boards. The family resemblance to other Rovers was obvious. Even so, the headlamps were almost completely recessed, and when Maurice Wilks was interviewed by *Motor* magazine in 1949 he gave a definite impression that he had been prepared for drastic modernisation of the shape before it was actually tooled for sale.

The M-Type, unlike the Scarab, was a very serious project, but was overtaken by events. Changes in car taxation laws, the government's pressure on all car firms to adopt a 'one-model' policy, the export possibilities and problems, *plus* a start-up of the Land-Rover project, all helped to seal its fate. By the spring of 1947 the project had been cancelled. The last of the three prototypes was finally run into oblivion by Jess Worster as recently as the 1960s.

Linking Scarab with the M-Type, and even with the later Rover 2000s, is a whole series of odd engines. Odd because of their physical layout and not because they were operationally peculiar. Jack Swaine, recently retired from Rover, joined the company in 1934 as a development engineer and remembers many of them. 'Round about 1935/36, Maurice Wilks was looking around for a bigger engine than the existing "fours" — one bigger in capacity, but shorter than the equivalent "six" would have to be.' (Wilks wanted this engine to replace the Poppe-designed Meteor unit, designed in the mid 1920s).

'The first thing we therefore looked at was a 60 degree vee-8 — not a 90 degree vee-8 because we thought that with a two-plane crank this might give difficult carburation problems; the 60 degree engine, on the other hand, would really be two four cylinder units clamped together at 60 degrees, not as much of a problem.

'We never actually made one, just sketched it out on paper — then, eventually, in the course of discussion, we conceived a 90 degree vee-6. We thought we'd been very clever in this, but subsequently found out that diesels with this layout already existed. So really we just re-invented the idea!

'The cars were fairly narrow-bonneted then, and I had to try to keep the engine narrow. So I decided to use one camshaft in the vee of the block, operate side exhaust valves directly from it, with overhead inlets — and to get the compactness I needed I thought it reasonable to tip the angle of the top face of the cylinder block towards the centre of the engine, and pull the inlet valves across to suit. That way we could tuck the exhaust valve into a pocket of the chamber.

'As it happened, Maurice Wilks then decided to hold off the vee-6, and soon afterwards we did a new straight "six" based on the existing "four", but he loved the combustion chamber idea, and asked me to do "in-line engine" versions of it. That's how the famous i o e Rover engine scheme was born.

'We had the i o e cylinder engines running just before the war started, but for all the usual reasons we couldn't start building them to sell until 1948.

'In 1945, for a while we concentrated on designing that little M-Type engine, which also had the i o e head arrangement about which everyone was completely convinced, but once that had been dropped, and the sloping head P3 engines were ready for production, we picked up a vee-6 design again.'

From then until the early 1960s there was always at least one vee-6 engine under development at Solihull. The story was even complicated in the early 1950s when a vee-4 version was made as well! Over the years the desired engine capacity varied quite a lot depending on the car or cars for which it might be intended. The consulting firm of Ricardo were also asked to comment on designs at the end of the war, and shocked even Rover by talking about two-stroke engines with sleeve valves.

It certainly took up a lot of Swaine's time. 'We started new designs again in 1950. They didn't have much relation to the one I had schemed up before the war, because we had refined the sloping head a lot, but there were similarities. We were on this path for another five years or so; the first engine we designed was a 3-litre, the second, much more compact, was a 2-litre, and the last one was a 3-litre again. In each case, there could be underbored, smaller capacity units, of course.

'This engine was really for a new P5, which at one time was comparable in size with the Rover 2000, but it grew a lot over the years. We mounted the carburettors so that they faced outwards and the manifolds fed downwards into the heads; the exhaust came out into the vee, and we got rid of the pipes down the back of the engine. We were disappointed with the performance, because the power peak was at 4,000 rpm. We had big problems with the induction system and breathing.

'The 2-litre vee-6 was for the smallest scheme of P5, but then as it grew up we had to enlarge the engine again. To get the breathing right in the later engines we ran an inlet gallery along the side of the heads, just below the ports, with SU carburettors stuck out in front of the unit, and air cleaners on each side of the car's radiator.

'But we were still struggling with power and breathing, and had to go wilder and wilder on valve timing. In the end time was running out on us, we had to drop the vee-6, and I asked Norman Bryden to produce the 3-litre version of the P4 engine instead.'

When development ceased, the engine was of 2,960 cc (88.9 mm by 79.37 mm bore and stroke), and produced 100 bhp at 4,000 rpm. At least 15 engines were either in cars, or running on test beds, by this time. When Jack Swaine was asked as to their welfare by Robert Boyle in 1962 he found all of them, including some 2-litre versions, still safely in store.

That was the last of the serious vee-6 studies, but even as late as 1964 Swaine's team of designers were still attracted to the concept. Having bought the rights to the ex-Buick aluminium vee-8 engine, they were allowed to start sketching up a vee-6 cousin to it, but with a cast-iron block, and specifically intended for a higher powered Land-Rover. This never progressed beyond the drawing stage.

Higher powered, or larger Land-Rovers, have often been in the wind. The Land-Rover itself, conceived 30 years ago, gets more and more power every time its sponsors can get permission to do another engine transplant. The Range Rover, of course, started life as the 100-inch Station Wagon project, and in its way was a direct lineal descendant from the Road Rover.

Road Rover was a continuous project for much of the 1950s, and was first formally noted by the directors in 1952. S. B. Wilks gained approval for its production in 1953, and in 1956 was forecasting its launch for the following year. The project was put 'on ice' in 1958 and quietly forgotten a year later.

Road Rovers were essentially large estate cars (on the P4 passenger car chassis — much modified) rather than 'go-anywhere' vehicles. The first prototype, called the 'Greenhouse' because of its very basic styling, was followed by heavier and yet more complicated devices. The definitive machine, with only two-wheel drive and the latest in Land-Rover four-cylinder engines, had a big and ungainly two-door body with large estate car tailgate, and was copied from the themes of mid-1950s Chevrolets. David Bache, who had arrived at Rover well before then, assured me that he *definitely* had *nothing* to do with it!

Gordon Bashford reckons that the original Road Rover concept was better than the final one. 'Despite Dick Oxley's efforts to maintain the original simple concept, his brief from management escalalated. They thought the original was too austere and asked for changes involving the shape which needed complicated pressings. In this way it got bigger, grander, heavier and more costly.'

It was also in the early 1950s when the company dabbled with the idea of marketing a special-bodied, exclusive and very expensive version of P4, with drop-head coupé or fixed-head coupé bodies by Pininfarina. Discussions with the Italian coachbuilder began in 1952, and were reported to the other directors, but no decision was taken to put such a car into production before public reaction could be gauged.

The completed Pininfarina prototype was shown at Earls Court in 1953 and, in some respects, really pointed the way to the lines of P5, which was to follow five years later. Looked at from the mid-1970s, it even has lines and masses in common with more recent Rolls-Royce convertibles (the Corniche cars), which is a good enough recommendation by any standards.

There were no mechanical differences between this prototype and the newly announced Rover 90s, but the body shell was unique and considerably longer at 15 feet 11.2 inches than the standard car. Only two doors were provided, and the car was in all respects more advanced in its looks than the P4.

The company were interested in public reaction, and they duly got it. There would have been custom at the right price, but they could not guarantee one so that was that. Another interesting 'might have been' for the Rover enthusiasts to mourn.

Mechanically, of course, there have always been oddities around the place. A licence to make the Hayes automatic transmission (in the mid-1930s) was quickly forgotten, and proposals to use ZF 5-speed gearboxes in the first Rover 3500 received short thrift. The P6 came in for a lot of attention after it had been announced. Faster versions were soon in demand, and before the Buick vee-8 came along they had engine ideas of their own.

P7 projects generally were re-engining exercises in the P6, along with some suspension work, the object in each case to make as few changes to quantity-produced base-unit structures as possible. Apart from tuning the existing 2-litre engine, which was done, the next obvious move was to make a 'six' version of the 'four'. To save time, Solihull engineers did this by the skilful application of 'back-street bodging' — heads and blocks were fabricated by cutting off one cylinder from two 2000TC units and welding the three-cylinder sections together again! The idea was that existing transfer-line tooling could be used, even though the new engine was much longer. However, there must have been some misunderstanding somewhere; later it was discovered that not enough reserve capacity in terms of engines per shift had been allowed for to deal with an incremental model.

Six P7s with this 152 bhp single-SU engine were built, and had a performance equally as impressive as that of the vee-8 car, though the weight was up, and considerable change would have been needed to the base unit and front styling. One car was actually sold off (to Ted Eves of *Autocar*) and is now owned by a Rover Sports Register member.

However, not discouraged, Wilks, King and Jack Swaine then took their reputations in their hands and decided to try for a five-cylinder layout, after Brian Silvester had given valuable technical advice on balance and in-car mounting. Even today, of course, there are very few 'fives' in private cars; in the 1960s there were none at all. This 2,472 cc 'five' could just about be squeezed into the existing base unit. Balance was not a major problem — that honour fell to the carburation. In Jack Swaine's own words:

'First of all we made a three-carb version which was a bit comical. One SU fed one cylinder, while the others fed a pair each. Manifolding and the head were easy because we cut and welded as with the 'six'. We then conceived a layout with two SU carbs, one at each end of a longish gallery, one pointing forwards and one backwards. It was logical to do this, but a bit on the bulky side. Using constant-depression carbs there was a problem — that we had, effectively, an infinitely long balance pipe. The engine never really knew which carb piston to lift first! We only built a couple of these, then began to concentrate on the vee-8.'

One Rover 2000TC-based project, in which the company was interested up to a point, was the very special two-door coupé-bodied 2000TC built up by Carrozzeria Zagato in Milan. It was very much lighter than the standard product, lower and more streamlined, and had some obvious family likeness with the Zagato-bodied Lancia Fulvia Coupé which was current at the time. At least two were built, of which the first was on a structure provided by the company, but there is no evidence that there was ever a firm intent to market this car in quantity. The problem, as with the Farina-P4 of the 1950s, was that there was an enormous amount of extra work, expense and specialisation in the body, and it was not at all clear that the public would back it with orders sufficient to justify the risks. After just two cars had been built, therefore, the project was dropped. Incidentally, some have said that they can see likenesses between this car and the new 3500 car. David Bache, I know, would be insulted by such inferences, as he spent much time on the 3500 in developing its package from scratch.

There is one other 'might-have-been' in the 2000 story — the Alvis GTS. This was a fastback coupé based on the standard car, and came about because Alvis themselves had no new car plans. Rover took control of Alvis in 1965, and discovered that although the 3-litre had been running since 1950 there were no plans to replace it. The existing TF21, with its elegant Park Ward coachbuilt body, was built in very small quantities, and was hopelessly uneconomic. The last sanction was due to run out in mid-1967, and David Bache was asked to propose a replacement.

Using a P6 3500 base unit, the same mechanical parts, and many unchanged inner panels, Solihull's stylists produced a sleek two-door coupé shape with (in 1966) a hatchback which predated the Scimitar GTE and its imitators by years. Scuttle and lower panelling was shared with P6 but the rest of the skin was new. The nose had much in common with outdated P7 proposals, and the carefully faired-in headlamps were carried forward in essence to the new Rover 3500 of 1976.

A careful look at the GTS, which David Bache now owns himself, shows a nagging resemblance to other coupés of the day. David Bache doesn't think he was directly influenced by another car, but admits that it is difficult to remain aloof . . . some might see suggestions of Plymouth and other American coupés in the roof shape.

Why didn't the GTS appear? Look at a few dates and consider. The GTS was conceived in 1966, and built up in the winter of 1966/67. The Rover-Leyland merger happened that winter, and product plans were revised soon afterwards. In the event there were no more Alvis cars, the last of the TFs being built in 1967. Incidentally, and no-one knows why, this car has always been nicknamed 'Gladys' by the styling department!

At the same time that Solihull were heavily committed to the new P8 saloon (already described in Chapter 11), in one small corner of the Solihull factory Spen King and Gordon Bashford were hatching out something else that might just have been made at the Alvis works. Gordon Bashford wryly points out that most of Rover's really exciting project engineering has been carried out either at his or at Spen King's home. The new car, very dear to their innovative ways, was no exception. Under Bill Martin-Hurst, Rover were thrust firmly towards a more sporting image. Rally cars were one thing, and the Rover-BRM was another, but where was the sporting car in the range? Without being offered a big budget, or even any sizeable development resources, Spen King was asked by Peter Wilks to rectify this.

P6BS was its project title, very unwieldy, because the car had elements of the P6 (Rover 2000) and B (Buick-based vee-8) in it, and was a sporting car (S). At Rover it has always lovingly been called the 'BS', never anything else; not, that is, until styling took an interest. King and Bashford collected together all sorts of bits and pieces, put them down in a corner of the jig and pattern shop (they were kept well away from the normal experimental department facility), and settled down to examine their philosophy. Racing practice, the latest motoring fashion and good old-fashioned engineering principles were all stirred in to a very deep design discussion. Whatever Spen King might now insist (and he has said more than once that older Rovers did not influence him over the BS), there was much distinguished history from the turbine cars and the King-Wilks-Mackie Specials to be drawn upon as well.

Basic design was settled in 1966, and as soon as the prototype Range Rover had been handed over to Tom Barton's Land-Rover team detail work got under way. The one and only prototype was built in 1967, significantly enough *after* the Leyland take over had taken place. As is well known, the car relied on a mid-mounted vee-8 engine with ingeniously arranged transmission, soft suspension including a De Dion rear end evolved from the P6, and a two-plus-nearly-one seating package. Wheel rims and tyres were fatter at the rear than at the front, and the accent was on good ride and refinement.

The 'styling' of the prototype was very much of an 'instant' job. Spen King tackled this himself, as the official styling department were much too busy on other projects, and his principle was to wrap the chosen mechanical components and the seating packaging as closely as possible. The extra bit of flair was offered, part-time and usually out of office hours, by Geoff Crompton of styling. One aspect, quite unexpected but very welcome at the time, was that it had the finest all-round visibility of any known Rover.

The car itself was assembled at the Alvis works in Coventry in great secrecy, and was always tested on private ground at first. It is doubtful if it ever turned a wheel on the public highway during 1967. So careful were the team about security that the car was always transported to and from Alvis in a closed truck.

The car worked well, and handled beautifully, but its approval as a production project did not mature. As conceived, it was meant to be assembled in quantity at Alvis, alongside the Alvis GTS, once the last of the Park Ward bodied TF21s had gone. According to official costings made at the time it could most certainly have been sold at Rover 2000TC prices — which would have meant that it could have undercut Jaguar E-Type prices by around £500. However, at this time the company was embroiled in mergers and attempted rationalisation, and there is no doubt that both Triumph *and* Jaguar were jealous of this new competitor. For these reasons, and the fact that the company was just bracing up to big capital expenditure on the Range Rover and P8 models, the BS was an 'off-on-off-on' project for some months. Before the finally cancelled car was shown to the public at the New York motor show in the spring of 1968, it had already been cancelled a couple of times and revived once.

Tony Poole of styling recalls. 'One day, rather later, we suddenly had a very abrupt request to come up with a production style for the car. I remember this panic very well, because the order came down on a Tuesday and we had to have sketches ready on the Wednesday.'

(In fact Bruce McWilliams of Rover's North American subsidiary had been proud of the exhibited car, and had also let it be known that a car looking rather like Ferrari's mid-engined 250LM would be very popular with the Americans).

'We had just one day to do the job. Up to then, mind you, we hadn't been thinking about the car at all — we were busy, as usual, and anyway we thought the project was dead. Of all our suggestions, really the body that won out was a thoroughly cleaned-up version of the job Spen had built.

'Then it all went quiet again. Suddenly, months later, it was abruptly resurrected — that would be in 1969 — and we had to make a full-sized clay model for a viewing. We then took all the dimensions off this, so that the car could be made official — and the urgency died again. I'm sorry to say that it never came back.'

The prototype, with its ingenious 'back-to-front' engine, compact transmission, superb ride and roadholding qualities, happily lives on in original King-Bashford guise. The specialist press were allowed a few days of glory in it (one particular high speed journey from London to the Midlands will live with me for ever), and it has been displayed to motoring enthusiasts all round the country. Its home, alongside the only remaining P8, and several of Rover's much older but historic vehicles, is now in the British Leyland Collection at Donington Park. It is really rather sad. Nobody, not even in the higher echelons of Leyland management, argues with my own opinion — that it was a unique motor car, which probably would have been a very profitable world-beater.

Which brings us up to the present — or as near to the present as British Leyland's security curtain will allow us to see. Has modern product planning, design and styling now reached the stage where such fascinating 'white elephants' can no longer occur? Thank goodness — no! Any company, or talented bunch of people, which could seriously consider a road-going version of the Rover-BRM turbine car, or have its Range Rovers considered fine enough to be exhibited in the Louvre as 'modern works of art', or turn its hand to ultra-modern versions of the Leyland National coaches and turbine trucks, or continue to develop the weirdest variations on a Land-Rover theme will surely do it again? Who knows, perhaps they already have?

2 Rover since the start. Who has run the company?

These are the people who have held top executive positions in the last 100 years, and the date of their appointments.

In 1877 John Kemp Starley and William Sutton joined in their original partnership as

Starley and Sutton. This partnership was dissolved in 1888, and the first true ancestor of Rover, J. K. Starley and Company Ltd, was founded.

	Chairman	Managing director	In charge of design/engineering
1888	J. K. Starley	J. K. Starley	J. K. Starley
1896	Sir F. Dixon-Hartland	J. K. Starley	J. K. Starley
1902		Harry Smith	
1903			Edmund Lewis
1906			Bernard Wright
1909	Col W. F. Wyley		
1910			Owen Clegg
1912			Mark Wild
1919			J. Y. Sangster
1923		J. K. Starley (Jun)	
1924			Peter Poppe
1928	W. D. Sudbury		
1929		Col F. Searle	C. T. Newsome
1931	Alex Craig		Maurice Wilks
1932	E. R. Harrison		
1933		Spencer B. Wilks	
1954	H. Howe Graham		
1956		Spencer Wilks and Maurice Wilks	
1957	Spencer Wilks	Maurice Wilks and George Farmer	Robert Boyle
1960	George Farmer became deputy chairman until 1963, when the post was abolished	Maurice Wilks	
1962	Maurice Wilks	William Martin-Hurst	
1963	George Farmer		
1964			Peter Wilks
1969		A. B. Smith	
1971			Spencer King
1973	A. B. Smith	Bernard Jackman	
1974			John Lloyd

In 1975, following the partial nationalisation of British Leyland, and the foundation of Leyland Cars, Rover (even as Rover-Triumph) ceased to exist as a separate entity. The individual positions listed above were also abolished at the same time.

Note: *Spencer Wilks retired from the chairmanship in 1962, and retained his seat on the Rover board until 1967. He then retired, becoming the company's president. Following his death in 1971 this position was abolished.*

3 The important milestones — who, what, when and where?

1877	John Kemp Starley and William Sutton join in partnership, to make bicycles at West Orchard, Coventry
1884	The 'Rover' name first appeared — on a pedal tricycle
1885	At a London exhibition, the very first Starley Safety Rover bicycle was exhibited
1888	William Sutton withdrew from the partnership. Starley then formed J. K. Starley and Company Ltd

1896	Starley converted his business to a public company, The Rover Cycle Company Ltd £150,000 Ordinary Share capital
1898	Factory moved from West Orchard to nearby Queen Victoria Road
1901	Death of Starley at the early age of 46 years
1902	The first engine-driven Rover announced — a 2¾ hp motor cycle (price £55)
1904	The first-ever Rover motor car announced — the 8 hp (price £200)
1906	The company's name changed to: The Rover Company Limited
1919	Purchase of Tyseley factory, followed within a year by announcement of the Tyseley-built air-cooled 8 hp Rover
1924	Motor cycle production finally ended. Total production 10,401
	Pedal cycle production finally ended. Total production 426,530
1929	J. K. Starley (Jun) resigned the managing directorship — this cut the last family link with the 1877 partnership, after 52 years
1931	Brief appearance of air-cooled rear-engined Scarab — meant to be Britain's first under-£100 car
1933	Appointment of Spencer Wilks as managing director. The 'quality-first' approach was born
1936	Rover invited to join other motor industry companies in the Air Ministry's 'shadow factory' scheme. Acocks Green building built first. The Solihull 'shadow factory' followed in 1939/40
1940	In conjunction with Frank Whittle's Power Jets concern, Rover began development of gas turbine 'jet' engines. Barnoldswick, Clitheroe and other ex-cotton mills requisitioned for this and other war work
1942/43	Jet engine interests released to Rolls-Royce, in exchange for production rights to vee-12 Meteor military engine
1945	Return to civil production of private cars. All cars now to be assembled at Solihull. A start made on gas turbine car/boat projects
1948	First public appearance of the Land-Rover
1949	Announcement of the Rover P4 car — a start to the 'Auntie' era
1950	Rover's first turbine powered car (the world's first) demonstrated
1957	Spencer Wilks became chairman, Maurice Wilks and George Farmer joint managing directors
1962	Spencer Wilks retired after more than 30 years' service
1963	Announcement of the Rover 2000, first 'new generation car'
	Rover-BRM gas turbine car raced at Le Mans
1965	Rover take over Alvis Ltd, with factories in Coventry
1967	Rover absorbed by Leyland Motors (who already controlled Standard-Triumph). First public appearance of the company's new vee-8 engine. Spencer Wilks became company's life president
1968	Leyland (including Rover) merged with British Motor Holdings, to form British Leyland Motor Corporation
	Mid-engined P6BS Coupé prototype revealed
1970	Announcement of Range Rover, the 'second generation' all-purpose machine from the company
1971	Death of Spencer Wilks
1972	British Leyland announced plans to combine Rover's operations with those of Triumph
1975	British Leyland in severe financial trouble. This led to massive Government support and injection of funds. The Ryder Report recommended setting up of Leyland Cars, and submerging of old individual company identities. A start made on this project at once
	Vast new Solihull factory block completed
	Solihull chosen as executive centre of Leyland Cars' design/styling operations
1976	Millionth Land-Rover manufactured
	Very successful launch of new Rover 3500 car. Other versions expected to follow shortly

4   The Rover Owners' Association

Rovers, like other cars with a fine pedigree, soon achieve enthusiastic support among new customers. However, the Rover Owners' Association, founded in 1955, was really a wider development of the Land-Rover Owners' Club, which had been set up in 1949.

The ROA, nowadays, is a company-supported organisation, with headquarters at Solihull, and company PR man Brian Sperring as its chairman. In total there are more than 33,000 members — equally split between British and overseas members.

Anyone reading this book, and wanting to join the ROA, as British Leyland hope they will, should contact Brian Sperring at Solihull.

5   The Rover pedigree

A chronological list of all Rover production cars made since the first 8 hp model of 1904.

Model	Years produced	Engine	Comment
8	1904 - 1912	1-cyl 114 x 130 mm 1,327 cc	Backbone chassis
6	1905 - 1912	1-cyl 95 x 110 mm 780 cc (Later 97 x 110 mm 812 cc)	
10/12	1905 - 1906	4-cyl 75 x 100 mm 1,767 cc	
16/20	1905 - 1910	4-cyl 95 x 110 mm 3,119 cc (Later 97 x 110 mm 3,251 cc)	1907 TT winner
12	1908 - 1910	2-cyl 97 x 110 mm 1,624 cc	
15	1909 - 1911	4-cyl 85 x 110 mm 2,488 cc	
8	1911 - 1912	1-cyl 101.5 x 130 mm 1,052 cc	With Knight sleeve-valve engine
12	1911 - 1912	2-cyl 96 x 130 mm 1,882 cc	With Knight sleeve-valve engine
12	1912 - 1924	4-cyl 75 x 130 mm 2,297 cc	Famous 'Clegg 12'
18	1912 - 1913	4-cyl 90 x 130 mm 3,307 cc	Bigger version of 'Clegg 12'
8	1920 - 1925	2-cyl 85 x 88 mm 998 cc (Later 85 x 100 mm 1,134 cc)	Air-cooled flat twin
9/20	1924 - 1927	4-cyl 60 x 95 mm 1,074 cc	
14/45	1925 - 1927	4-cyl 75 x 120 mm 2,132 cc	Poppe o h c-engined car
16/50	1926 - 1928	4-cyl 80 x 120 mm 2,426 cc	Enlarged Poppe engine
10/25	1928 - 1933	4-cyl 63 x 95 mm 1,185 cc	Enlarged 9/20 engine
2-litre (and Light 6)	1928 - 1932	6-cyl 65 x 101.6 mm 2,023 cc	First Rover 'six'
Meteor (also Light 20)	1930 - 1933	6-cyl 72 x 105 mm 2,565 cc	Larger version of 2,023 cc 'six'
Pilot	1932 - 1933	6-cyl 59 x 86 mm 1,410 cc (Later 61 x 90 mm 1,577 cc)	Thomas-designed 'six' — related to 10/25 'four'
P1 10	1934 - 1936	4-cyl 66.5 x 100 mm 1,389 cc	Wilks/Boyle '100 mm' engine
P1 12	1934 - 1936	4-cyl 69 x 100 mm 1,496 cc	Enlarged '100 mm' engine
P1 14 (and Speed 14)	1934 - 1936	6-cyl 61 x 90 mm 1,577 cc	
Speed 16	1934	6-cyl 65 x 101.6 mm 2,023 cc	
Speed 20	1934 - 1935	6-cyl 72 x 105 mm 2,565 cc	
P2 10	1937 - 1948	4-cyl 66.5 x 100 mm 1,389 cc	
P2 12	1937 - 1948	4-cyl 69 x 100 mm 1,496 cc	
P2 14	1937 - 1938	6-cyl 61 x 90 mm 1,577 cc	

Model	Years produced	Engine	Comment
P2 16	1937 - 1948	6-cyl 67.5 x 100 mm 2,147 cc	
P2 Speed 20 (and P2 20)	1937 - 1940	6-cyl 73 x 100 mm 2,512 cc	
P2 14	1939 - 1948	6-cyl 63.5 x 100 mm 1,901 cc	
P3 60	1948 - 1949	4-cyl 69.5 x 105 mm 1,595 cc	First i f s Rover — sloping head engine
P3 75	1948 - 1949	6-cyl 65.2 x 105 mm 2,103 cc	Same chassis as 60 — sloping head engine
P4 75	1950 - 1954	6-cyl 65.2 x 105 mm 2,103 cc	First full-width body
P4 60	1954 - 1959	4-cyl 77.8 x 105 mm 1,997 cc	
P4 75	1955 - 1959	6-cyl 73 x 88.9 mm 2,230 cc	
P4 90	1955 - 1959	6-cyl 73 x 105 mm 2,638 cc	
P4 105R	1957 - 1958	6-cyl 73 x 105 mm 2,638 cc	With Roverdrive semi-automatic box
P4 105S (later 105)	1957 - 1959	6-cyl 73 x 105 mm 2,638 cc	
P5 3-litre	1959 - 1967	6-cyl 77.8 x 105 mm 2,995 cc	First chassis-less Rover car
P4 80	1960 - 1962	4-cyl 90.5 x 88.8 mm 2,286 cc	
P4 100	1960 - 1962	6-cyl 77.8 x 92 mm 2,625 cc	
P4 95	1963 - 1964	6-cyl 77.8 x 92 mm 2,625 cc	
P4 110	1963 - 1964	6-cyl 77.8 x 92 mm 2,625 cc	
P6 2000	1963 - 1973	4-cyl 85.7 x 85.7 mm 1,978 cc	Base-unit body, de Dion rear suspension
P6 2000TC	1966 - 1973	4-cyl 85.7 x 85.7 mm 1,978 cc	
P5 3½-litre	1967 - 1973	V8-cyl 88.9 x 71.1 mm 3,528 cc	Ex-GM vee-8 engine
P6 3500	1968 - 1975	V8-cyl 88.9 x 71.1 mm 3,528 cc	New engine in P6 shell
Range Rover	1970 to date	V8-cyl 88.9 x 71.1 mm 3,528 cc	4-wheel-drive estate car
P6 2200 (and 2200TC)	1973 - 1976	4-cyl 90.5 x 85.7 mm 2,205 cc	
3500	1976 to date	V8-cyl 88.9 x 71.1 mm 3,528 cc	New SD1 5-door car

The Land-Rover family

Model	Years produced	Engine	Comment
SI	1948 - 1958	4-cyl 69.5 x 105 mm 1,595 cc (77.8 x 105 mm 1,997 cc from 1952) (diesel, 85.7 x 88.9 mm 2,052 cc from 1957)	80, 86, 88, 107, and 109-inch wheelbase
SII	1958 - 1961	4-cyl 1,997 cc petrol and 90.5 x 88.9 mm 2,286 cc petrol and 2,052 cc diesel	88-inch and 109-inch wheelbase
SIIA	1961 - 1971	4-cyl 2,286 cc petrol and 2,286 cc diesel 6-cyl 77.8 x 92 mm 2,625 cc from 1967	88-inch and 109-inch wheelbase
Forward-control	1962 - 1972	4-cyl 2,286 cc petrol and 2,286 cc diesel, plus 6-cyl 2,625 cc petrol	109-inch and 110-inch wheelbase
SIII	1971 to date	4-cyl 2,286 cc petrol and 2,286 cc diesel, plus 6-cyl 2,625 cc petrol	88-inch and 109-inch wheelbase
Forward-control 101-inch	1975 to date	V8-cyl 88.9 x 71.1 mm 3,528 cc	Exclusively for military use. 101-inch wheelbase

Index